T0284949

DESOLATION

A HEAVY METAL MEMOIR

MARK MORTON

WITH BEN OPIPARI

 hachette
BOOKS

NEW YORK

Hachette Books
Hachette Book Group
1290 Avenue of the Americas
New York, NY 10104
HachetteBooks.com
Twitter.com/HachetteBooks
Instagram.com/HachetteBooks

First Edition: June 2024

Published by Hachette Books, an imprint of Hachette Book Group, Inc. The Hachette Books name and logo is a trademark of the Hachette Book Group.

The Hachette Speakers Bureau provides a wide range of authors for speaking events. To find out more, go to hachettespeakersbureau.com or email HachetteSpeakers@hbgusa.com.

Books by Hachette Books may be purchased in bulk for business, educational, or promotional use. For information, please contact your local bookseller or Hachette Book Group Special Markets Department at: special.markets@hbgusa.com.

The publisher is not responsible for websites (or their content) that are not owned by the publisher.

Print book interior design by Bart Dawson.

Library of Congress Cataloging-in-Publication Data has been applied for.

ISBNs: 9780306830983 (hardcover); 9780306836749 (signed edition); 9780306831003 (ebook)

Printed in the United States of America

LSC-C

Printing 1, 2024

To my family . . . to everyone I've ever jammed with . . . and to everyone who has ever listened. Thank you.

CONTENTS

Contents

DESOLATION

GOD, PLEASE GET ME THROUGH THIS

I t's 1 a.m. and my heart is thumping so hard in my chest I can hear it. My hands are shaking. My chair feels like a roller coaster. Waves of vertigo flood my head, and my stomach is in a free fall. I'm scared. Sweat pours down my face in recurring hot flashes. My vision fades in and out, a blurry tunnel narrowing from all sides.

I stare at the desk in front of me, trying to focus. Over on the hotel table there are one and a half turquoise 80 mg Oxycontin pills left over from the five I'd scored earlier that afternoon. These are among the heaviest of pharmaceutical opiates, pills normally prescribed to treat extreme pain in terminally ill cancer patients. But I don't have cancer.

I calculate the math through the fog in my head. I've taken 280 milligrams. I'm still under my self-imposed but loosely observed daily limit of 300 mg. Even for an experienced pill junky like me, that's a dangerous limit. It could easily be a lethal dose, and it most certainly

1

would be to someone without my level of opiate tolerance. But that blurry boundary I've set is an attempt to manage my addiction. It's an attempt to feel like I'm in control. It's an attempt to stay alive. Because I don't want to die.

The bottle of Absolut Vodka I pulled from my tour bus earlier and shoved into my backpack before checking in is on the desk. I've put a pretty good dent in that too, but a little more than half the bottle remains. There was a time when I used to only drink beer with these strong pills. Another attempt at a boundary. But lately I've started drinking hard liquor with my Oxys to jump-start the effects. And though I typically prefer the strongest pharmaceutical opioid pain-killers, when I can't find the right pills, I'll snort heroin or do any other opiate I can get my hands on. Sourcing my habit feels like a full-time job. It consumes a great deal of my time and money. I've accepted the lifestyle. I know I'm an addict and I live with it.

But tonight, it's all turning on me. I'm not doing the alcohol and drugs—they're doing me. And now I'm panicking. "Fuck. Is this what an overdose feels like?" I think to myself. "I thought I'm not supposed to feel it coming."

The veins in my neck throb. My arms and legs are numb. "Calm down," I tell myself out loud. "Take a deep breath. You're just freaking out."

My eyes start to feel heavy. My head snaps upright, adrenaline and fear pulling me back from another involuntary nod into unconsciousness. So many times before, I've eagerly anticipated the soft, slow drift past the wandering carefree daydreams and into the gentle dreamy Eden that heavy opiates create. But this time, something is wrong. I'm not sure why, but the drugs are hitting me different. It feels erratic. I'm anxious and agitated. I stand up and pace frantically around the room, hoping to snap out of it.

My posh Midtown Manhattan hotel suite is a short walk from Madison Square Garden. My band Lamb of God will be playing there the next two nights after today's day off. We're in the middle of the biggest tour we've ever done, opening for Metallica, the world's biggest metal band, across three continents. Early in our career, we would've scoffed at the idea of playing huge stages all over the globe with some of the world's biggest bands. For a band as extreme as ours, that would have been unthinkable. But now we're doing it. This should be a triumphant moment.

Fifteen years earlier in Richmond, Virginia, we had started out jamming in basements and garages with little aspiration to do much beyond the punk and hardcore underground. In those early days, we were as much a drinking club as we were a band. But when we did play, it was furious and intense. Blending the influence of local math metal heroes like Breadwinner and Sliang Laos with more conventional thrash influences of bands like Slayer and Pantera, we wrote our own music from the start. Stitching together massive grooving riffs with off-time, tightly syncopated rhythmic cadences and blistering blasts of pure noise, we began as an artsy, instrumental grindcore band. To characterize the extremeness of our sound, we cheekily named ourselves Burn the Priest—not exactly a brand for mainstream consumption.

Imagine a steel box full of nails and broken glass. Now douse it with kerosene, light it on fire, and roll it down a long, steep, winding staircase. That's what we sounded like. After a short time performing at local parties and warehouses as an instrumental act, we added a singer. Randy Blythe's infernal scream not only completed the sonic elements of the band, but he was also the physical and visual embodiment of the chaos we had been creating musically. We renamed ourselves Lamb of God.

It was magical. We were a burning car crash: jarring, unhinged, and impossible not to watch. Somewhere between the cases of beer and the bong hits, we had created the cornerstone of our sound, a sound that would carry us far beyond any level of success we could've imagined. We went from a dingy Richmond basement full of empty bottles and cigarette butts all the way to Madison Square Garden and beyond.

But that *beyond* is now coming down fast as I struggle to remain conscious between realizations that I might be in trouble. I pace around my hotel room trying to walk it off, then look in the mirror. My pupils are pinpoints. My face is bright red, splotchy and sweaty. My heart is still pounding, my arms still tingling. I'm scared. Dizzy, I sit on the bed, lay back and lose consciousness again. Jolted awake, I snap back up and taste vomit burning the back of my throat.

God, please get me through this. It's funny how people get religious when shit hits the fan.

Three months earlier, I said a similar prayer in desperation. My firstborn daughter, Madalyn Grace, had contracted a rare and still largely unexplained bacterial infection during delivery. Doctors struggled to find out what was wrong as she deteriorated rapidly in the hours after her birth. Once her condition was properly identified, she was airlifted by helicopter from Richmond to Charlottesville, Virginia, for further treatment. Watching the medics wheeling her into the ambulance for the short ride to the helipad, I ran to my truck to make the drive while they flew. I drove 90 mph down I-64 west and got to the hospital in Charlottesville before they did. I watched the helicopter land. They told me later that she died twice during the flight.

God, please get her through this.

For a short time after arriving in Charlottesville, Madalyn was stabilized as we hoped for some sort of recovery. But that hope didn't last long. In the late afternoon of August 14, 2009, I sat in the neonatal intensive care unit at University of Virginia Medical Center on a chair in front of a window with a panoramic view of the Shenandoah Mountains. The medical machinery in the room hummed and beeped, but everything still felt quiet. As I cradled her tiny body wrapped in a hospital blanket and whispered to her how sorry I was that this world had made her so sick, my two-day-old daughter Madalyn died in my arms.

In the days after Madalyn died, I had no clue what to do. Nothing could've prepared me for the despair I felt. What began as a leave of absence from a thrilling world tour to be home for the joy of Madalyn's birth had turned into a nightmare of death, anger, and sorrow. It was excruciating to sit still in all that grief. So fifty days after my daughter's death, I rejoined the tour to escape the reality that was consuming me at home.

Back on the tour, everyone was still having a blast. Lamb of God was attaining unimaginable new heights as a band, and people were celebrating. But I was crushed by grief and trauma. My bandmates were loving and supportive, yet nobody really knew what to do with me. I don't blame them. I didn't know what to do with myself. I disappeared into a black hole of drugs and alcohol.

Now back in this New York City hotel suite, I'm sinking deeper into that void. I wretch and try to clear my throat of the lingering taste of stomach acid. Hoping to break the heat flashes and to shock myself into coherence, I strip down and stagger to the shower, turning the water as cold as it will get. I stand as long as I can under the cold water. The heat flashes finally subside, and I stare at the shower tile thinking about how pathetic this is. I wrap myself in a large bath towel and lay on the bed, still soaking wet, staring at the ceiling. I wake up shivering a few hours later. It's over. But it's a long way from being finished.

Madalyn's death didn't turn me into an addict; I was already well into that process by the time she died. I had been drinking for decades, and my hard drug use had progressed from being sporadic and recreational to being commonplace. The fire was already lit. But the trauma of my infant daughter's death, coupled with my own inability to process the accompanying grief, poured gas on the flames of my steadily progressing addiction.

Horrible things sometimes happen to good people. And when a horrible thing happened to me, it accelerated a descent that I have come to believe was already inevitable. I don't blame the depths of my addiction on Madalyn's death. My short time together with my first-born daughter is not reduced to the nightmare of self-destruction that followed her passing. That's only part of the story.

CHAPTER 1

COLONIAL MOMMA'S BOY

"FOOL YOURSELF"
LITTLE FEAT

One of the most magical things about music for me is how it stirs powerful emotional responses. Stevie Ray Vaughan can make me shed real tears, awestruck by the uninterrupted flow of energy between his pensive soul and his instrument. Billy Gibbons can make me laugh out loud with the playful, cocky swagger of his playing style, jabbing back and forth in a bluesy banter with his rhythm section. Duane Allman makes me feel free and inspired, suddenly aware of the endless possibilities. The right song can take me to a different place in time and can trigger powerful emotional and sensory reactions.

Little Feat's "Fool Yourself" is one of those songs. It feels and sounds like my childhood. It puts me in touch with the earliest versions of myself that I can just barely remember. This isn't because of a specific incident associated with that song. It's broader than that. It's the entire texture and mood. The instrumentation, the tones, the production and the mix, the vocal melodies and swell of the chorus: all these elements exemplify the sounds of the early and mid-'70s imprinted somewhere deep inside my consciousness.

In the late 1990s, I was a regular customer at Plan 9 Records, an independent music store in Richmond, Virginia. I could easily spend an hour flipping through their racks of used LPs, and I usually bought a few. I had been loosely familiar with Little Feat, having heard their hits "Dixie Chicken" and "Fat Man in The Bathtub" all my life. But after exploring Frank Zappa's Mothers of Invention and learning of Lowell George's association with that band, as well his work with the legendary Captain Beefheart, I was interested in digging deeper into George's own band, Little Feat. I bought a beat-up copy of their Dixie Chicken album for $3.

When I flipped the record and dropped the needle on the vinyl for the start of side two, through the pops and crackles a funky drum beat and electric piano riff emerged, setting up Lowell George's soulful interpretation of Fred Tackett's beautifully written song. I was captivated and moved in that supernatural way that music can do. The groove, the arrangement, the melodies, and harmonies made me feel like a young child. I sat crossed legged in front of the record player and soaked up the song and all the feelings it stirred up.

I don't know for certain what inspired Fred Tackett's lyrics, and I'm not sure I ever want to. Often learning what a song is about ruins our own connection to it. For me, "Fool Yourself" is about struggling to navigate life when it's moving faster than we want it to.

On a large peninsula in southeast Virginia, between the James and York Rivers, sits the small town of Williamsburg. Founded in 1632, Williamsburg was a center of early American colonial government. Its residents included founding fathers George Wythe, James Monroe, and Patrick Henry. Along with the nearby landmarks of Jamestown and Yorktown, Williamsburg completes Virginia's "Historic Triangle," a trio of loosely connected living history museums, preserved Revolutionary War battlefields, and restored colonial era settlements. Together with the Busch Gardens theme park, these attractions make Williamsburg the most visited tourist destination in the state, drawing history buffs from all over world.

Williamsburg is also home to the College of William & Mary. Founded in 1693, William & Mary is the second oldest college in the United States. Notoriously selective in its admissions, the college boasts alumni Thomas Jefferson along with other US presidents, Supreme Court justices, and dozens of US senators.

Williamsburg's surrounding areas are much more modest. In contrast to its highbrow identity as a cornerstone of American history and academia, out of view from the picturesque college campus and seasonal tourist attractions, the adjacent communities in outlying James City County have a slow, quiet, small-town feel. Suburban subdivisions mingle with expanses of farmland and forest. Narrow two-lane roads wind through swamps and fields where Revolutionary and Civil War armies once camped. Trailer parks, churches, and cemeteries hide behind strip malls, discount shops, and chain restaurants. Working-class locals earn their living in service and hospitality jobs stemming from Williamsburg's tourist industry or in the massive Anheuser-Busch brewery outside of town. Locals dress head to toe in the colonial-era costumes they wear while working at the historic attractions and then order dinner at drive-thru windows on their way home: the ghosts of our founding fathers ordering a cheeseburger and fries. The pungent, sour smell of fermenting malt and hops periodically blankets sections of town. Nobody seems to mind.

It was here on a Saturday morning, November 25, 1972, that I was born, the third of three boys born to Raymond and Marianne Morton. The first of us, Michael, died a few days after birth from what I've been told was a heart condition. My brother Allan came a year after Michael, and I was born seven years after that. I was a "surprise," which is just a gentler way of saying I was a mistake. But my parents took to the news of an unplanned child excitedly, and my brother was ecstatic to have a little brother.

My father was a quiet and stern man. He had grown up poor in rural Maine, one of five children in a tiny house with no plumbing. There aren't many details of his childhood. My dad rarely spoke about his father, who died when he was twelve. When he did, it was clear my dad and his siblings had grown up with alcoholism and domestic violence. He once told me about a time when, after committing some minor childhood infraction, his drunken father chased him around the backyard, swinging an axe and threatening to kill him. Several years after my father's death, while I was in Maine for some studio work, I visited an elderly aunt who told me how bad the abuse was. It had been directed most intensely at my father and his two brothers.

"You can't even begin to understand the hell those boys went through," she told me. I asked for more details. My aunt stared out of the window of her small, shared room in the residential care facility where she lived.

"You *really* don't want to know," she said.

I took her word for it.

Sadly, the wrath of my dad's father was not softened by his mother, whom I only met a few times. She was reserved and cautious. She showed little outward affection since she was likely in perpetual survival mode because of the abuse she suffered. Even so, despite not having spent much time together, I did feel an unspoken bond with her. She looked me straight in the eye when she spoke to me. More than a few times she mistakenly referred to me by my father's middle name, Russell. I never corrected her. I actually kind of liked it. She was attentive during the few times we were together. But she always struck me as being haunted.

As a teenager, my father couldn't wait to escape, so he dropped out of high school and joined the Army. He was assigned to serve in the military police and was stationed in Frankfurt, Germany. It was there, during his decorated service as a sergeant providing security for supply missions throughout the Berlin blockade crises, that he met my mother in 1959.

My mother was born in Danzig in 1942 during the height of World War II. The city has a complicated history and has long been a part of Poland. However, my mother was born to German parents when the city was considered, at least by Germans, to be part of Germany. She has always identified as German.

My mother grew up during the collapse and aftermath of Nazi Germany, and her earliest memories are of living in makeshift refugee camps. The war left masses of German citizens destitute and homeless, helpless bystanders whose lives had been uprooted in the wake of Hitler's evil. Routinely shuffled from one remote farm town to another, my mother, her siblings, and their mother lived for several years on the charity of farmers and financially well-off families who had more successfully weathered the storm of war. Her father was a conscript in the German army and had been lucky enough to be captured and held as a prisoner of war for much of his time as a soldier. When he was released after the war, he reunited with the family. They settled in Frankfurt to build a new life amidst the reconstruction of post–World War II Germany.

Like my father, my mother experienced significant abuse growing up. Also like my father, she never discussed her trauma with me. But I knew enough about their upbringings to realize that when my mother and my father met, they found in each other a partner in kind. And even though in the beginning they could barely speak each other's language, together they shared a dream of running away somewhere as far away as they could get from everything they had ever known.

That somewhere turned out to be Williamsburg. When my father's deployment to Germany was over, he was transferred to Fort Eustis in Newport News, Virginia. He brought my mother to America with him, and they married immediately, staying in the area after my dad's honorable discharge. Following stints at a freight train company and later as an auto mechanic, my dad took a job at the Ball Metal factory in Williamsburg on a beer can manufacturing line, where he worked for four decades.

By the time I was born, my parents were establishing a comfortable life. They had just bought a modest but newly built house on a quiet cul-de-sac cut into a massive expanse of forest just outside Williamsburg. My mother stayed home with me for the first few years of my life, earning extra money by babysitting other kids during the day. She was the first to notice my interest in music.

My parents weren't musicians, but there was always music in our house. They loved early rock and roll from the 1950s. "Stagger Lee" by Lloyd Price was one of my dad's favorite songs, and my mom loved Elvis Presley. We had a gigantic combination television and record player in the living room. As a toddler, I sat in front of that monstrosity of an entertainment center wearing headphones way too big for me. I listened to everything from rock 'n' roll and classic country from my parents' record collection. I even listened to classical music recommended by our neighbor in a futile attempt to culture me early.

My mother told me that I impressed her friends with my ability to pick out specific Elvis records by song title long before I could read the titles on the label.

When I was three, my mom took a job at a local bank, so I started spending my days at the home of a close family friend who also watched several kids during the week. I transitioned easily to my new babysitter. There were plenty of kids to play with. We watched *Mister Rogers' Neighborhood* and *Sesame Street*. We had full reign of their fenced-in backyard.

Our small, middle-class, multiracial neighborhood was full of kids of all ages. We used the vacant lot near our house for pickup football games and as a meeting spot. Neighborhood dogs, including ours, roamed freely, and nobody seemed to mind. Older kids raced go-karts back and forth down our street. On summer evenings, county service trucks drove down our street, spraying a thick fog of mosquito repellant, often with a small group of us neighborhood kids following close behind on our bicycles. We liked the smell of the chemicals.

The forest and long stretches of land along the power lines adjacent to our neighborhood were our big playground. We built elaborate forts, digging trenches and covering them with scraps of wood from nearby building sites. We played war and had dirt clod fights. We gathered around drainage ditches and watched with morbid curiosity as older teenagers with pellet guns killed defenseless frogs one after another. We picked wild blackberries by the bucket, our hands stained by the indigo juice of the ripe berries and by our own blood drawn by the unavoidable thorns. We ate tomatoes and cucumbers pulled from the large garden that my father kept at the back of our yard.

In the fall, my dad spent many weekends deep in the woods near our house, cutting firewood to heat our home during the upcoming winter. Allan helped by stacking the cut logs onto the pickup truck and sometimes even wielding the chainsaw. I was allowed to tag along but was too young to help, so I'd wander into the woods and play.

My brother and my dad were close. They were always working on some project: stacking firewood, changing the oil in the car, tuning up a lawnmower. They were a team, one I longed to be a part of but felt disconnected from. Allan was our father's apprentice, absorbing everything our dad taught him. But I was different. I was much more outwardly sensitive. I was anxious and clumsy, not as rugged and not as tough, but more timid. I was a momma's boy.

My dad was stern and unaffectionate, but I knew that he loved me. He always made himself available, and he treated my brother and me fairly. I don't recall my dad ever spanking us or using any physical discipline on us, likely due to his own childhood spent on the receiving end of physical violence. (My mom gave out the spankings.) My dad was a provider and a protector who made me feel safe. But I could feel that my father was more in tune with my brother than he was with me. I always felt like I wasn't living up to his expectations. The close connection that my brother and I shared helped to bridge that gap. Being significantly older than me, Allan was as much a role model for me as my father was. But I longed to have a closer bond with my father. I wanted him to be proud of me.

But whatever disconnection I felt from my father growing up was offset by my close bond with my mother. She was loving and affectionate. She cooked dinner and baked desserts and kept our house immaculate. She loved sewing and knitting, making dresses from patterns, and crocheting blankets. She kept plants in every room and always had an arrangement of fresh flowers on the kitchen table. My mother found beauty in the everyday things and reminded us to keep that perspective.

My dad's job at the beer can factory paid well. His own strong work ethic had him climbing the ranks at the company, moving from entry level assembly line work into a management position with his own office. His career success coupled with my mom's entry into the workforce at the bank afforded us some small luxuries. One of those was travel.

Because she lived so far away from her homeland, regular trips back to Germany were important to my mother. My dad didn't share this desire to stay in touch with his roots and rarely returned to Maine, but he supported my mom's need to stay in touch with hers. And she usually took me with her. Some of my earliest memories are from Germany: the playground behind my grandparents' Frankfurt apartment complex, the smell of my grandfather's cigar, the sound of the European ambulances. My uncle, a successful businessman in the trucking industry, took time off from work to drive us into the countryside to see castles and landmarks.

Back at home things were changing. I was too young to understand why, but the mood around our house was becoming tense. There was a feeling of discordance. My dad spent longer hours at work and more time in the garage. Conversations were short and cold. My mom had become rail thin. My parents laughed less and argued more; this tension took its toll on me emotionally. I became more and more anxious as I carried the burden of my parents' unhappiness. The carefree, naive bliss in my childhood faded away quickly and was replaced by fear, uncertainty, and self-criticism. I thought that perhaps if I could stay quiet and out of the way, maybe my dad might be less frustrated. If I could be more helpful and less needy, my mom might not seem so sad and overwhelmed. I wanted things to be like they used to be, but I didn't know how to get that back. My life was transitioning into something different, and that scared me.

DESOLATION

My dad's upward mobility at work meant that we would be moving into a new—and nicer—neighborhood. It also meant I would be starting at a new elementary school without my friends from our old neighborhood. My brother was a junior in high school and had plans to go away to college soon, so it didn't affect him as much. But my whole world was changing, and I didn't want it to.

Our new house was a custom-built brick ranch-style home in the upscale neighborhood of Windsor Forest. Though it was only a couple of miles from our old neighborhood, there was a different vibe. My ramshackle forts and drainage ditch playgrounds were replaced by tennis courts and a swim team at the private neighborhood pool. But I didn't play tennis, and nobody talked to me at the pool. I didn't fit in. I was too nervous to try to make any new friends. I was lonely and sad.

My parents were lonely and sad too. They were having marital issues. My dad was always working. My mom's bank job and duties as a homemaker kept her busy. They were losing connection with each other, and the stress of moving into an expensive new house while preparing to pay for my brother's college made it worse. I didn't know how to process the changes. Why did we have to move away? What was wrong with our old house? Why were my mom and dad fighting? How can I make it stop? Did I do something wrong? I wanted to disappear.

I reacted to these heavy concerns by isolating with my new best friends. But these new friends didn't go to my school: my new best friends were food and television, both easy fixes for boredom and loneliness. Food—sugar in particular—was my first drug. Compulsive eating was my first display of addictive behavior. I sought comfort in food. I wasn't eating out of hunger but instead to soothe myself, to change the way I felt. Food provided a dependable distraction. It gave me pleasure. This fundamental component of addiction—reacting to an emotional state by taking or consuming something to alter that state—reappeared later in my life in far more dangerous and consequential ways.

We eventually settled into our new life. My parents busied themselves establishing our new household, meeting our neighbors, and finding new routines. Landscaping projects and decorating our new house kept them distracted from their marital problems. Meanwhile, I ate junk food and played video games on the Atari 2600 gaming system I'd gotten for Christmas.

Although we were all navigating the challenges that come with change, life wasn't all bad. My dad started buying used cars at auction and fixing them up to resell, which turned out to be a good supplement to his already respectable income from the can factory, but I think he just did it because he enjoyed it and because he liked the hustle. His favorite cars were Lincoln Continentals and Cadillac Coupe DeVilles. Every few weeks my dad drove a different Lincoln or Cadillac, and he always had a fat wad of hundred-dollar bills folded up in his pocket, quick cash from his car dealing.

The best part about all of this was that I felt included. On Saturdays, my dad took me to a car auction in Chesapeake, about an hour from where we lived. I walked through the rows of cars with him as he took notes and jotted down the numbers of the cars he intended to bid on. Sometimes he sent me across the large lot full of cars to verify a detail on a specific car. I was thrilled to be his assistant. I was great at identifying cars by their year, make, and model. Standing next to him during the auctions, I learned to understand the rapid, rolling flow of the auctioneer's voice. Old men chewed tobacco and spit in the gravel. I studied my dad's subtle nods and slight hand gestures as he committed to each rising price or withdrew from the bidding completely. My dad was stone faced and stoic, and I was proud to be next to him. He was my hero.

At the end of the summer of 1982, my father, mother, and I drove my brother four hours west to start his freshman year of college at Radford University. I was almost ten years old and probably a little too old to cry the way I did when we dropped him off. But my dad didn't scold me for it. He was probably hurting too.

CHAPTER 2

THE FAT KID

"NERVOUS BREAKDOWN"
BLACK FLAG

Black Flag's "Nervous Breakdown" is the perfect punk rock song. Fans and critics can debate the significance of British punk versus American punk, question the authenticity of the Sex Pistols' calculated tantrums, and even argue about what does or does not qualify as true punk. The beauty of these abstract deliberations is that everyone can be right and wrong simultaneously. But for me, "Nervous Breakdown" has all the elements that make punk rock thrilling. Greg Ginn's sharp cornered guitar riff struts and stumbles with a pulse that feels both confident and agitated. His tone and attack are abrasive and bark out a steady, impatient cadence that demands reaction.

Ginn's swaggering riff is a hook by itself, but it's Keith Morris's manic vocal performance that propels the intensity of the song. The singer's panicked confessions of mental instability sound urgent and genuine. I believe him. Yet Morris delivers his open vulnerability with a bold, confrontational sneer. He embodies the flawed hero. Morris is actively falling apart in front of us, but we still want to be like him because he makes it look and sound so fucking cool.

"Nervous Breakdown" will forever remind me of being a kid skateboarding through the streets of Williamsburg, gliding through our little suburb of nowhere just barely beginning to understand that I wasn't the only one that felt confused and overwhelmed by anxiety. Punk rock music carried the message that we were all a little twisted. And sometimes it felt good to shout about it.

The first time someone called me fat, I was eleven or twelve years old. I was walking with a couple of kids from my neighborhood. Trying to be funny, I was teasing a scrawny kid about the perils of moving on to a new school and being picked on by older kids.

"You'd better start pumping some iron!" I laughed, showing off for a girl walking with us.

But my intended barb didn't work as planned. The girl quickly chimed in, defending her friend. "Yeah, but you're fat! What are *you* going to do?"

I was speechless. I tried to mask my embarrassment with a nervous laugh. I was fat? How did this happen? *When* did this happen? Had everyone been laughing at me behind my back all this time? I wanted to run away and hide.

I don't think I knew that I had put on quite a lot of weight in a fairly short period of time. Physical and emotional changes were happening fast, so it hadn't occurred to me that I was becoming the "fat kid." But now I was, and apparently I was the last to know.

Of course, most kids get teased or taunted at some point. It's a part of growing up. You learn to shrug it off, you toughen up, and you move on. And this event was not some unimaginable trauma. It was an ordinary jab that I had coming to me: I had been dishing it out, and you shouldn't talk trash if you can't take it too.

However, the revelation that I was now the fat kid went far deeper for me than just a playground insult. It was a pivotal turning point in the way that I would perceive my own self-worth from that day on. The disproportionate significance of what should have been an incidental slight was that, for the first time, I felt an all-consuming sense of inadequacy. The embarrassment of a physical flaw pointed out in public unlocked overwhelming fear, self-doubt, and self-loathing that had been lurking under the surface.

In that moment, my mind shifted. I saw myself as not good enough and as unworthy of being loved. I convinced myself that I was a disappointment to my parents and my friends. I blamed myself for not being as good at sports as my peers, for not being popular, for not being cool. And while I had already been carrying those emotions, I had never been able to characterize my discomfort, to put a label on it. But now I had a clear reason to despise myself.

These were unreasonably severe reactions to being called fat, but reason played little part. What should have simply been an innocuous insult instead started the psychological war that I would wage against myself for decades. The self-obsession, self-hatred, and self-pity that emerged from this war was the groundwork for the mindset that fueled my addictions later in life.

Soon afterward, my behavior changed. I began wearing the same clothes all the time, convincing myself that certain outfits made me appear thinner. Oversized shirts, I reasoned, made my body look proportionately smaller, and there were a couple of favorites that I believed hid me the best. Of course, I didn't appear any different.

I just looked like a chubby kid wearing the same muumuu he wore yesterday. And while showing up to school every day in the same shirt from the day before certainly didn't earn me any cool points, the repetition made me feel safe. I was terrified of being noticed, yet I convinced myself that if I always looked the same, everyone would stop noticing me. But this had the opposite effect: the very thing I was doing to avoid attention was likely drawing unwanted attention to myself.

Besides trying to hide in my clothes, other strange behaviors emerged. I developed odd body postures. To make my bulging stomach appear flatter, I would suck in my gut and hold it in as tight as I could for as long as I could. For a while, whenever I stood or walked, I'd hold my breath with the futile hope of changing my appearance into something I thought would conceal my true body shape. It hadn't yet occurred to me that this uncomfortable stance made my soft, pudgy chest protrude more than usual, accentuating the flabby breasts I had developed because of being overweight. Before long, some classmates publicly pointed this out, adding to my embarrassment.

My reaction was to continue to alter my posture, but this time it wasn't as much of a deliberate strategy as it was a subconscious reaction. Imagine trying to stand in a way that made you invisible. I was so terrified of being seen that I was trying to use my own body to hide itself. With my head down, my back rolled forward, and my shoulders pushed up to my ears, I lumbered through the school halls, eyes fixed to the floor, anxiously hoping to reach my next class without making any eye contact or talking to anyone.

Over time, my fear and anxiety manifested in new ways. Dressing the same every day had served a practical purpose, but now I began to compulsively act out routines that reflected a growing obsession with symmetry and balance. If I opened a cabinet door, I had to open the opposing door, shut them both, then repeat the process in reverse order. I'd start the entire process again, in the opposite order, and finally a third time in which I opened and closed both doors simultaneously. This kept all things correct, balanced, and equal. I'd nervously tap out rhythmic sequences with my teeth using either side of my jaw to complete the pattern, reverse the order, then start the process again in opposite order to keep it balanced. This ritual could go on for indeterminate lengths of time until some distraction mercifully pulled me out of it.

Although I've let most of these behaviors go, some of them are still there: all light switches in my home have to be pointed in a certain way. When I'm pulling items off the shelf in the grocery store, I still stick to certain specific patterns and feel uneasy if I ignore the impulse to do so. And I still usually wear the same clothes every day. If you look in my dresser, you'd find a few pairs of black jeans and seven or eight versions of the same plain black T-shirt.

Yet as gloomy as all of this sounds, there were also some exciting changes. It was the mid-1980s, and skateboarding culture was having one of its heydays. Ramp skaters like Tony Hawk and Christian Hosoi had become mainstream celebrities. Their daredevil athleticism and West Coast punk rock brand of cool made them heroes to me and to my small group of relatively marginalized friends. We loved that skateboarding and its culture had an air of defiance. The fashion was ragtag and sloppy, leaving ample room for creativity and self-expression. Even the act of skating itself felt subversive. With our duct-taped shoes, oversized T-shirts, and army surplus jackets, we turned the sleepy streets of Williamsburg into our own skatepark. I was not the best of the bunch. While my friends were learning acrobatic tricks, it was all I could do to push along and keep up with the pack. But it hardly mattered that I sucked at skateboarding. The camaraderie I felt was a lifeline because for the first time in my life, I had an identity.

In addition to my newfound infatuation with skateboard culture, another force was beginning to take hold in my life, one that was far more powerful: music. As a young child, I was enamored with the sounds of Kiss, Van Halen, Lynyrd Skynyrd, and other great '70s bands coming from the 8-track tape player in my older brother's bedroom. Thanks to him, a solid education in great hard rock music had long been in place.

My taste in music by this time had expanded to include more modern metal bands like Iron Maiden, Def Leppard, Twisted Sister, and Mötley Crüe, all of whom were enjoying mainstream success. Up until this point, I just listened to music. But then it occurred to me that I might actually be able to *play* music. Not music like I had played back in fifth grade when I was a nervous and mediocre third chair snare drummer in music class. Instead, I wanted to play music like the type I had been listening to and had started to see on television.

At this time in the 1980s, MTV, which had only recently made it into my neighborhood, actually played music videos all day every day. It hadn't yet become the home for fake drama and scripted "reality" television. Each afternoon, I came straight home from school and watched masters like Eddie Van Halen and Prince exhibit effortless command over their instruments. I couldn't get enough of it. For me and millions of other young music fans, MTV created a new, more direct relationship between the music we loved and the people who made it. There was something captivating about seeing the artists performing. Watching band members interact, each playing their own integral role toward a common purpose, looked magical to me.

I was particularly mesmerized by guitar players. Steve Stevens's blistering solo in Billy Idol's "Rebel Yell," Gary Richrath's soaring leads in the live video of REO Speedwagon's "Ridin' the Storm Out," and Brian Setzer's hip, throwback swagger in Stray Cats' "Stray Cat Strut" all captivated me. I wanted to be in a band and I wanted to play guitar. I believed these things might be possible. And I was twelve years old.

There was one small problem: I knew nothing about guitars. Grateful to see me exploring different interests, my parents supported my quest to buy one. I scanned ads in a local newspaper and found a modest beginner model guitar that my parents bought. For the reasonable price of $15, my entire life changed.

I didn't realize that this nylon string classical-style guitar was an odd choice for an aspiring rock musician, but it didn't matter. I didn't even know how to tune my new instrument, but that didn't matter either. I was still figuring out how to just make sounds with it. Once I figured out where to put my fingers between the frets to properly sound a note, I was off and running. I plucked out what I thought sounded like "Should I Stay or Should I Go" by the Clash. My one string rendition, complete with the percussive string scrapes between the notes, had me feeling pretty accomplished. The Kinks' "You Really Got Me" followed, on one string and very likely in the wrong key. But I didn't care because I was becoming a guitar player.

Yet despite my progress, I was still unsatisfied. I couldn't make the guitar sound like I wanted it to sound. All the music I liked had a heavy guitar presence that somehow sounded...loud. For that, I was going to need an electric guitar. My parents came through again, so after a few months of plucking relentlessly on that little nylon string acoustic, I leveled up to my first electric guitar and a small practice amp. Another odd choice for a beginner, the guitar was a Hondo replica of a Gibson Explorer. It was massive, heavy, and awkward to handle. I absolutely loved it. The amp was a small Crate practice amp. This new equipment was much better suited to my goals, but it still left me searching for the perfect sound. Turns out that sound was called *distortion*. That's what makes guitars sound heavy and overdriven. I added a distortion effects pedal, and things fell into place.

The only problem was that I didn't know how to properly play any-thing. I needed lessons.

I started taking beginner's guitar lessons from a local Williams-burg musician named Cabot Wade. Cabot was a phenomenal first teacher. He was patient, encouraging, and enthusiastic. He played in a local working band with a massive repertoire of covers and originals. Cabot was a full-time musician with plenty of experience playing gigs, and he also had some studio experience. He had briefly been married to the actor Glenn Close in the early '70s when they had both been a part of the Up with People performing arts collective.

I took lessons with Cabot for the next year and a half in a side room at a local recording studio called Fresh Tracks. I was an atten-tive student, though as we progressed, I did what most guitar students end up doing: I began practicing what I wanted to practice instead of what I had been assigned. Trying to figure out AC/DC and Van Halen riffs was more appealing than learning basic music theory and scale modes. Still, I was moving forward, gaining a decent foundation of basic chord and scale structures from my lessons while keeping it fun by learning some cool riffs and songs. Cabot even arranged my first gig. He put together a group of kids he had been teaching into a little pickup band to perform at a local arts festival in Williamsburg. I played bass because another one of his students was a little further along than me on guitar. But that hardly mattered. I could've played the triangle and I would've been happy.

By now, you may sense a paradox. Aspiring to perform on stage was—and still is—contradictory to my self-conscious and introverted nature. I have yet to figure out this paradox, but it's not that uncom-mon among musicians. This strange drive to be on stage under the lights while simultaneously being terrified of being seen under those same lights will probably never make sense to me. Psychological conundrums aside, our little pickup band played "Every Breath You

Take" by the Police and "Wipeout" by the Ventures. It was both terrifying and exhilarating, even though I'm sure we weren't very good.
The only thing that mattered was that I finally felt like I was on my
way to getting good at *something*. I was committed. Thanks to my
parents' support and Cabot's patience, I was learning to play.

My newfound obsession with the guitar and my acceptance
among a small group of skater kids were welcome developments.
Though I continued to suck at skating, it was fun to be around friends,
and the culture made us feel like we were part of something. I also
gravitated toward other kids who were musical and jumped at any
chance to make noise with them. My friend Clark had a drum set and
a keyboard and was decent at both. My parents let him bring over his
kit, tolerating the noise for a few hours in the room above the garage
when we got together. Another friend, Joel, was already a skilled pianist
by junior high. He could easily play Van Halen's "Jump" and Mötley
Crüe's "Home Sweet Home" on his keyboard, which was more than
enough motivation for me to learn the relatively rudimentary guitar
parts to those songs. Some weekends I spent the night at Joel's house,
and we'd play those songs over and over. He was more advanced than
me, but he always patiently indulged my requests to play it some more.

Skateboarding and music inevitably led me to punk rock. As the
home to the College of William & Mary, Williamsburg had a hip
local record store and an equally cool college radio station. Both were
rich resources in my punk rock education. I dove headfirst into Black
Flag, Circle Jerks, Dead Kennedys, Sex Pistols, and anything else that
seemed aggressive and subversive. The timing was perfect. Most punk
rock required fairly minimal technical skills to play. The song structures tended to be simple, but their aggression was fun to play along
with. Black Flag's "Nervous Breakdown" was an immediate favorite.
Greg Ginn's fuzzed out and boxy riff combined with Keith Morris's
unhinged performance, a seemingly self-diagnosed psychotic break,

encapsulated everything that thrilled me about punk rock in just over two minutes.

It was also around this time that I took my first drink of alcohol. It was relatively uneventful. I've heard alcoholics in recovery share that their first drink was life changing, an instant solution to what had been a disconnected existence full of anxiety and self-loathing. I find these testimonies to be compelling. I almost envy the profound relief that these people felt in that moment. However, that was not my experience. On that fall afternoon when a handful of my skate punk friends and I made our way to the old abandoned, overgrown amphitheater adjacent to the William & Mary campus, armed with a couple six-packs of beer, some wine coolers, and some cigarettes, I found no guiding lights or solutions to my anxiety and self-doubt. The shitty beer tasted like shitty beer, and the wine coolers tasted like juice that had gone bad. The cigarettes stunk and made me feel dizzy and a little queasy.

However, what I did find that day was acceptance. I had been allowed to participate in our adventure. I was part of the pack. We were misbehaving, and this misbehavior made me feel independent and mature. Most of all, though, I felt validated. My inclusion implied trust. Trust that I wouldn't tell. Trust that I could handle it. And all of these things were true. Soon after, I smoked pot for the first time with a friend after school, huddled under the back porch of my house, awkwardly holding in the stinging smoke, waiting for something magical to happen. Nothing did. I didn't feel high at all. But I did feel cool.

CHAPTER 3

CHEESE
AND BUTTER

"DRIVER 8"
R.E.M.

By the 1990s, R.E.M. was one of the biggest bands in the world. Releasing chart-topping albums, dominating airplay at MTV and rock radio, and selling out arenas, the band had become a household name. But in the early and mid-1980s, R.E.M. was a college rock band. They were a jangly blend of classic rock, folk, punk, and country with genuine vulnerability and threads of Southern culture running through it all. This was the R.E.M. I knew first.

I don't remember where I first heard R.E.M., and that may be because they have always sounded so familiar to me. R.E.M. had a depth to their sound that was beyond just rock for the sake of rocking. The lyrics seemed more like poetry than a rock song. It was perhaps slightly pretentious at times, but when it worked they had a fragility and level of introspection that set them far apart from their peers.

Growing up in a small town in southeast Virginia, I had few options for seeing live music. We didn't have much of a local music scene. The few young bands around had to be creative about finding ways to put on shows. When I was in eighth grade, one of those bands was the Eddies.

The Eddies were a three-piece band made up of students from our local high school. They played mostly covers of songs by their own punk and alternative heroes. I first watched them perform an all-ages show at the Williamsburg Regional Library in front of a small gathering of local kids, and they became our heroes. I had barely started playing guitar, but I was already realizing that music was all I wanted to do. The rock stars I was seeing on MTV might as well have been from another planet. It all looked magical and unattainable. But watching the Eddies that night made music feel possible. These were kids from my town, going to the same schools I was going to. They were playing "Driver 8" by R.E.M. right in front of me. And they were good.

A year or two later, the Eddies' guitar player Mike Derks moved from Williamsburg to Richmond and joined a new theatrical band called Gwar. They went on to massive international success and eventually took my band Lamb of God out as a support act on our first national tour. The Eddies' bassist Bobby Donne also moved to Richmond after high school and formed the pioneering instrumental math metal punk hybrid Breadwinner. Their oblong grooves and angular, off-kilter rhythms were a huge influence on the early Lamb of God material and played a major role in developing our own sonic identity.

Standing in the library watching the Eddies play "Driver 8," I couldn't have imagined all of that was going to happen.

A t the end of summer 1986, I began my freshman year at Lafayette High School. My hometown of Williamsburg is small. In the 1980s, it was even smaller. It was the kind of place where kids graduated high school with a lot of the same people they started kindergarten with. Williamsburg moved slowly, in a way that made it feel disconnected from the cities and towns around it. It was a suburb without a city. Changes were few, like the occasional new shopping center or preplanned housing development carved into the surrounding sprawling forests. But while Williamsburg may have felt frozen in time, I wasn't. I was determined to change. I had never been good at anything, but I was focused on finding something that would change that.

I briefly attempted reinvention as I prepared to enter high school. At the end of eighth grade, I was approached by a couple of classmates who were already training with the high school junior varsity wrestling team. They were athletic and competitive, but they were also nice kids who I'd always gotten along with growing up. There was an opening on their wrestling squad, they explained, and they needed someone to compete in one of the unoccupied weight classes. I could barely believe my ears when they told me I would be perfect for the position. I was being recruited! As it turned out, what they were actually saying was that there was no other kid around who was *heavy* enough to meet the weight requirement for that class but who also might still be able to learn basic wrestling techniques just well enough to fill the slot. This was not a glorious introduction into my wrestling career. But despite the humbling circumstances, it was an opportunity to be a part of something. I also knew that practicing with a sports team would get me into better shape. And it would be fun. Maybe I would even win some matches!

I started attending daily workouts with the team shortly before the beginning of my freshman year. I learned some beginner's wrestling moves, but more than anything, I ran. And ran some more. We ran lap after lap around the school, then we ran more. Long after I assumed that we must have done enough running, we continued to run. I had never experienced that level of physical exertion. But I promised myself that I would stick with it for at least a little while. I didn't want to quit immediately. The workouts never got any easier, but they did get slightly less shocking once I started to know what to expect.

As soon as I knew a few basic moves, I was put into scrimmage matches with some of the better wrestlers on our team. My teammates took great joy in quickly tying me up like a pretzel whenever they wanted. They laughingly mimicked the exasperated sounds I made as the breath left my body during these scrimmages. Still, I wasn't disheartened. I was new to all of this and hadn't set high expectations. And despite their mimicking, my friends on the team supported me and tried to teach me how to wrestle, so I didn't mind laughing along with them at my ineptitude. It *was* actually pretty funny.

I was entered into a couple of matches as the season began. I started my wrestling career with an undefeated record. Admittedly, the other team didn't have a wrestler in my weight class, so it was victory by default. But in my first actual competitive match, my opponent quickly defeated me. Learning from my scrimmage experiences, I tried my best to maintain my dignity by keeping my gasps and groans to a minimum.

However, as the novelty of the wrestling team started wearing off, I realized that it wasn't for me. The workouts weren't the issue; they were brutal, but I could tolerate them. And it wasn't my teammates either. They were cool and helpful, which I appreciated. I didn't even mind not being good since I was used to not being good at much of anything. The simple fact was that I just didn't look forward to any of it. Nothing about it intrigued me. It was clear that I just wasn't a wrestler, so I quietly quit the team. I don't think anyone even noticed.

As my freshman year established its rhythm, I trudged through Lafayette's mazes of windowless hallways drenched in harsh, fluorescent light, feeling as awkward and self-conscious as ever. My attempt at wrestling had fallen flat, but fortunately a greater calling was becoming louder and louder: my passion for music. I was always thinking about exploring new bands and artists, analyzing the styles and repertoires of legendary guitarists, and learning to play my own guitar. My parents had set me up with good beginner guitar gear, and I was taking regular lessons from a great teacher. I was learning quickly. Music was taking over.

In addition to my parents' backing, my brother Allan, seven years older than me, was a huge supporter of my musical ambitions. That age difference seemed more pronounced when we were young. Allan was a mentor to me growing up. I looked up to everything he did. Our bond was tight, and Allan happily included me in many of his pursuits. He'd take me riding on his Honda XR75 motorcycle down the winding trails and along the stretches of power lines just beyond our tiny cul-de-sac. I'd sit cross legged on the gas tank, hands gripping the cross bar of the handlebars, hanging on for dear life. I'd howl with excitement over the growl of the small four-stroke engine. I felt like Evel Knievel.

"Quit pulling!" he'd yell when my exuberance convinced me that I was the one steering our course. "You're gonna wreck us!"

One time, his predictions came true. Allan was thirteen, so I was only six. Anxiously anticipating a curve in the trail ahead of us, I pulled sharply at the handlebars, which caught Allan by surprise. With no warning and no time to counteract my impulse, he was unable to correct what I had done. We veered off the worn-down clay path into the briars and brush alongside the trail. Allan slammed on the brakes, and the bike tipped over sideways, coming to rest flat in the weeds. One of my legs was pinned under the weight of the motorcycle as the scorching exhaust pipe burned into my skin. I yelled, half from pain and half from fear. Realizing what was happening, Allan threw the bike off me, picked me up, and checked me over for injuries. I had just a minor burn on my leg and a couple of tears. We picked ourselves up and rode home.

"You're alright," he reassured me. "But how many times do I have to tell you to stop pulling?"

Besides our shared love of motorcycles, Allan and I also listened to a lot of the same music. Like everyone else in my family, Allan wasn't a musician, but he loved hard rock, Southern rock, and early heavy metal. By the time I began to pick up the guitar, his taste in music had already influenced my own tastes. He took pride in watching me learn how to play some of his own favorite songs. Van Halen's "Ain't Talkin' 'Bout Love," Lynyrd Skynyrd's "Sweet Home Alabama," and Ozzy Osbourne's "Crazy Train" were some of the first riffs I mastered.

On weekend evenings, Allan often drove me to the neighboring cities of Hampton and Norfolk to explore musical instrument stores that were larger than the friendly but tiny family-owned music store in Williamsburg. We'd drive an hour down I-64 East, blasting cassette tapes on the Pioneer tape deck in his little red Toyota 4×4 pickup truck. On the way down, I dissected the differences in the tones and techniques of the masterful guitarists coming out of the speakers. There was Boston's Tom Scholz with his anthemic melodies and multiple harmonies stacked in thick layers on top of one another; Aerosmith's Joe Perry with his fluid, slippery swagger; Dokken's George Lynch with his modern, acrobatic flash and speed; and ZZ Top's Billy Gibbons with his authentic Texas boogie and soul-crushing blues. All were masters of their craft, but they were so different from one another. I recognized early on that the guitarists who moved me the most had their own unique voice on the instrument.

As much as I enjoyed our interstate listening sessions, the payoff came at the music store. I felt like a kid in a candy store at places like Alpha Music in Virginia Beach and Three Guys Music in Newport News. All I wanted to do was listen to the questions the customers asked the store clerks and watch the players show off their latest riffs. I absorbed everything. Allan was endlessly patient as I drifted slowly around the store. I stared at the walls of guitars, daydreaming about what they would sound like as I played them. Some had sharp, angular body shapes. They looked like weapons. Others were more traditionally shaped, with curved, flowing contours and deep, colorful sunburst finishes. I began to understand that a player's choice of guitar reflected their personality and style.

As my playing ability grew, so did my confidence. I began asking the salespeople if I could try out some guitars and amplifiers. After a while, once Allan and I had become regular visitors at several of the stores in the area, the staff let me play anything I wanted. This gave me access to all the latest pro quality gear, even if only for an hour at a time. Classic guitars like Gibson Les Pauls and Fender Telecasters, popular modern guitars of the day made by Kramer and B.C. Rich, and the Marshall amps that my favorite guitarists played on MTV were now within my reach.

But one guitar caught my attention. It was a Tobacco Sunburst Gibson Les Paul Junior, just like the guitar made famous by Leslie West of Mountain. Most of my guitar heroes played hot-rodded modern variations of the classic Fender Strat design, and I typically gravitated toward those. Yet there was something special about this particular Les Paul. It felt good in my hands, and I looked forward to playing it. With a Marshall amp next to me, I'd post up on a stool and pound out the riffs to Led Zeppelin's "Whole Lotta Love," Jimi

Hendrix's "Purple Haze," and Black Sabbath's "Paranoid." It was like being in a trance. And sometimes I'd lift my head up to realize that people had gathered around to watch me play. I was young and had gotten good quickly. I found these situations to be both terrifying and thrilling. The paradox of being a self-conscious introvert while simultaneously feeling compelled to nervously perform in front of people would prove to be a lifelong riddle.

These weekend trips to the city convinced me that I was going to need some better gear. That would require money—which meant I needed a job. And finding a job as a ninth grader in a small town meant I needed rides. Once again I had to count on my parents' support and assistance.

At first, my parents didn't see eye to eye on this. My mother was apprehensive. "It's still a little too early for you to start working a real job," she warned me. "You don't have to be in such a hurry. Those days will come soon enough without you rushing into it."

My father, however, was less concerned. He had grown up dirt poor in a house without plumbing. He had worked harder as a child than some people ever do as adults. He saw having a job as a good thing, a character builder. "It'll be good for him," he countered. "It's not too soon for him to start learning what it takes to put a couple dollars in his pocket." After some deliberation, my mother relented, and I was given the green light to make some money.

My first attempt at a job was as a laborer at a local produce farm, where my friend Geoff had been working. *It was hard work but fun*, he promised. I liked Geoff because he was independent and confident without being particularly popular or even concerned about being popular. He was from northern England and had spent most of his childhood there. Until Geoff, I had never heard anyone pronounce the *th* sound as an *f* sound, so my *thing* was his *fing*. At first, I thought Geoff had a speech impediment. I never said a word about it because

I didn't want him to feel self-conscious. Only later did I learn that it was a part of the dialect from where he grew up.

What I also liked about Geoff was that England had given him early exposure to a world of metal that I was not too familiar with. Geoff was a massive Iron Maiden fan. I was somewhat familiar with Maiden and particularly liked *The Number of the Beast* and *Piece of Mind* albums. The elaborate interwoven guitar compositions and operatic vocals were top tier in their musicality but still maintained a vital heaviness. Bruce Dickinson's lyrics tell vivid stories of mythological heroes and wartime legends, all of which captivated my adolescent imagination.

But Geoff's knowledge of hard rock and metal ran deeper than just Iron Maiden. He was also into less mainstream bands like Savatage, Grim Reaper, and Motörhead. Geoff was also the first person I knew who was a King Diamond fan. He knew the band members' names, all the lyrics, the stories behind the lyrics, everything. While I didn't like those smaller bands as much as he did, I liked that he knew so much about them.

It was on Geoff's recommendation that I applied for the job as a farmhand the spring of my freshman year. On our work days, a small group of us rode the bus after school and got dropped off at the farm to work a few hours until dinnertime, when our parents picked us up. The bus rides were more enjoyable than the job. On the way to work, Geoff and I talked music, debating the appeal of Mercyful Fate versus King Diamond and imagining an alternate universe in which Bruce Dickinson had not replaced Paul Di'Anno in Iron Maiden.

One day, after a few shifts of picking and sorting vegetables and cleaning up the barn, I was sent out to the field with a group of young farmhands. Our job was to grab the fresh bales of hay as the baling machine spit them out. We were supposed to throw them onto a flatbed trailer that was being pulled by a separate tractor. Simple enough.

But as the operation began, I realized that this would be harder than it sounded. The bales were heavy, and the tractor's machines were loud and intimidating. Everything was also happening fast. I tried to keep up with the others, who had all done this before. Geoff encouraged me by showing me how best to grab the bales and how to position myself next to the trailer to ensure I hit my target. I wanted so badly to be as good as the others, but it was difficult to keep up with the pace.

Soon there was a more debilitating obstacle, separate from my anxiety and inexperience. As the dust and dirt swirled through the air, my face began to itch. My eyes swelled each time I rubbed them. My nose was gushing, my eyes were watering, and I couldn't stop sneezing. This was literal hay fever. I was supposed to be hurling heavy bales of hay onto a moving flatbed trailer; instead, I could barely see in between sneezes. I must've looked as helpless as I felt. It wasn't long before the head farmer mercifully yelled for me to head back up to the barn.

It was my last day on the job. Blaming my allergic reaction, the farm boss gently broke it to me that I wasn't going to work out. I'm sure if allergies had been the only issue, he could've suggested some Benadryl. This one hurt. I once again felt inadequate.

My failure as a farmhand was a letdown, but I rebounded quickly because my broader objective was all about funding my musical pursuits. I started asking around about another job. A couple of my skateboarding buddies had summer jobs as busboys at a seafood restaurant in town. There was a position open in the kitchen, and on their dual recommendation, I got the job. I oversaw the cheese and butter trays!

My routine was simple. When diners first arrived, they were brought a serving tray with crackers and two glass bowls, one filled with a processed cheddar-like cheese spread and the other filled with a whipped butter-like substance. They snacked on cheese and butter and crackers until their food came out, at which point the trays went back to the kitchen. This is where I came in: I refilled the bowls of cheese and butter. Finally, here was a job I could handle.

During my training, I learned of an alarming—and disgusting— part of the job. I was explicitly instructed *not* to empty the bowls before refilling them. Apparently, that would've been a waste of good cheese and butter (or whatever those substances were). I was instead told to layer new cheese and butter directly over whatever remaining portion was in the used bowls, cavalierly slathering over cracker crumbs and whatever else might have made its way into the bowls. We couldn't even be bothered with removing the crumbs from the used bowls.

This was the routine, table after table and night after night, for a week or more at a time. The bowls were rarely emptied and cleaned. It was awful. But it was a job, and I kept going by keeping the endgame in sight: new guitar gear. I was making decent money too because at the end of each night, every server tipped me a couple of bucks for keeping their trays full. This often meant $30 for every shift, plus my minimal hourly wage. Working a few nights a week had me earning $400 a month or even more. At this rate, I figured I could start investing in some quality gear by the end of the summer.

Another upside to my gross job was working alongside a couple of my friends, one of whom shared my obsession with music. Ryan Lake had moved with his family down to Williamsburg from the Washington, DC, suburbs of northern Virginia the year before and had found his way into our misfit clique of skateboarders. A foil to my anxious brooding, Ryan was upbeat and positive. He was gentle and well mannered but had a lively sense of humor. Like me, he wasn't a particularly good skateboarder, but he was a phenomenal guitarist.

Ryan and I bonded over music. We spent Saturday nights at his house playing guitar, listening to music, and discovering new bands. I watched him figure out new songs by ear and tried to follow along as he learned the guitar riffs in real time. Ryan was never arrogant about his skill level and paused patiently while I caught up on whatever song we were learning. I don't know that either of us realized it, but he was giving me guitar lessons.

It was in Ryan's bedroom that I first heard Metallica and Megadeth. It was life altering. Those two bands combined the aggression and defiance of the punk rock music I loved with the musicianship and technical prowess of bands like Iron Maiden and Judas Priest. I listened for hours on end, memorizing every lyric, analyzing rhythm patterns, noticing studio overdubs and subtle changes in tempo. I soaked it all in. Heavy metal had created a world that I finally felt comfortable and welcome in. I didn't want to leave.

Years later, Lamb of God toured all over the world with most of the bands I was discovering. Ryan would go on to write, record, and tour internationally as a member of the renowned doom metal band Alabama Thunderpussy. But all of that was still a long ways away.

CHAPTER 4

AXIS

"SOMEBODY SAVE ME"
CINDERELLA

Cinderella gets a bad rap. It's easy to understand why. Their debut album, Night Songs, *released in the summer of 1986, was drenched in the over-the-top, hair metal styling that was trending with popular hard rock bands at the time. Gliding around the stage in glitter trench coats, polka-dot pants, and shiny cowboy boots, they referenced a movement of glam bands from a generation before, bands like Sweet, Slade, T. Rex, and New York Dolls. Naming themselves after a fairy princess made it clear upon arrival: Cinderella was all in on the glam. But there was more to this band than teased hair, pouty lips, and campy videos.*

Front man Tom Keifer stood out. His raspy, growling vocals channeled Dan McCafferty from the '70s hard rock legends Nazareth. But Keifer was also an adept guitarist, incorporating slide guitar and traditional blues elements to his tasteful playing. Wielding his scarf-adorned microphone stand and his low-slung Gibson Les Paul with equal

41

proficiency, Tom Keifer's stage persona blended Aerosmith's Steven Tyler and Led Zeppelin's Jimmy Page.

And underneath all the flashy imagery and trendy marketing was great songwriting. All the lipstick in the world couldn't overshadow Keifer's driving guitar riffs and undeniable vocal hooks. Their classic rock influences were always referencing bands like the Rolling Stones, Led Zeppelin, and Aerosmith.

Night Songs was a smash hit and marked the beginning of a three-album run that established Cinderella as one of the bigger hard rock bands in the world. On those following albums, 1988's Long Cold Winter *and 1990's* Heartbreak Station, *the classic rock, blues-influenced underpinnings of the band became more pronounced. Despite massive commercial success and their evolution into a straightforward, blues rock band, Cinderella is far too often remembered as a hair-sprayed, high-heeled '80s act. And that's a bad rap.*

By the beginning of tenth grade, music had become my primary focus. I played guitar every day. Living out my own version of the Bryan Adams's song "Summer of '69," I really did play until my fingers bled. Sometimes I fell asleep at night playing guitar, and my mother had to wake me up to tell me to go to bed. My part-time job smearing cheese and butter had allowed me to save enough money to buy some respectable gear. I had a couple of nice guitars: a white Kramer Focus and that Gibson Les Paul Junior that had captivated me in the music store. Unknown to me, my brother Allan had selflessly set aside some money from his golf course job. He used it to buy the Gibson for me as a mind bogglingly awesome Christmas present.

42

I also upgraded my amplifiers. I bought a used 50 watt Marshall amp head, much like the ones I'd seen some of my guitar heroes playing through. I paired that with an off-brand speaker cabinet loaded with the same Celestion speakers that many of my favorite players were using in their more expensive, name brand amp rigs. I even managed to scrape up the money for a 4-track cassette recording machine and a rudimentary Roland drum machine to start experimenting with songwriting and recording demos. With some decent gear and my playing skills improving, I set my sights on finding a band.

My buddy Ryan was already playing with some guys a couple years older in a band called Axis. They had learned some songs by Black Sabbath, Mötley Crüe, and Rush. They were sounding pretty good, but Ryan thought they could use a second guitarist. Conveniently, Axis practiced in my neighborhood, so I started hanging out at their jam sessions, partly because it was fun, but more importantly so I would be around just in case they asked me to jam with them. And eventually they did. There were a few false starts. The guys would invite me to jam with them a time or two and then they wouldn't. Though it was frustrating, the uncertainty was a strong motivation for me to practice even more on my own. I learned the songs inside and out. After a few more chances to prove myself and some heavy lobbying by Ryan to his bandmates, I joined Axis.

Joining a band was the greatest thing that had ever happened to me. I couldn't wait to go to band practice. Though at first we didn't know many songs, we played the ones we did know over and over, and we slowly added new cover songs to our repertoire, like Ozzy Osbourne's "Crazy Train" and Metallica's "Ride the Lightning." We were pretty good! And we were committed to improving.

Our rehearsals in our bass player Lance's basement became a hangout for a few older kids from our school. When Lance's parents were out for the evening, band practice became a party, so kids came over to listen to us play. Alcohol and weed popped up sometimes. The forbidden element of being around booze and drugs struck me as cool and dangerous in a thrilling sort of way, but I wasn't much interested in participating. I was far more intrigued by the girls who came around than I was in the drugs and alcohol, even though I was inexperienced there too.

I was a shy kid, a couple years younger than everyone around our band scene. Even Ryan, who was in my grade, was a year older. With that age difference, I was always worried about saying the wrong thing, so I kept my mouth shut as much as possible because I was just happy to be present. I observed intently and learned as much about teenage social interaction as I did about playing in a band.

"Hey Mark. How old are you?" a girl once asked me while the band took a short break from playing. I knew her just a little bit. She was a senior and lived in a far corner on the other side of our neighborhood. She was sitting up against the basement wall with a couple other girls and drinking a Sun Country wine cooler. She seemed so cool.

"Fifteen," I answered abruptly. My mind shifted into overdrive, trying to think of something interesting to add, but I had nothing. I wisely kept my mouth shut.

"Well, maybe one of these days," she said, smiling flirtatiously. She took a swig of her wine cooler and returned to her conversation with the other girls who had barely noticed our brief interaction. But I was over the moon just thinking of the possibilities.

Axis made good progress. We practiced a lot and built a decent catalog of songs, but there was one problem: we didn't have a singer. Until now, we had been playing entirely instrumentally. We knew that to be a *real* band we needed a singer, so we pieced together a beat-up PA system and started our search.

Our lead guitar player Ryan tried out first. Though he was able to make it through a few songs singing and playing guitar simultaneously, the burden of singing lead vocals left his guitar playing less dazzling than usual. Because we were a two guitar band, we probably could've worked around that problem, but even beyond that, his voice didn't fit. It had a bit of a Mickey Mouse quality to it. Ryan was one of the best guitarists I'd ever seen, but he wasn't our singer.

Next was Bryan, our drummer. He couldn't wait to sing. I say this with love, but drummers are an interesting breed. Many of them choose the instrument at the back of the stage and then spend the rest of their lives overcompensating, trying to make sure the audience notices them. True to form, Bryan was ready for his spotlight. He was a better singer than Ryan and less cartoony, but he still wasn't great. He was sort of shouting somewhere close to being in key, as opposed to actually singing. But even if Bryan *was* our man, who wants to see a band with a drummer as a front man? You can't lead the show from the back of the stage. Phil Collins and Steven Tyler started out as the drummers for Genesis and Aerosmith, but they had sense enough to ditch the drum kit and grab the mic stand. They found someone else to hit things with sticks behind the rest of the band. Bryan was a good drummer. He was more valuable to our band holding down the beat than he would be shouting into a microphone.

As for me, I had no interest in being our singer. I was terrified enough just playing guitar in front of people. I wouldn't have made it anyway. My singing voice is unremarkable; I've never considered myself more than a mediocre background singer, and even that I struggle to do while playing guitar at the same time. So it was three band members down, one to go.

Out of all of us, our bass player Lance had the best *personality* to be the front man. He was good looking, charismatic, and had a great sense of humor. He was a cross between Bo Duke from *The Dukes of Hazzard* and Jeff Spicoli from *Fast Times at Ridgemont High*. Lance always dressed cool and was popular with the girls. He even drove a Camaro! But everyone involved, thankfully even Lance, knew that he was tone deaf. We were going to have to look outside the band.

We tried out some friends who had been hanging around band practice, but they were even worse. It's one thing to imagine yourself as the lead singer of a rock band: wide stance, long hair blowing in the wind, arms outstretched while you belt out high notes and soaring melodies over the top of your band. It's another thing to do it. We all watched as several of our would-be rock star friends' fantasies went belly up. One by one, they stepped up to the microphone, only to wilt immediately when they heard themselves wailing atonally through our raggedy PA system. After this failed experiment, we had just one prospect left.

Chris Marrow was a new kid at school. He had just moved from the neighboring city of Newport News. Chris was a fifteen-year-old bona fide rock star. He looked and dressed like Nikki Sixx from Mötley Crüe, except with bleached blond hair. Every girl in school wanted his attention, and every guy in school either wanted to be his friend or beat him up.

Lafayette was a small school where like-minded kids stuck together. Chris gravitated toward our blended social circle of metal heads, punkers, skaters, and Deadheads. Upon meeting Chris, I instantly started working on him about joining our band.

"We're really good! With you as our front man, we'll be the best band in town!" I told him. I believed this. Never mind that there were at most four actual bands in town.

"I'm a bass player, man," Chris said. "I'm not even sure I can actually *sing*."

"That doesn't even matter. You'll figure it out. It's gonna be great!" Chris was unswayed. He wanted to start a band where he could play bass. This was a problem. The last thing Axis needed was the school's biggest rock star starting a band that would compete with us.

I kept chipping away. One day at the lunch table, Ryan and I were showing off our latest musical accomplishment: my 4-track recorder that I had been using to record our band practices. I had even learned how to set up microphones to capture good quality audio recordings. I had no clue that what I was doing was a rudimentary version of audio engineering. I just wanted to listen to my own band.

Axis had recently learned Cinderella's "Somebody Save Me," the third single from their debut album *Night Songs*, which was popular at the time. Somebody at our cafeteria table had brought a small Panasonic cassette player to school, and we were all listening to music. Trying not to seem overly enthusiastic, I suggested we check out a recording of our most recent band practice. Ryan and I sat back proudly as our friends listened to my recording of our impressively executed instrumental version.

"Whose Cinderella tape is that?" Chris asked from a few seats down, only halfway paying attention.

"That ain't Cinderella! That's us! That's Axis!" I boasted, shooting a quick smile at Ryan who was already grinning back at me.

"That's y'all's band on that tape?"

"Hell yeah! The only thing we're missing is a singer!"

Chris caved. "Okay, okay. I'll try out. Damn, you guys sound *good*."

He was right. We did sound good. All we needed was the right front man, and we were sure that Chris was our guy. He followed through within a week and was instantly in the band.

Despite his uncertainty, Chris was a pretty good singer. He had a strong midrange and a raspy growl, comparable to Ian Astbury of the

Cult. He could hold out notes with powerful sustain and had a decent understanding of pitch and control. His range was a bit limited, at times getting cracky and squeaky in the higher registers. But the rest of us just looked the other way whenever things got a little dicey. He was putting in a lot of effort and took his new role as the singer for Axis seriously. Whatever reluctance he'd had about being our singer disappeared as soon as he joined. Chris was as committed as the rest of us. But Chris also looked great, almost as if he'd walked in straight from a video shoot. He sported messy long hair, cutoff T-shirts from all the coolest bands, ripped up jeans, and floppy white Reebok high tops.

The rest of us were nowhere near as stylish, so we were going to have to work on our image as we prepared for Stockwood, our first big show. It was the upcoming local battle of the bands, and we planned on being a contender. But first we had to be chosen to compete. Stockwood was held at Bruton High School in nearby York County. It was unique in that anyone of any age was eligible to try out. Most of the bands that entered were rock and metal bands from all over the region, varying greatly in age. Tenth graders in their first bands auditioned alongside weekend warrior garage bands made up of moms and dads well into their thirties and forties. Local amateur musicians took Stockwood seriously, and winning the competition was an honor. The winner, chosen by a panel of judges, was evaluated on their sound, performance, and crowd response.

The event began with a full day of auditions, from which five bands would be selected to compete in the actual show. The Bruton High School auditorium was buzzing with bands loading in and out. Most were complete strangers, giving the event a suspenseful feel to me. I was consumed with an odd feeling that I was starting to love: equal parts panic and thrilling adrenaline rush.

We were all quieter than usual most of the day. This was serious business, and we loaded our gear in as efficiently as we could. We took the stage with "Crazy Train" by Ozzy Osbourne. We were nervous, but we were well rehearsed and we knew it.

Firing up with the distinctive rhythm progression of the intro from "Crazy Train," Lance, Bryan, and I locked in tight, establishing the simple, heavy groove. Ryan slid in shortly after, tastefully executing Randy Rhoads's iconic guitar riff over top of our driving cadence. Chris stood tall and cool, center stage, confidently hoisting the mic stand and pounding his fist to the riff. By the time the first verse hit, we had momentum. I was terrified and thrilled at the same time. I could tell we were playing great, so I didn't want to screw it up. And I didn't. As we finished, we got a short round of applause. My nerves eased a bit. One down, one to go.

Next was "Smokin' in the Boys Room" by Brownsville Station, a song also famously covered by Mötley Crüe. Our take more closely resembled the Mötley Crüe version, and we nailed it too. Chris sang well and moved as if we were playing a real concert. Bryan and Lance were locked in with no stutters or mistakes. I played my rhythm guitar parts accurately, with just enough added flavor to sound interesting but not stand out. And Ryan's solos were outstanding. After our tryout, we packed up our gear and hung around, checking out some of the other bands. Other band members stopped to compliment us on our playing.

A week later we got the call. We were in. We spent the next few weeks rehearsing for the show and dialing in the details of our upcoming performance. We chose songs for the set list, which we repeatedly sketched out, scrutinized, and revised. We added Iron Maiden's "Wasted Years," Megadeth's "Peace Sells," and Poison's "Talk Dirty to Me." I'm still not sure who suggested that last one, but I know it wasn't me.

Placed strategically among these covers was an Axis original. I'd put together the music and lyrics for a song called "Open Your Eyes." I presented it to the rest of the band, who took to it immediately. It was the first song I'd ever written, and it was not great. The lyrics were my fifteen-year-old mind's attempt at sociopolitical, environmental commentary. I even included a reference to my favorite Bad Religion album.

The sky is black and the fields are gray,
They don't see, they look the other way,
Open your eyes, it's our own curse,
How could Hell be any worse?

People only hear what they want to hear,
People only fear what they want to fear,

Tell us what we want to hear,
Show us things we do not fear,
Close your eyes and you won't see,
The darkening reality.

The music to "Open Your Eyes" was only a little better than the lyrics. But it was our song.

The last detail left was our wardrobe. We needed to look like a pro band, and pro bands always had good style. We didn't want to take the stage looking like we'd just walked out of study hall. Chris was easy because he already looked like a rock star. Lance got a pair of black, fringe leather, knee-high moccasins. He paired them with a cut-off shirt, ripped jeans, and his low-slung bass. Bryan didn't do much to style up his image, but it didn't make much difference. Except for his arms whirling in the air and his shaggy haired head bouncing to the beat as he played, his massive chrome Ludwig drum set kept him mostly hidden. Ryan raided his mother's closet and found a pair of turquoise, quilted polyester pants from the '70s. They fit tight, even on Ryan's beanpole frame, and the fact that they were a bit short only helped to accentuate his gleaming white, high-top sneakers. He added a Whitesnake tour shirt to complete his ensemble.

But I was struggling to come up with something to wear. I was overweight and uncomfortable in my body. I didn't know how to feel cool about clothes. I usually did everything I could to get people *not* to notice me, so dressing up to be noticed was unsettling and unfamiliar. Nonetheless, I was committed to our cause. I borrowed a pair of glammy, black leather boots from Chris. They had shiny pointed toes and a low heel. I tucked my ill-fitting black jeans into the boots and put on an oversized Cinderella T-shirt. Topping it off was my black leather Members Only jacket.

I looked ridiculous. Making matters worse, my ongoing battle with my dad over the right to grow my hair long left me with a dreadful bowl cut that framed my round, chubby face. The night of the show was terrifying as we waited to play. I lumbered around anxiously backstage in my silly boots, chewing my fingernails off. The auditorium was packed. We had friends and classmates in the audience, which was both comforting and disconcerting. My parents were even there. It wasn't lost on me that my dad's presence at the show was his quiet, simple way of showing support for my musical ambitions.

As we took the stage and launched into our first song, some kids jumped out of their auditorium seats and rushed to the front, rocking out in the small orchestra pit. We all traded thrilled looks as we played. We were putting on a real rock show! The show was a blur. I was nervous and focused on playing all my parts correctly. I didn't move around much, partially due to my concentration on playing but also because those stupid boots were hard to walk in. But the rest of the guys were full of energy. Axis won the Stockwood battle of the bands contest that night.

After the show, we headed back to Bryan's house, which was empty because his parents happened to be out of town for the weekend. We seized that opportunity to have a victory celebration. A bunch of our friends showed up, all as proud as we were. There was beer and weed. I had drunk beer and smoked pot before, but that was because I had wanted to fit in: the kids I'd been with were doing it, so I reluctantly figured I should too. But this time was different. I liked it this time. I liked the buzz. I wasn't stumbling around or throwing up in the bushes like some of the other kids. I was holding it together. I felt cool. I liked myself. For one of the first times in my life, I wasn't nervous or anxious. I wasn't scared of doing or saying the wrong thing.

Late that night, a much older, straggler Deadhead at the party offered me a hit from his small glass pipe. It was weed, but he mentioned something about a little bit of opium. I took a hit. An L.A. Guns video flickered on the television. I was pretty sure this was the greatest night of my life.

CHAPTER 5

KILLING CYCLE

"CALL OF THE WILD"
CIRCUS OF POWER

In the late 1980s, when overproduced, hair metal dominated MTV's pro-
gramming, Circus of Power were an anomaly. Fusing elements of classic
Southern rock, blues, and punk with heavy metal–style production and
authentic, grimy New York City aesthetics, they were a mangy, snarling
mongrel next to a pack of primping poodles. But their songwriting was
inconsistent. And as their relatively short career progressed, the band's
music videos began to suffer from some of the clichés of cheesy plots
and video models. But on Circus of Power's self-titled 1988 debut album,
they caught lightning in a bottle. "Call of the Wild" and "In the Wind"
were damn near rock 'n' roll perfection. It was everything I wanted.

During my senior year in high school, my band Killing Cycle was in
full swing. Williamsburg didn't provide us with a lot of options to play
shows, but we tried our best to make up for it. We begged club owners
in nearby cities to let us sneak in and play despite being underaged. We

played high school band competitions, house parties, and even rented community centers. We played anywhere and everywhere, as often as we could.

In the summer of 1990, shortly after I graduated high school, I went with some of my bandmates to see Faith No More and Circus of Power at The Boathouse in Norfolk, Virginia. After Circus of Power's set, their guitarist Gary Sunshine was hanging out at the soundboard. Thrilled at the chance to speak to one of my heroes, I nervously approached Gary and told him how great I thought their set was. I also told him that my band covered "Call of the Wild" and "In the Wind." He was genuinely surprised and told me how cool it was to hear that younger bands were playing Circus of Power songs. He was stoked. I was too.

Over three decades later, while writing this book, I found Gary Sunshine's account on a social media app. I messaged him and told him how I'd approached him at that show so long ago. Gary wrote me back and, to my surprise, he remembered our encounter. I'm still a fan.

As my tenth grade year ended and the summer of 1988 began, I faced a harsh reality. The most important thing in my life was coming to an end: Axis was breaking up. Lance and Bryan were both going away to college, while Chris, Ryan, and I were still in high school. Their colleges were far away, so getting together to practice wasn't realistic. For a little while we tried to ignore the inevitable, playing parties that summer and talking optimistically about continuing to jam during their semester breaks, but all that faded away as soon as the guys left for school. The band was finished, and it was time to move on.

As one of the best guitarists in town, Ryan had plenty of options. He immediately started jamming with a few different groups around town, one of which was a bassist and drummer duo in their late twenties. Ryan played with them long enough to get a set of cover songs up and running and quickly brought Chris in to sing. This left me out of the mix, but only for a short time. They had played a few house parties together, but when Ryan started focusing on a different group he'd been playing with, Chris immediately suggested me as Ryan's replacement. Though I didn't have Ryan's skill level as a guitarist, I'd been steadily progressing since Axis and felt more confident. I was ready to be the sole guitarist in a band. I had briefly met the older guys once at one of their practices with Ryan and Chris, but I was formally reintroduced and immediately invited into the band. It was a new beginning. We called ourselves Damage.

Damage introduced me to a new, and much more adult, world. My time in Axis had been a gateway into hanging out with older kids from my school, but they were still kids. The bassist and drummer in our new band were in their mid- and late twenties. Conscious of our new environment and our age, Chris and I did our best to avoid conducting ourselves like goofy teenagers, always mindful not to do or say anything stupid. We got good at playing it cool.

Our bass player, Matt, was kind and thoughtful. Tall with a thick build and a heavy, furrowed brow, he had a brooding appearance. Despite his resting scowl, Matt's sharp, sarcastic sense of humor often quickly snapped him into a gentle laugh. Matt worked as a server in one of the popular taverns in the tourist area of Colonial Williamsburg. His long bushy hair pulled into a ponytail only accentuated his colonial-period costume, which he would sometimes show up wearing, fresh from a shift.

Matt was a good bass player. He played like he actually wanted to be playing the bass, not as if he wanted to be playing guitar. Matt was well versed both in college rock bands like R.E.M. and Hüsker Dü, and also in classic and hard rock. He drove a comically beat-up Datsun 280Z that was my ride to and from band practices since I didn't have my license. His polite nature helped to relieve my mother's concerns about this new older friend who was regularly picking me up to go jam.

And then there was our drummer, Chopper Dale. In contrast to Matt's low-key aura, Chopper Dale was a giant, hippie biker. Dale stood six-foot-four and usually wore tattered cutoffs, a handmade tie-dyed T-shirt, and construction boots. His voice toggled between a low, mellow timbre with a slight Southern drawl and a thunderous boom that could explode in an instant. While I had heard some stories and occasionally saw small signs of Dale's potential for violence, I never felt threatened. If anything, Dale was protective of both Chris and me.

Chopper Dale was also a drug dealer, mostly weed and LSD. In hindsight, I'm surprised that as a naive sixteen-year-old I wasn't more taken aback by this. Even when I'd see pounds of marijuana and sheets of LSD at one time, it seemed matter of fact. It was just something that happened in the back room in between sets. I was there to play music and didn't care about getting high. Dale rarely ever addressed the drug stuff, and he never encouraged me to do any drugs. Maybe that was his way of being protective. Or maybe he just knew that I didn't give a shit about anything but playing music. Both were probably true.

As his nickname implied, Chopper Dale was a Harley-Davidson enthusiast. Walking into band practices at his house involved stepping over piles of motorcycle parts. The short hallway filled with Dale's procrastinated motorcycle rebuild opened up to a spacious living room arranged entirely around the centerpiece: Dale's colossal drum kit. Flowing tapestries with tie-dye patterns and mandala designs hung from the walls and ceilings. Nag Champa incense burned, and live Grateful Dead recordings played from the stereo. Dale was a Dead-head, as was most of the regular crowd hanging around the house. I had heard the Grateful Dead, but it wasn't until I started hanging out at Dale's that I developed my love for Jerry Garcia's spontaneous, expressive guitar style and the humble authenticity of his voice. Jerry's playing spoke to me.

But Dale's house wasn't all hippie vibes. His taste in music was diverse. He introduced me to *The Age of Quarrel*, the pioneering album by New York hardcore legends Cro-Mags. The opening track to that album, "We Gotta Know," was one of the first songs I learned with Damage. Even more impactful was when Dale played me the album of one of his new favorite bands, Circus of Power. Their grimy blend of bluesy Southern rock influences mixed with hard rock and metal riffing hit me just right. We covered "Call of the Wild" and "In the Wind" from Circus of Power's self-titled debut album.

Band practices at Dale's house were a blast. Most of our rehearsals had a built-in audience of friends and house regulars. Referring to our practices as "rehearsals" is a bit of a stretch, though. We weren't ever *rehearsing* for anything. We played once outside Dale's house, a fraternity party at the College of William & Mary up the road. But I never felt like we were wasting our time or falling short. Chris and I spent countless afternoons and weekend nights in late 1988 and early 1989 at Dale's house. We played music, and I was having the most fun I'd ever had.

Drugs and drinking were part of the scene around Dale's house, but it usually stayed mellow. Although Dale drank beer and smoked a lot of weed, I never saw him sloppy or belligerently drunk. There was a lot of LSD too, but that drug normally doesn't lead to aggression. And I was uninterested in any party scene that didn't involve me play-ing music. One particular weekend, however, stands out.

In the 1980s, small towns in southeast Virginia were the types of places where medical facilities might keep their supplies unlocked. They might even keep those supplies behind a building without any security. And some of the supplies might even include bulk stocks of medical grade anesthesia. I won't pretend to know where it came from. I also won't pretend to know who acquired it. But one evening, a full, five-foot-tall tank of medical grade nitrous oxide showed up at Chopper Dale's house.

Known in some circles as hippie crack, but more widely known as laughing gas, nitrous oxide is an anesthetic most used during dental procedures. It quickly produces a euphoric and disassociated state. When properly administered by medical professionals, the gas is trickled out through a mask in measured doses, just enough to keep the patient sedate and distracted from whatever uncomfortable procedure is happening. When recreationally abused by a house full of metal heads and hippies, the contents are inhaled and held in as long as possible to maximize the effects. There's an immediate tingling, lightheaded, full-body euphoria, accompanied by a strange ringing in the ears. Another bizarre side effect is that it dramatically lowers your voice. After a hit, you sound like a slowed down recording, adding to the silliness of the experience. Then it all disappears as quickly as it happened. The whole trip takes about thirty seconds. Then you do it again. You tolerate the headache and nausea, convincing yourself that the fun house, body buzz, rollercoaster, head ringing trip is worth it.

That weekend, Dale's house was more crowded than usual. Word spread around our social circle that there was a nitrous party happening. Deadheads, punk rockers, and thrash metallers sat around all weekend inhaling balloons full of hippie crack and giggling for thirty seconds at a time. I did my share. Maybe a little more than my share.

Sitting on Dale's choppy waterbed and coming down from a hit, I watched my friend Jacob inhale a massive nitrous balloon. His eyes rolled back into his head as he leaned to the side, creating a violent wave in the cheap waterbed. Jacob then vomited all over the bed. Unbothered, Dale nonchalantly sucked in a balloon. Glancing at the contents of Jacob's stomach now splattered all over his bed, Dale saw a piece of undigested hot dog. In a calm, deep, Darth Vader voice, artificially pitched octaves lower than normal from a nitrous hit, Dale thoughtfully suggested, "Jacob, you should really chew your food more."

Over time, Damage's lack of purpose began to take its toll. Our party vibe practices lost their excitement. The attention spans of the band members began to wander. Matt had his sights set on moving an hour west to Virginia's capital city of Richmond. Some of his friends had already moved there and were gaining traction in Richmond's thriving music scene. As soon as Matt got the chance to join a band playing on the club circuit there, he jumped at the opportunity.

Chopper Dale had been playing with other people all along. His primary "occupation" left him with time to play drums with several bands, one of which played a lot of Grateful Dead songs. Between Matt moving to Richmond and Dale's hippie band, Damage fizzled out. There were no bad vibes. Damage had just run its course—a loud, fun, chaotic, psychedelic, anesthetized course. This put Chris and me back at square one, with one difference: we were an established team now. But we needed to rebuild.

Around this time, I was introduced to a newcomer to our town. John Peters had recently moved with his family from Houston to Williamsburg. Standing in the parking lot of an apartment complex where a party had outgrown the building and spilled outside, John and I bonded over our shared love of classic muscle cars and heavy music. We both owned early '70s Chevy Chevelles and loved thrash metal music. How I got my Chevelle is a story in itself.

Earlier that year, while riding with friends down a narrow country road in Julie Watson's 1984 Dodge Colt on the way to a cornfield party, we rounded a sharp left curve and into the path of a speeding pickup truck. Julie swerved in a panic, jerking the steering wheel hard to the right. The car careened off the road and into a large cedar tree. I was in the passenger seat without a seatbelt. People didn't wear seatbelts then like they do now. Especially teenagers because it wasn't cool.

But face planting into a car windshield isn't cool either. I remember almost nothing of the actual accident. Upon impact, I was hurled forward and upward into the dashboard and windshield of the car. The force of my head and body pushed out the passenger side of the windshield and bent the dash. I landed sideways on the floorboard of the car with my head at Julie's feet and my legs in the passenger side floorboard. Julie's shirt and most of the front seat were splattered with blood from where the windshield had sliced my forehead. My friend Jeff, who had been riding in the back seat and had broken his leg in the crash, later told me that when they climbed out of the car to wait for an ambulance, he thought I might be dead.

After the crash I woke up with a horrible headache, made even more painful by the roaring sound of some kind of engine. That noise, I later learned, was the jaws of death they used to cut the door off the car to get me out. Opening my eyes, I couldn't see anything because of all the blood that had run down from my forehead into my eyes. I heard the welcome sound of an EMT telling me that I had been in a car accident and that I was going to be okay. She was a calming presence in a terrifying situation, and everything she told me turned out to be true. I ended up with a concussion, a stitched-up forehead, a broken toe, and a body full of bumps and bruises.

The following week a representative from Julie's insurance company showed up at our house with a check for $1,500 to help compensate for any inconveniences that might arise from my injuries. My parents interpreted this as being "please don't sue" money. Not too long after that, I used that same exact $1,500 to buy my first car, a faded blue 1972 Chevy Chevelle with Cragar S/S mag wheels and dual exhaust.

Standing in a light rain in the parking lot of that apartment complex, John and I made small talk about our Chevelles and drank cheap keg beer out of plastic cups. I had been starting to drink more regularly, usually keeping an ear out for parties on the weekends. There were almost always a couple of options. Drinking was fun. I liked the buzz. When I drank, I felt loose and comfortable. It made me happy. My anxiety lifted and I relaxed. I also felt cooler when I drank. And everyone did it, so it seemed normal.

John and I discussed the merits of our shabby hot rods. His was faster, but mine looked better. As we talked, we discovered that not only were we both proud Chevelle owners, but we also liked many of the same bands. John's favorite Slayer album was *Reign in Blood*, mine was *South of Heaven*. He had a fake ID, which meant that he could buy alcohol. And to make a cool situation even cooler, John played bass. He had some decent gear and was looking to join a band. This was perfect. With John on bass, all we needed was a drummer for our new band.

Word had spread quickly around our tiny music scene that Chris and I were looking to start a new band. Some friends suggested we check out another relatively recent transplant named Joey Huertas. Joey grew up in New York City in a blue-collar, Bronx neighborhood. His family had moved to Williamsburg just a couple of years earlier, and he finished his last two years of high school across town at Bruton High. We initially spoke by phone and discussed our goals. We were both serious about putting a real band together. I could tell by talking to him that he was a good drummer and that he had confidence.

When Joey and I first met in his small garage practice space to play together, I was a bit overwhelmed. He was a tornado of energy and unrestrained creativity. He talked as fast as he could think and had a new idea every other minute. He was loud and opinionated, sometimes even a bit overbearing. His New York mannerisms felt brash to my much slower, small-town Virginia sensibility. But I liked him. He was funny, with a morbid and bizarre sense of humor. Most important, Joey was a good drummer, easily the best metal drummer in our town. I was surprised I hadn't heard about him sooner. After a couple of exploratory jam sessions in his garage during which Joey and I auditioned each other, it was clear that we were a great fit. We both had solid groove and lots of ideas, and we were ambitious and excited.

When John, Joey, and I played together, the chemistry was there. It felt like we'd been a band for years. We intuitively understood each other's musical style. We improvised together in free-form jams that often ended up sounding rehearsed. We were locked into each other's playing, simultaneously anticipating the next change and predicting the next freestyled riff. It was thrilling. I'd never felt such a connection to other musicians. Chris watched it all happening and was just as ecstatic. We dove headfirst into rehearsing and learning songs for our new band, which we called Killing Cycle.

We held band practices every Friday night in Chris's large, walk-out basement recreation room. We moved in and took up the entire room. Joey's drum set was massive: a shiny, black Pearl brand kit with double kick drums and cymbals anywhere he could fit one. John's job detailing cars at a local Honda dealership allowed him just enough financial independence to secure a loan for a new Ampeg SVT bass amp and a powerful, matching speaker cabinet. Chris had saved up enough money to buy an old, beat-up PA system from the 1970s. It still worked well and was loud enough for him to be heard over the rest of us. I still had the same gear I'd been using since before I'd joined Axis: my white Kramer Focus 2000 guitar and a 50 watt Marshall JCM800 plugged into a Sonic 4×12 cabinet with Celestion speakers.

Unlike Damage band practices at Chopper Dale's house, Killing Cycle practices had no party atmosphere. While getting drunk was becoming increasingly common for most of my bandmates and me (except for Joey, who rarely drank and didn't do any drugs), we only did it after rehearsals. We were focused as we put together a set of cover songs. We kept some of the songs that Chris and I had been playing in Damage, including the two Circus of Power songs, along with "Love Removal Machine" and "King Contrary Man" by the Cult. We added "Bloodbath in Paradise" by Ozzy Osbourne, which was great fun for me because the song features blistering guitar work by Zakk Wylde. We worked up our own heavy interpretation of Billy Idol's "White Wedding," and we played versions of "Nobody's Fault" and "Time" that were far closer to the much heavier Testament and Wrathchild America versions than they were to the Aerosmith and Pink Floyd originals.

The big difference between Killing Cycle and my previous bands was that we also wrote our own material. I had been experimenting with songwriting since my early days in Axis, but by the time Killing Cycle was formed I was writing my own riffs. We were all becoming adept at arranging and structuring songs. Bolstering our songwriting efforts were lyrical contributions from Joey and Chris. Joey was an active lyricist, with notebooks of stories and off-the-wall lyrics rooted in his dark sense of humor. Our song "Apology Accepted" explored the guilt, shame, and remorse of running over the neighbor's dog. (I never asked Joey if he wrote that from personal experience.) "Deep Freeze" was the imaginary story of a terminally ill patient who is cryogenically frozen, hoping that he can be thawed and cured once medical technology can treat his disease. "Landslide Suicide" was an antidrug song loosely inspired by a family friend of Joey's who died of an overdose. Chris wrote the lyrics for "Eye of the Storm." Taking a less narrative approach than Joey's contributions, Chris opted for more abstract, impending doom themes arranged over my very Led Zeppelin "Immigrant Song"–influenced musical composition.

In short time, Killing Cycle had pieced together a strong repertoire of covers and a handful of original songs. Once we got comfortable playing together, our practices loosened up, and friends came by to listen. After band practice, we'd usually head out to a party or find a way to make one.

I was beginning to drink regularly on the weekends. Miller beer, Everclear grain alcohol, and Jack Daniel's were mainstays. Drinking made me feel relaxed and confident. I could finally talk to girls without second-guessing every word. And they even talked back! Plus, teenage growth spurts and a lot of self-imposed meal skipping had left me much thinner. I was no longer the fat kid. My dad had also finally relented and stopped forcing me to get my hair cut. It was longer and shaggy now, hanging well past my shoulders. I wore ripped jeans and heavy metal concert T-shirts with a black leather jacket. I finally felt cool. Partying felt to me like it was a part of that metamorphosis. It was a component of my new identity. But the band was still my priority.

As good as we were, Killing Cycle faced the obstacle of being stuck in our dead-end town. There weren't a lot of places to play. Taking a cue from the time Chris and I spent in Axis, we put on our own show at the local recreation center. We entered local band competitions, winning first place at the Lafayette High School Battle of the

Bands. We also entered the famed Stockwood competition at Bruton High that Axis had won a couple years earlier and were shocked when we did not win. We laughed it off. We knew we were the best band that night. We also knew we had to think bigger than high school band competitions. It was time to go after some real gigs.

About an hour's drive from us, in the Norfolk and Virginia Beach area, there was a small but active metal club scene. Popular local bands played the circuit all week long. Traveling regional acts came through to headline on the weekends, often playing with smaller local openers. We were dying to be a part of it. We knew that if we wanted to play in clubs, we needed a proper demo tape to submit to the talent bookers. Fortunately, I'd become acquainted with Ronnie, the owner and studio engineer of Fresh Tracks Recording Studio, when I took guitar lessons there a few years earlier. Ronnie remembered me when I stopped by, and he kindly gave us a discounted rate on some studio time to record our demo.

Killing Cycle's recording sessions at Fresh Tracks were like nothing I had done before. They were serious and professional. The small, strip mall studio was divided into three sections. There was a live room, just big enough for John, Joey, and me to set up to record the basic rhythm tracks. In the corner of the main room was a small, soundproof booth where Chris sang his isolated vocal takes. On the other side of the live room was a large glass window looking into a long, narrow control room where Ronnie worked at the 16-channel mixing board. Next to the board was a large reel-to-reel tape machine loaded with two-inch tape to record the sessions. The studio walls were covered with acoustical tiles, foam soundproofing, and cedar wood panels.

It was a modest, low-budget recording studio, but to us it might as well have been the most modern, cutting-edge facility in Hollywood. We were all well rehearsed and worked efficiently to make good use of our studio time. Ronnie was patient and attentive, educating us about basic recording techniques. He gave us honest critiques of our performances to help us get the best takes possible onto tape. I had already gained some rudimentary experience in multitrack recording with the 4-track cassette recorder I'd used to make practice demos. But recording at Fresh Tracks was a whole new level. Its sixteen separate tracks opened possibilities for adding extra layers of guitars, overdubbed solos, harmonies, and background vocals. If I could hear it in my head, I could try it in the recording. If I didn't like the sound of something, I could do it again. I knew as soon as we started that the studio was where I felt most at home. It still is, and that's because recording is still my favorite part of my job.

We recorded four original songs that Ronnie mixed down to a cassette tape that we could copy. We wrote a short band bio, printed it out with a list of all our songs, and submitted it along with our demo tape to clubs. They must've liked it because we started getting offers to play shows. But they were very entry level. Most of the invitations made clear that we would not be paid. As a new band on the club circuit, we had to start by playing short sets for no money and opening for other bands. But we knew if we went over well, we could move up the ranks. We'd caught our big break and were finally turning pro. Or at least that's how I saw it.

One club was particularly exciting to me. On Stage was a dingy metal club nestled among used car dealerships and pawn shops that lined a shabby commercial avenue in downtown Virginia Beach. Miles away from the scenic, tourist-dominated oceanfront area, On Stage catered to young, heavy metal loving military personnel stationed at several nearby bases. Of all the clubs on the circuit, On Stage booked the most traveling bands and even sometimes featured up-and-coming national touring acts. The club manager was a tall, barrel-shaped guy named Bear, who was likely in his mid-thirties but who looked much older. He always looked like he'd just woken up in the same clothes from the night before, which may have been true. Bear was in charge of everything at On Stage, including booking and scheduling bands.

Joey had made the forty-five-minute drive to the club to drop off our demo tape and bio a few weeks earlier. Bear liked what he heard. He offered us an unpaid time slot on a Wednesday night opening for local circuit stalwarts Jinx. We were thrilled. As far as we were concerned, we might as well have been opening for Iron Maiden at Madison Square Garden. This was the biggest thing any of us had ever done musically. But there was one small problem: our rock star breakthrough moment was on a school night. I nervously pled my case to my parents, explaining what a huge opportunity this was. I pointed out that I'd been keeping my grades up, and I promised to come straight back home as soon as we were finished and had our gear packed. Because they had always supported my musical ambition, they let me play. My dad didn't have much to say. He listened, thought for a minute, then nodded his head and said, "Okay." Chris got a green light from his folks as well. Killing Cycle was going to play a real club.

The afternoon of the show, we met up as soon as Chris and I got out of school. We were nervous. We piled as much of our gear as we could into Joey's Chevy Chevette and John's recently acquired Honda Prelude. (The engine in his Chevelle had died not long before.) The club would provide some in-house speaker cabinets we could use to plug our amps into. When we arrived at the club, we parked by the back load-in door and started unpacking our gear. John's anxiety got the best of him. He staggered over to a nearby dumpster and threw up next to it. "Dude, I don't know if I can do this," he said to me, eyes red and watering from having just vomited.

"I'm nervous too, man," I confessed. "But we're here. We worked hard for this. Don't worry. We're gonna be great." I wasn't sure if I believed we were actually going to be great. It just seemed like something I was supposed to say.

Once we got our gear inside and stacked next to the small stage, we walked over to the club office in the front corner of the building and introduced ourselves to Bear.

"Hey, Bear! We're Killing Cycle from Williamsburg. Thanks for giving us a slot," Joey said, trying to sound cool and not overly excited.

"Uh, yeah. Nice to meet you guys. Glad you could make it," Bear replied uneasily. He looked us over one at a time, eyes returning to Chris and me. "How old are you two?" Bear asked suspiciously.

"I'm sixteen," Chris answered nonchalantly.

"I'm seventeen," I followed.

Bear stared at us blankly. On Stage was a night club that served alcohol. We were too young to be in the building without a legal guardian. None of us had thought about this before, and Bear hadn't thought to ask. Evidently he didn't get a lot of high school kids auditioning to play his club. "Y'all are just fuckin' kids," Bear groused. "I could get in a lot of trouble for this."

Bear nervously scratched at the balding spot on the top of his head and gazed up at the grimy, drop ceiling tiles, deep in thought. "Okay," he barked. "Here's the fuckin' deal. You two will sit *right here*," he said sternly to Chris and me, motioning to a small table just outside his office door. "When you're not on that stage playing your set, your asses will be right fucking here at this table where I can keep my eye on you. The other two can get your gear out of here as soon as y'all are done playing. Understand?"

We understood. Bear was taking a real risk letting us play. We were grateful for the opportunity and followed his instructions. Chris and I stayed at our assigned table and drank free sodas until it was time for us to go on. It was a Wednesday night and we were opening for a local act, so there wasn't much of a crowd. But we played as if it were a packed house. Joey twirled his drum sticks high above his head in between snare hits while his feet hammered out rhythms on his kick drums. John lunged back and forth to the rhythm in the widest stance he could hold, bass slung low, down to his knees. Chris confidently stalked the narrow stage, whipping the microphone cable into the air in between vocal lines and engaging the small audience. And I was on fire. My nerves melted away by the second song of our eight-song set. My guitar felt like it was playing itself and I was just along for the ride. It was magical feeling, one that I still experience when everything flows without much effort.

Bear was impressed with what he saw. He immediately offered us more shows on much better nights. One Friday night a couple of months later, we opened for a traveling band from Florida called Last Child. Bear had grown to trust that we wouldn't try to drink alcohol or do anything stupid to get him in trouble, so we got there early and casually hung out with the Last Child guys. They were a few years older, but we hit it off. They told us about their life on the road, traveling from town to town in their van. They'd usually play Thursday through Sunday nights at a club and then move on to the next club in the next town and do the same thing. It all sounded like a dream to me. I couldn't imagine anything I'd want to do more.

That night, not far from us in neighboring Norfolk, the Arizona-based thrash metal band Flotsam and Jetsam was playing at The Boathouse. I had a couple of their albums and was a fan. Whatever competition that show posed didn't hurt our turnout because On Stage was packed. Chris introduced a song and dedicated it to Flotsam and Jetsam, boasting that we would've gone to their show but we were playing our own instead. We launched into our version of Flotsam and Jetsam's cover of Elton John's "Saturday Night's Alright for Fighting." The Last Child guys watched our whole set and complimented us when we finished. We stayed after and watched their set. They were phenomenal. I thought for sure they were on their way to being the next Skid Row, but I never heard anything more about them.

That summer, we played a few more club shows around the area, including a brutal weekend of woefully unattended shows at The Crystal Inn in Newport News. But a familiar sense of doom was creeping into our band. I had been accepted to Virginia Commonwealth University in Richmond. It was the only college I'd applied to, and I wasn't particularly confident that I'd get in. I wasn't sure that I even wanted to *go* to college. But one thing was certain: I would've done just about anything to get out of Williamsburg, and college was a fast ticket out.

Toward the end of that summer, Chris stunned all of us by enlisting in the Marines. His plan was to defer for a year and start boot camp shortly after graduating from Lafayette High. With that, Killing Cycle's fate was sealed. We played a few more parties and even popped up at the Stockwood competition the following year. We won this time. But the dream we'd shared was dying. It had been the greatest thing I'd ever experienced, and I had no idea how I could ever match it. At the end of August 1990, my parents and I made the hour-long drive up I-64 to Richmond. I moved into my shared room on the fifth floor of VCU's Johnson Hall and prepared to start my freshman year of college.

CHAPTER 6

LAUGH SPELLED BACKWARD

"MOUNTAIN SONG"
JANE'S ADDICTION

Jane's Addiction's Nothing's Shocking album was a cultural signal flare. When it was released in the summer of 1988, thrash metal and glam metal were peaking as the dominating forces in heavy metal and hard rock. Jane's Addiction had created a stir in their hometown of Los Angeles as a pillar in an underground alternative rock scene that was rooted in L.A.'s infamous club Scream. But outside of Southern California, the band was largely unknown.

The first time I ever heard Jane's Addiction was when I saw the video for "Mountain Song" on MTV. It was like nothing I'd ever seen before. It's a cliché to say that, but it was true. Watching that choppy, low-budget video for the first time, I felt like I was peering past a slightly *opened door, sneaking a glimpse into an undiscovered, exotic world of music and counterculture. Equal parts punk rock, heavy metal, and carnival sideshow, the band grooved a heavy riff that felt like Led Zeppelin's iconic "Whole Lotta Love" played backward. Drummer Stephen Perkins pounded tribal rhythms that locked in with Eric Avery's loping, hypnotic bass line. Perry Farrell howled over the driving music, singing abstract lyrics referencing the conflicts between individualism and capitalistic greed. Young women danced on stage wearing diapers as a frenzied club crowd whirled and moshed. It looked like a punk rock, heavy metal circus.*

But it was Dave Navarro who caught my attention the most. In the middle of all the psychedelic, alt-rock, fun house lunacy was a guitarist who I immediately related to. His tone, his guitar of choice, and the amps behind him all made sense to me: he had to be a metalhead. After listening to the entire album, my suspicions were confirmed. Over the course of the track list, Navarro's adept playing references metal pioneers Eddie Van Halen and Randy Rhoads as much as it does alt rock heroes Mick Ronson and Daniel Ash.

Dave Navarro and Jane's Addiction were an early look for me at the possibilities for unlimited creativity, even within the context of heavy music. Their fusion of punk, metal, folk, and psychedelia was confrontational and celebratory. In a few years, the alternative and grunge explosion would envelop the entire world. But it was never any better than Nothing's Shocking.

Unpacking my belongings in my dorm room at VCU, I regretted my decision to go to college. I thought that going away to school would be a one-way ticket out of Williamsburg, but I was immediately homesick. Everything I'd ever known was in Williamsburg. I'd never lived anywhere else. Most of my friends were still back home, going to a local community college and hanging out together just as much as we had in high school. Worst of all, the most important thing in my life had disappeared when Killing Cycle broke up. I felt like I was starting all over from nothing.

I didn't have a roommate my first few days in the dorm, so I had time to adjust to my new environment and process the change without anybody else around. But it also left me feeling isolated. I had brought my guitar and a small practice amp to Richmond, so I did the one thing I knew would make me feel normal: I plugged in and played. Classes didn't start until the following week. I spent my first few days in Johnson Hall moping through whatever freshman orientation meetings were required and playing guitar in my free time. That week, blues guitar legend Stevie Ray Vaughan died in a helicopter crash. I heard it announced on the radio the morning after.

One evening as I jammed in my empty room, someone walked past my open doorway and immediately walked backward, returning into my view. The tall shaggy haired kid stuck his head in and greeted me.

"What's up man? You sound pretty good. What kind of stuff are you into?" he asked, smiling.

"Thanks man. I'm into all kinds of stuff, mostly thrash metal, I guess," I replied nervously.

His face lit up. "Sweet! Me too! We should hang out. I play bass. I brought one with me. I'm in 524, down the hall on the other side of the building. Come by anytime. We should definitely jam!"

"Awesome. I'll come by for sure," I answered.

And with that, I'd met my first friend at VCU. His name was Chris Adler.

Shortly after meeting Chris, I got paired up with my new room-mate, Mike Ryan. Mike had come to VCU from Roanoke, Virginia, a small city between the Blue Ridge and Appalachian Mountains. Mike was a metalhead. He was small and impossibly skinny, with long thin blonde hair cut into an impressive mullet. He had a strong mountain accent that, along with his excited optimism about being in Richmond, created a calm, friendly aura. We hit it off instantly. Mike's funny, country boy sensibility felt familiar. We also liked a lot of the same music. Not only did we share a love for heavy metal, but we were into rap artists like Public Enemy, N.W.A, and Cypress Hill. We also both liked newer hard rock acts like Alice in Chains and Soundgarden. Mike didn't play any instruments, but he was a talented visual artist majoring in fine arts. Shortly after we'd settled into our dorm room, Mike drew a rendering of us leaning up against a detailed Slayer pentagram with "Welcome to the Abyss" written above it. We proudly hung it on our door.

Just across the hall from our metal headquarters, a much differ-ent scene was coming together. Two kids from the Washington, DC, suburbs of northern Virginia were establishing room 519 as the social and cultural epicenter of Johnson Hall's fifth floor. They'd somehow fit a full-size couch into their room. They also had a record player and the floor's only coffee maker, which was always brewing. The residents of room 519 were an odd couple. They were both named John, so everyone called them by last names only. John Partin was reserved and cool. He had long dark hair and a Jim Morrison quality, minus the leather pants and LSD. An English major, John read Jack Kerouac and Allen Ginsburg. He listened to Bad Brains and Rites of Spring. His tastes in music and his interests were artsy and of a counterculture nature in ways that I'd never even been exposed to. But none of it was for show. If the fifth floor of Johnson Hall had a mayor, it would've been Partin.

Partin's roommate was John Campbell, a high-energy kid with a mischievous personality. He stayed up all night and often skipped class. John was much more interested in hanging out than doing schoolwork. He was constantly up to some kind of bullshit. One morning as I walked from my room to the floor's shared bathroom to begin my day, Campbell came flying through the air like an NFL linebacker, grabbing the bottom of my boxer shorts and pulling them down to my ankles as he fell. He'd pantsed me first thing in the morning, and I barely even knew this dude. Campbell was well versed in DC punk and hardcore bands like Minor Threat, Fugazi, and Scream, and he had been going to punk shows in DC all through high school. The sounds of DC punk blasted nonstop from the record player in room 519.

As the fall semester began, I kept up with my class schedule and school assignments. But along with my required freshman courses, I was getting another education in my dorm. The music coming across the hall from Partin and Campbell's room was new to me. The unpolished authenticity of bands like Kingface and Soulside resonated just like Circus of Power had a couple years earlier. Adding to that excitement was that most of these bands were largely undiscovered and rooted in a music scene that was just a couple hours north of us in DC. I was captivated by the idea of entire communities of bands with sizable fanbases operating outside of the mainstream, with no radio, MTV, or major touring exposure.

In addition to introducing me to underground music, Partin presented me with another equally exciting opportunity. He was the vocalist in his own punk rock band back home in Manassas, Virginia. He wasn't the greatest singer, but he had charisma. The band was called Hgual, which is *laugh* spelled backward. It was a terrible name. Partin had to say it out loud to me at least three times before I would even attempt to pronounce it. Hgual had recently released an album on a Minneapolis-based independent label called Skene! Records, which had also recently put out an EP by future punk rock superstars Green Day. Skene! had a small roster of bands and was working to organize a low-budget tour of the East Coast featuring Hgual and a few other bands on the label. But Hgual had a problem: they'd lost their bass player when he went away to college. His choice of school was too far away to commit to any consistent rehearsal schedule, so he quit the band.

Partin and I had become friends quickly over the first few weeks of school, and he knew I could play guitar pretty well. To salvage their slot on the tour, Partin asked if I would join Hgual as their guitarist. He told me that their previous guitar player, a kid they called Hose, was willing to play bass. Hose was apparently a good bass player and didn't mind making the switch.

I had heard the Hgual album a few times blasting across the hall out of room 519. I wasn't really a fan. The music veered all over the place, switching styles from bashing mid-tempo rock to hyper fast punk to white boy reggae. The vocals ranged from talking to shouting and weren't pitched in any discernible key. It all seemed random and confusing. But despite my lack of enthusiasm for their music, when they asked me to join the band, I said yes. It was a no-brainer. Hgual was a band that had real things happening. An album? A tour? These were massive opportunities. I wasn't going to let the minor detail of not actually liking the band's music get in the way of all that!

Partin and I started making the ninety-minute weekend trips from Richmond to Manassas for band practice. I felt excited to be in a band again. Hose was an easygoing slacker kid who lived for music. We got along well. He was remarkably talented but humble.

Though not the most technically precise player, his intuition for composition and song structure was more advanced than mine or anyone else's I'd ever played with. He patiently showed me the ins and outs of the Hgual songs, most of which he'd written the music for. I had learned several of them off the CD before our first practice, but once we started playing together, Hose pointed out nuances in the songs that I'd overlooked. Hgual's music had more depth and detail than I'd first given them credit for.

Rounding out my new band was drummer John Skaritza. He was yet another kid named John, so we usually referred to him by just his last name too. Skaritza was an excellent drummer. He had played in his high school marching band, which came through in his drumming. He hammered out fast rolling beats and extended fills that morphed into reimagined rhythm patterns, shifting the groove without warning. His style was more akin to Jane's Addiction's Stephen Perkins than to any punk rock drummers I could think of. He was studious and kind of nerdy, but also cool in a subtle punk rock kind of way. His taste in music seemed hip and exotic, and he regularly talked about bands I hadn't yet heard of like the Jesus Lizard and Wire.

I gained an appreciation for the Hgual material as we dug into it. The stylistic diversity of their songs started to feel more like a unique strength. It was different than anything I'd ever been a part of. We learned a set's worth of songs quickly and even started writing a couple new ones.

My periodic trips to Manassas were a welcome distraction. But back in Richmond, my freshman year of college was in full swing. I've always been terrible at retaining information from reading, so I barely cracked open a book. Nonetheless, I did a decent job keeping up with my class work. I was diligent about attending class lectures and took thorough notes. When I wasn't in class or hanging out in 519 with Partin and Campbell, I often headed down the long hall across the building to Chris Adler's room. He had a bass guitar and small practice amp. I'd bring my guitar and amp with me, and we played along to albums by Dokken and Danzig. We shared a love for the Chicago-based doom metal band Trouble and were both massive Megadeth fans. The day Megadeth's *Rust in Peace* album was released in late September of 1990, Chris and I gladly walked the two miles from our dorm building to Plan 9 Records to buy it.

Most weekends, if I didn't have band practice with Hgual, I'd find a ride back to Williamsburg. I was still a bit homesick. My friends there were hanging out and partying every weekend, and that's where I wanted to be. I'd started dating Sarah, a girl from Williamsburg whom I'd met the year before when we had both worked in the same strip mall. I was a dishwasher in a sandwich shop, and she worked at a lingerie store a couple of doors down. Sarah was older than me. When we started dating, I was seventeen and she was twenty-four. She was short and curvy, pretty with long wavy hair, light brown eyes, and a slight Southern accent. She'd already been married and divorced, which I found exciting. I felt an odd sense of pride about dating an older divorcée. But despite her age and marital history, Sarah was far from worldly. She was a simple, small-town girl who hadn't seen much beyond Williamsburg.

My drinking was also beginning to accelerate. Alcohol was forbidden in our dorm at VCU, so we didn't have too many chances to get drunk. But my weekends in Williamsburg revolved around partying. More and more, I drank until I passed out. That wasn't ever my intention; it's just what seemed to happen. Once I started drinking, I rarely stopped until I shut down. Even worse, sometimes I'd drink until I'd black out, remaining conscious but ultimately losing track of where I'd been or what I'd done. I'd wake up in the morning unsure whose couch I was sleeping on or how exactly I'd gotten there. None of this struck me as alarming. I was having fun and enjoyed the way alcohol made me feel. I felt cooler and smarter when I drank. I looked forward to partying with my friends and didn't feel like anything I was doing was a problem.

In the first couple of weeks of 1991 during my freshman year semester break at VCU, I embarked on my first music tour. At least "tour" is what we called it. It was actually just a four show run down the East Coast over the course of a week, spanning from Massachusetts to North Carolina. We were joined by Long Island hardcore band Bad Trip; New Jersey punkers Sticks and Stones; and a noisy, grimy punk rock / hardcore hybrid from Connecticut called Beef Trust. The bands had different musical styles, but we had all released music on the Skene! Records label, which was ostensibly helping to promote the shows.

Leading up to the tour, I don't recall us ever discussing how we would be traveling from show to show. Transportation is a vital component of any tour, and it seems impossible that we wouldn't have talked about our travel arrangements. But somehow, up until a few weeks before we were set to leave, we had no plan. Fortunately, Sarah possessed two valuable assets that helped us make the shows happen: a strong wanderlust and a gray, four-door, 1985 Mercury Topaz. We squeezed all five of us—the four band members plus Sarah—into that cramped sedan. Stuffed into the trunk of the Topaz was Hose's bass, my white Kramer guitar, my 50 watt Marshall JCM800 amp head, Skaritza's snare drum and kick pedal, and all of our sleeping bags and backpacks full of clothes for the week. There wasn't any space to spare, but we didn't mind. We were all thrilled to be leaving town to play music. We arranged to borrow the rest of the gear we'd need for the shows from the other bands traveling in tour vans and carrying all their own equipment. They were generous to help us out. There was a spirit of community among the groups.

Our first couple of shows were at Club Babyhead in Providence, Rhode Island, and at the historic Bunratty's club in Boston, where our bill was merged with another show that night featuring underground thrash metal legends Only Living Witness. I was thrilled watching the local heroes pound through their riff-heavy set, which was much more in my musical wheelhouse than the band I was in. But I was happy with what we were doing. We played for gas money to the next show and crashed on a different floor every night. We continued on with a decent show at home in Richmond in front of a small but friendly audience, followed by a smaller, matinee show in a storefront space in Greensboro, North Carolina. Hgual didn't bring the house down anywhere along the way, but we were always at least pleasantly received.

Those few shows in early 1991 were the beginning of a lifetime of touring. I'd already played a few clubs with Killing Cycle, which were great learning experiences. But the Hgual tour was a level up. The smell of grimy clubs, anxious anticipation before the doors opened, camaraderie between the bands, cramped travel conditions, lack of privacy, miles rolling by on the interstate: I didn't know it at the time, but those elements were part of an all-encompassing lifestyle that would end up consuming large portions of my life. Over time, I would develop a conflicted relationship with touring, often bemoaning the exhausting and uncomfortable conditions that inevitably came with it yet simultaneously feeling compelled to go back out and play more shows. But in the winter of early 1991, it was all still brand new.

CHAPTER 7

GRACE STREET GUMBY

"DO YOU COMPUTE"
DRIVE LIKE JEHU

As far back as anybody knew, my older brother and I were the first members of our family to attend college. When I started applying to schools, my dad laid out his deal: he would pay my tuition, but there were no breaks. No semesters off, no part-time class schedules. It was a damn good deal, and I was happy to take him up on it. But he did have one other stipulation. His offer was off the table if I intended to major in music.

"That's a waste of money," he told me flatly. "I'm not paying for that."

I didn't have a lot of leverage to argue. Though I had been considering VCU's well-respected music program, I wasn't sure what that meant or even what I wanted to do with it if I got accepted. I just knew that music was what I cared about most, and it made sense to me to dive deeper.

With the option of majoring in music a nonstarter, I enrolled in VCU's College of Humanities and Sciences. Initially, I majored in mass communication, but I switched to political science by my sophomore year. I'd been an average student at best in high school, just barely satisfying VCU's grade point average and SAT admission requirements. But by the time I was taking upper level political science courses in college, I excelled. I got an education in a field that I hadn't ever intended to major in.

I also ended up getting an education in music. Moving to Richmond put me in touch with a world of independent, underground music that I never knew existed. Growing up, I had been exposed to punk rock in the form of Sex Pistols, Black Flag, and some smaller bands known in the skateboarding circles. But my understanding of punk music was narrow.

When I got to Richmond, my new friends exposed me to bands like Fugazi, Sonic Youth, the Jesus Lizard, Shellac, and Drive Like Jehu. These bands made chaotic and noisy music. The guitar parts were often atonal and "wrong" from a technical perspective. But their layered and abstract soundscapes had depth. The songs were exponentially greater than the sum of their parts.

Influenced by what I was hearing, I felt compelled to unlearn so much of the technical precision I had gained from being a thrash metal player. I tore down my philosophy that the more technical or skill dependent a piece of music is, the better it is. I learned to play with more spontaneity and emotion. I wanted to channel my energy straight from my spirit to my instrument, ideally bypassing the brain completely. And sometimes I succeeded.

The influences of punk and post-hardcore bands like Shellac and Drive Like Jehu came full circle for me, eventually impacting my *songwriting in Lamb of God. The uncomfortable, stuttering interval of Shellac's "Pull the Cup" echoes in Lamb of God's "Descending." The brittle, staccato guitar pattern that opens "Do You Compute" by Drive Like Jehu is referenced in our song "The Subtle Arts of Murder and Persuasion."*

I believe one of the things that has always set Lamb of God apart from our peers is the strong punk rock component in our creative DNA. I'm grateful for my formative years in the clubs of our city. The authenticity and pureness of the music that I discovered in Richmond has informed my creative process ever since.

By my sophomore year at VCU, I was less concerned with what was going on back in Williamsburg and increasingly engaged with my new life in Richmond. I was enjoying school and was particularly interested in the government courses that I had been required to take as a freshman. I was anxious to sign up for more of them, so I decided to major in political science.

The early '90s was an exciting time to be a newly independent, young adult. Popular culture was shifting in ways that felt urgent. The glossy aesthetics of '80s music and style were falling out of fashion. Young America's celebration of wealth and excess was disappearing. A new purpose-driven mindset was spreading. It was now *cool* to have a social consciousness. It was *cool* to be aware of societal problems like racism, misogyny, homophobia, and homelessness. That growing cultural consciousness started influencing my goals. I felt motivated to become more educated. I believed that my generation could help make things better. Many of my peers shared that belief.

Music trends fell in line with this new cultural paradigm. Perry Farrell's traveling Lollapalooza music festival was taking off. I went with carloads of friends to see the Lollapalooza tour at Walnut Creek Amphitheater in Raleigh, North Carolina. The nationwide tour was loud in its promotion of diversity and inclusivity. With a lineup featuring Black artists and female-fronted bands, Lollapalooza pushed back against the white, male dominance in rock. The festival also featured promotional displays and points of engagement for environmental and political action groups. These things may seem normal today, but they all seemed radically progressive at the time. Nirvana and Pearl Jam were taking over MTV and radio, providing a dressed down, relatable counter to the glamorous rock star images of bands like U2, INXS, Mötley Crüe, and Guns N' Roses, who had been among the biggest bands in the world just a year or two before.

While I was a fan of many of the alternative and grunge bands taking over the mainstream, my real focus was on our local music scene. Richmond had always been home to a vibrant art and music community. VCU's renowned art school drew fresh waves of eccentric personalities to the city every year. This made it a fertile ground for creativity. There were warehouse art studios and dingy basement practice spaces all over the neighborhoods surrounding VCU. In the 1980s, Richmond had produced the mildly successful new wave bands Ten Ten and House of Freaks. It had also spawned the art metal, shock rock freak show Gwar. I was anxious to be a part of it all.

Hgual decided to get more serious after being inspired by the positive experience of our four show "tour." Our drummer John Skaritza relocated to Richmond and enrolled in VCU. Hose, our bass player, ultimately didn't want to leave his familiar surroundings of Manassas, so we amicably parted ways. The bass slot was filled by my friend John Peters, who had played bass in Killing Cycle. Bringing Peters into the band was a smooth transition. He and I already knew how to lock in tight with each other on riffs, and Skaritza's dynamic drumming added a welcome component of depth to our new song ideas. We started practicing as often as possible, setting up anywhere we could. Sometimes we'd borrow other bands' practice spots for a few hours. When we couldn't find a space in Richmond, we'd make the hour drive down to Williamsburg and practice in my parents' garage for an afternoon.

As Hgual, we began to establish ourselves as regulars on Richmond's punk rock club circuit. We opened for our friends in Avail, who were quickly becoming an international act. We also opened for more established touring bands that came through Richmond, like Milwaukee punk veterans Die Kreuzen and the Washington, DC, band Shudder to Think.

I paid close attention to the bands we played with. I watched how they interacted with each other, onstage and off. I asked questions to band members who seemed approachable—but this was usually not the singer. I noted how they traveled: typically a beat-up but well-maintained van with a "loft" in the back to store gear. I paid attention to who they brought with them and what roles they all played. Every show was an education, and Hgual applied what we learned. We printed T-shirts to sell at shows. We recorded a demo with Don Zientara at Inner Ear Studios. This felt like a big deal. Don was a major figure in the Washington, DC, punk and hardcore scene; he produced and engineered records by Minor Threat, Fugazi, Jawbox, and others.

Sarah's Mercury Topaz had gotten us through our first tour, but she and I had broken up and the band needed a better tour vehicle. I sold the 1986 Ford Escort station wagon I'd been driving and bought a 1977 Ford Econoline van. Hgual was doing the things that *real* bands did.

But creatively we were getting restless and needed to level up. Hgual did a short and dismally attended run of out of town shows with our friends in the band Groove. Not long after that, Groove broke up, leaving their singer Chris Wade without a band. Chris was a huge talent as a front man and lyricist, but he was also a close friend so we brought him into Hgual.

The summer before my junior year, Hgual moved into a large, shabby house at 2829 West Grace Street with a dingy but spacious basement where we could practice. Our plan was to start a new band with a new vibe and a new name. As a playful homage to Hgual's friend and founding guitarist Hose, we called our new band Hose Got Cable.

Hose Got Cable was a mess from the start. At least it was for me. The structure of the new band was chaos. For starters, our drummer now wanted to sing. This idea did make sense because he was the best singer in the group. So now we had three singers. To add to the confusion, Partin and Chris Wade both wanted to play guitar, which they had just recently picked up. So now we also had three guitar players, two of whom couldn't really play yet. We started writing songs that were bass and drum driven, with screamed vocals and noisy, textural guitars layered over top. It was reminiscent of bands like Sonic Youth and Drive Like Jehu. These were bands that I liked as a listener, but as a player I didn't know how to fit into that style. My technical ability had always been an asset; now it was an obstacle. The other guitarists weren't able to play the parts that I contributed, and I wasn't having fun joining in with the abstract feedback and single note drones that everyone else was gravitating toward. We tried for a few months to make it work, but I never found my space in the sound. I was clearly in the way. Not wanting to force the situation any longer, I bowed out of Hose Got Cable.

With me out of the way, Hose Got Cable took off. They became one of the most popular punk bands in Richmond, headlining well-attended shows around town. They released records, played huge out of town shows with Gwar and Avail, and developed their own following beyond Richmond. Admittedly, Hose Got Cable's rise was difficult for me to watch. I was genuinely happy to see my friends having success, but I was jealous. They were doing everything I wanted to be doing. I felt like we had all worked so hard to get in a good position, and then as soon as I was out of the picture, they found success. But there was no animosity. I cheered them. If anything, watching Hose Got Cable thrive made me more determined to establish a band of my own.

In short time, that happened. My old roommate from the dorms, Mike Ryan, had started playing guitar, and we began writing some songs with a couple other friends who played bass and drums. We called ourselves Nascar Drag. The stock car racing reference in our name was a cheeky nod to the small-town redneck-y upbringing that Mike and I shared. I also liked the potential interpretation of "drag" as in drag queens. Drag queens in race cars. Fuck yeah. Nascar Drag was a pretty good band too. Noisy, hard driving punk that was a mix of Shellac and Fugazi. Mike's brittle, unconventional playing meshed well with my cleaner, more riff-oriented technique. Nascar Drag kept busy playing shows around town, most notably opening for Alice Donut. We even did a few shows out of town opening for Hose Got Cable. It was all a lot of fun, and I was happy to be playing music, but something was still missing.

In contrast with my bumbling musical ambitions, my college studies were going well. I had become immersed in VCU's political science program. By my third and fourth year of college, my course schedule allowed me to minor in international relations and African American studies along with my political science major. I was particularly intrigued by the history of political protest and activism. The Black Power movement and the political revolutions in Central and Latin America fascinated me. It all seemed to fall right in line with the punk rock ideals that ran so strongly in our music scene. It was during all of this that a unique opportunity for some political activism of my own fell directly into my lap.

One afternoon, while my friend Tony and I sat on the front porch of the 2829 house killing a twelve-pack of beer, my house-mate Skaritza came home on his bike with a huge six-foot-tall stuffed Gumby doll tucked under his arm. He'd found it discarded in an alley on his way home from class and decided it would be a great addition to the house's decor. We agreed. Tony and I propped the Gumby up in one of the rusty porch chairs, and we continued drinking the afternoon away without thinking much about it.

The following night, a local television station ran a short tongue-in-cheek human interest story on its 6 p.m. broadcast about a missing Gumby doll. Gumby had been stolen from the owner's front porch in James City County, and the owner wanted it back. There was even a reward. I don't remember which of us first saw that broadcast, but by the time the story ran on the 11 p.m. news, our entire house was captivated. All five housemates and even some house regulars stood around the television like we were watching the moon landing. This was a story! Someone had stolen this Gumby and ditched it in Richmond. And even though we weren't the ones who *took* it, we were the ones who *had* it! We all felt compelled to turn this story into something bigger.

The first thing we did was bring Gumby in off the porch. We had a potentially valuable hostage on our hands and couldn't risk being spotted. We got straight to work. Our plan was to capitalize on the publicity of our accidental hostage by using it to raise awareness about homelessness in our city.

We chose a high-profile target. George Allen had recently taken office as the sixty-seventh governor of Virginia. The son of a legendary NFL head coach, Allen had won the 1993 election with a platform of aggressively conservative stances that included eliminating the monitoring of state water toxicity levels, stricter mandatory sentencing for first-time offenders, and time limits for welfare recipients. In the progressive but slightly naive eyes of my coconspirators and me, Governor George Allen epitomized the type of rich white dude, power baron politics that we detested.

We carried Gumby to the basement, where we bound and blindfolded him like a proper captive. Polaroids were taken as I sat down to write our manifesto. We called ourselves the Jehu Revolutionary Front. The name was an homage to one of our favorite post-hardcore bands, Drive Like Jehu. The manifesto read:

JEHU REVOLUTIONARY FRONT

In the early 1970s, a series of essays detailing the character of the modern revolutionary was published. The author of these works, a prophet named Julius Lester, examined the nature of the society around him and explained the steps necessary to overcome the intolerance, injustices, and oppression that continues to engulf us all. Julius Lester, Rudy Ray Moore, John Reis and other great thinkers of our troubled times have provided the inspiration for the Jehu Revolutionary Front. The JRF is growing by the hour. Our members come from all walks of life and share the common goals of peace, equality, and the right to self-determination for all inhabitants of the Earth. However, peace can never be peacefully attained. The oligarchic nature of the present power structure in this country has denied the people access to the institutions and officials that shape the conditions of our existence. These unfortunate circumstances have made violence a necessary strategy. JRF members are willing to fight and die for our cause.

There is great danger in organizing and participating in a revolutionary movement. Due to these dangers, the JRF is currently unable to disclose the identities of our organizers. (We have no "leaders"; humans have been made all too aware of the dangers that "leaders" are capable of.) However, we call on our brothers and sisters all over the world to join our movement. Anyone who believes in peaceful coexistence and the right to self-determination is already a JRF freedom fighter, whether they know it or not. Take it upon yourselves to carry out JRF terrorist operations. The first of our programs is already underway and you will be hearing about it soon. We can say now that it involves the kidnapping of a six foot "Gumby" doll from a yard in southeastern Virginia. This event has already received media attention (television and radio) and a reward has been offered for Gumby's return. Future operations are currently being planned by our Minister of Terrorism and her/his associates. We call on you to organize and carry out your own terrorist acts with the JRF in mind. We will hear of your efforts and know that you are with us. When the timing is right, we will unite and become even stronger. Our rulers have left us with no other alternatives. Let's fuck it up.

JRFM1
Minister of Propaganda

Reading the JRF "manifesto" now, almost thirty years later, the language is alarming. As a member of the generation who was there for the Oklahoma City bombing, the Columbine massacre, and 9/11, I realize any political statement flippantly referring to *terrorism* or a *die for the cause* ideology is jarring. If any college knuckleheads circulated our manifesto today, they'd probably have an armed government agency kicking in their door. But the early 1990s were different times.

Once we typed out our spirited, albeit recklessly worded, manifesto, we printed out copies at the local Kinko's. We stuffed the letters into envelopes, which also contained Polaroids of our hostage Gumby. Later that night, we paid a 2 a.m. visit to several nearby radio and television stations. As stealthily as possible, with the waiting car still running, I glided up to the building entrances, slid the envelopes in the mail slots, then disappeared back into the night. We laughed all the way home about how silly this was, but it felt like maybe we had a shot at pulling off something awesome.

The next step was to wait. We stayed quiet for a couple of days, vigilantly watching the local news and listening to the radio, hoping we'd hear some mention of our antics. But nothing happened. No news about Gumby. Undeterred, we moved on to phase two. A couple of nights after we'd first delivered the manifestos and Polaroids, we returned to the local media outlets, this time with a ransom letter laying out our one simple demand: we'd return Gumby if Governor Allen donated five dollars to the Daily Planet, a Richmond area homeless shelter.

It was a symbolic move, one that would certainly be an easy request for the governor to fulfill. Even in 1994, five dollars barely bought lunch. But our real point was to create a conversation about helping the homeless. Even if Governor Allen never ended up hearing anything about a stolen Gumby ransom—and it was hard to imagine that he would—we already felt victorious. We'd caused a bit of chaos and stimulated some relatively high-profile discussion about an important issue.

A night or two after we delivered the ransom letters, something miraculous happened. The story was back in the media! Local radio stations were reporting about the Jehu Revolutionary Front, and a local newspaper called us an "underground organization." We were official. News stations showed pictures of the manifesto and of Gumby in our basement. We were ecstatic. It got even better: a spokesperson for the governor soon released an official statement saying, "Although this may have been offered in jest, the governor will not pay $5 for several reasons, the first being that a crime was committed when the Gumby doll was stolen, and if he paid the $5 it could cause a copycat incident to occur. And we certainly don't want that to happen."

The statement indicated that in addition to the local authorities investigating the incident, the Virginia State Police were also getting involved. The Daily Planet shelter begrudgingly addressed the situation too, denouncing our mission in an area newspaper: "The Daily Planet is not in any way, shape or form involved in this. In fact, I had no knowledge that Gumby was missing until this morning when I was called by a radio station. We just aren't involved and we don't condone that kind of behavior, even if it's well intentioned."

Despite all the negative attention, or maybe even because of it, we accomplished our mission: we'd reached the governor's desk. From my young, activist viewpoint, Governor Allen's handling of our silly Gumby incident proved what I'd already suspected to be true. People in his position didn't give a shit about the underclass in America. The way I saw it, he couldn't put his pride aside for five minutes to give five fucking dollars to help desperate people in his own capital city. It disgusted me.

In the days that followed, it was reported that the Gumby had been returned to its owner, which was bullshit. I happen to know that the Gumby we'd been holding captive was last seen in downtown

Washington, DC, hand delivered and strapped to the back of a tour van belonging to the band Rocket from the Crypt.

Is it conceivable that there were many errant, unattended six-foot-tall Gumbys floating around the relatively short distance between Richmond and Williamsburg that week in 1994? Hardly.

Did the governor's office orchestrate the "Gumby Returned" story to take the heat off him about the $5 donation demand? I believe they did. I hope they at least bought those people a new replacement (and imposter) Gumby.

Years later, my housemate, JRF coconspirator, and former bandmate John Skaritza became acquainted with a man who had worked in the governor's office during the Gumby scandal. He confirmed that, for that one week in June of 1994, my roommates and I were a huge pain in Governor George Allen's ass.

CHAPTER 8

CHICAGO

"AXIS ROT"
SLIANG LAOS

In the 1990s, the music scene in Richmond, Virginia, was booming. Clubs like Twisters, the Metro, and Alley Katz had live music almost every night and leaned heavily on local talent to keep their calendars full. Abundant low-rent housing and plenty of vacant lofts and warehouses made it easy for bands to keep practice spaces. Recording studios like Montana Sound and David Lowery's Sound of Music offered reduced rates during downtime for local bands to record demos and independent releases.

Richmond's thriving music scene was stylistically diverse. Local bands blended odd combinations of influences into signature sounds. Alter Natives combined punk and funk into high-energy instrumental jams. King Sour, also instrumental, were an abstract fusion of jazz and metal that featured bassist Tom Peloso, who went on to big-time success as a member of indie rock heroes Modest Mouse. Hose Got Cable pushed the limits of post-hardcore, with droning, atmospheric sound sculptures while Avail kept their hook-laden punk anthems more traditional.

Situated between the larger, more populated metropolitan areas of Washington, DC, and Norfolk, Richmond was a place that many national touring acts tended to pass by. As a result, regional and local bands were often the main attraction. Our scene was insular and self-supporting. Local bands played to audiences full of members of other local bands. We influenced each other. We shared our environment and created a sound we could identify as music of and from Richmond.

In the earliest days of Burn the Priest, the bands we emulated and most admired weren't rock stars or even national touring acts. They were people we knew, or they were friends of friends. Sure, we loved Pantera and Slayer, but we listened to Richmond natives Breadwinner far more. Metallica and Megadeth forever had our respect, but underground math metal pioneers Confessor from just a couple hours away in North Carolina were musical sages in our eyes. Our heroes were close and within reach.

One of the most important Richmond bands for me was Sliang Laos. They weren't just my favorite local band but were my favorite band period. Sliang Laos were artsy and abstract, but with massive heavy riffs. Stilted, sparse drum patterns looped under grinding guitar rhythms, pushing and pulling, stretching out powerful grooves into lurching elliptical lopes. Singer Andrew Sigler maniacally paced the stage, howling and ranting about a dying planet that, at the time, still seemed far away.

Sliang Laos ending up being just a brief flash of genius. Shortly after recording an album's worth of material that had been slated for a label release, the band broke up without explanation. Those recordings were passed around in Richmond quite a bit but never made it very far outside of our circles.

In the spring of 2018, Lamb of God released an album under our old band name, Burn the Priest. The album commemorated the twentieth anniversary of the first Burn the Priest LP. The track list consisted of cover songs from some of our early influences. Included was a rendition of Sliang Laos's brilliant prophecy of doom, "Axis Rot." Honoring the influence and legacy of one of our favorite Richmond bands and biggest influences felt like the least we could do.

In the summer of 1994, I graduated from Virginia Commonwealth University with a bachelor of arts degree in political science and minors in both African American studies and international relations. I loved school. It felt comfortable and I was good at it. The thought of leaving the academic environment made me uneasy because it provided me with direction that I didn't have otherwise.

I'd been working as a line cook at Red Lobster during my last couple of years in college to pay rent and bills at the 2829 house. However, restaurant work wasn't exactly calling out to me as a career. Music was still my biggest passion, but the music scene I'd been operating in was independent and underground, so that didn't seem to be a viable career path either. Sure, some bands got big enough to pay the bills, but that seemed like a one in a million chance.

I wanted to stay in school. I was accepted to a master's degree program in international studies at Chicago's Roosevelt University. Roosevelt is a small school in downtown Chicago. Going to school there checked two boxes for me. The first was that it meant I could stay in school. I'd need to work part-time to supplement my student loans, but my primary focus would be school. The second and more important detail was that Chicago had a strong music scene.

Chicago was the adopted home of blues legends Buddy Guy, Freddie King, and Hound Dog Taylor. The city had also recently been churning out successful contemporary rock bands. The bands Urge Overkill, Veruca Salt, and Smashing Pumpkins were all enjoying hit singles and mainstream success. My interest, though, was in the underground scene. Chicago's ultrahip label Touch and Go Records was home to some of my favorite bands like the Jesus Lizard, Shellac, and Tortoise. Legendary clubs Metro and Lounge Ax had live music almost every night. I wanted to find my way into that scene the same way I had found my way into the Richmond scene a few years before. Anxious for change, Fergus and Todd, the bass player and drummer in Nascar Drag, moved in with me. Nascar Drag had kind of fizzled out, but we were all still good friends. I was relieved to have them along. It would be cool to have familiar people to jam with in a new city.

I enrolled at Roosevelt University for the fall 1995 semester. Our plan was that we would move to Chicago the summer before I started school, which meant I had about six months left hanging around Richmond. It was around this time that I got a call from John Campbell. Campbell and I had remained friends since the dorm days; he was also a regular at the 2829 house. He'd gotten pretty damn good at playing the bass too. We had played together a bit in an on again, off again party punk band with the ridiculous name Fatty Love. (Yes, a weed reference.)

Campbell invited me to join in with a jam group he'd just put together. He and our friend Matt Conner had been coming up with some heavy riffs with our old friend from the dorms Chris Adler on drums. I didn't even know that Chris played the drums. I only knew him to be a bass player, but I was happy to join in. I met up with them at Chris's house in Richmond's Church Hill neighborhood.

Setting up to jam with those guys in that cramped back bedroom felt inconsequential. The mood was casual. We were just some friends making some noise for fun. We didn't have a goal beyond that. The other three guys had played a couple times before. They showed me a couple riffs that they'd already worked out together, which I picked up quickly. Once we cranked up to full volume and locked into playing together, there was a surge of energy in the room. It was ear splittingly loud in that small room and we could all barely remember the next part to play, but there was an undeniable energy to the sounds we were creating. It was more than just loud and fast. It felt fresh and unique. Still, none of us could've known that we were laying the groundwork for a band that would eventually go on to sell millions of records and spend decades touring all over the world.

Jamming with Chris, John, and Matt was instantly great. In Nascar Drag, we'd labored over ideas and struggled to make things jell. With these new guys, it felt natural. Every idea was exciting. We strung riffs together into flowing instrumental songs that had the power and technicality of thrash metal but simultaneously felt unhinged and chaotic like the punk bands we loved. We wrote riffs and we partied. Cheap beer by the case and endless bong hits were as much a part of our jams as guitars and amplifiers. We'd finish playing a newly assembled song and I would burst into laughter, thrilled with how fun it had been to play and how heavy it sounded. After a particularly spirited performance of a new piece of music, we stopped tight and I immediately exclaimed, "Damn! That's the heaviest, most evil shit I've ever heard! That's some burn the priest shit!"

I don't know where that came from. I'd never put those three words together before in my life. We started calling ourselves Burn the Priest.

Together, we quickly wrote a handful of instrumental songs. Our music leaned heavily on the influence of local math metal pioneers Breadwinner who, before their breakup, had gained critical acclaim and a cult following with their Merge Records release *The Burner*. I listened to that album every day for several years, often over and over. Pen Rollings had been Breadwinner's guitarist, and though we had become friends I made no secrets about the fact that he was a musical guru to me. Another massive influence on our new project was the local band Sliang Laos. They too referenced Breadwinner's lurching, oblong grooves, but they did so in the context of fully developed songs with a grim industrial vibe and complex dystopian lyrics. Our biggest musical influences were our friends, and my new band was the most fun I'd had playing music in years.

In the spring of 1995, Burn the Priest played in public for the first time. We played three songs at a house party. It wasn't even planned. The four of us had wound up at a party together. When we saw there was a band playing, we decided to jump in. As they stopped for a break, we cavalierly asked if we could use their gear to play a few songs. While they hemmed and hawed about it not being such a great idea, we strapped on their guitars and blasted off like a bomb. We were fucking awesome. Matt played riffs with his left hand while chugging from an upright bottle of bourbon with his right. Chris broke the drummer's kick pedal and then just started actually kicking the bass drum with his foot. We were a spectacle of total chaos. It was perfect. And then it was over. All of it. I started packing up my life and prepared for my move to Chicago.

Leaving Richmond was more difficult than I'd expected it to be. By the time we moved to Chicago, a couple of other friends eager for a change of scene jumped on board with us, so that made five of us. Two of the guys and I moved into a house in Chicago's Lakeview neighborhood just off Ashland Avenue. Having friends from Richmond with me helped some, but that familiar feeling of homesickness again set in quickly. I questioned the decision I'd made. Burn the Priest was special. I knew it. Just when I'd gotten into a band situation that felt right, I bailed. Campbell told me they were going to carry on. Matt had quit when I left, but a new guitarist named Abe Spear joined in our place. I was a bit envious because I wanted to be there with them, but even more than that I was relieved that the project hadn't died when I left.

I found a job cooking at The Chicago Diner, a vegetarian and vegan restaurant on Halsted Street. I had plenty of cooking experience from previous jobs and I'd been a vegetarian myself for several years, so it was a good fit. The diner was in the middle of a neighborhood known as Boystown, the epicenter of the city's massive gay community. The social consciousness of the '90s had influenced me heavily by this point, and I considered myself to be open minded and at ease with anyone's lifestyle. But nothing I'd seen in Virginia could've prepared me for being dropped straight into Boystown.

Nights after work, I'd ride my bike home past block after block of packed gay bars and nightclubs, thumping with house music. Some of these places had comically aggressive names like Manhole. Posters for drag shows and pride events hung in nearly every shop window. There was a level of visibility and outness that I was totally unaccustomed to. It was a crash course in gay culture that I hadn't been expecting. But the shock of Boystown's flamboyance wore off quickly. I began to appreciate the vibrance of the neighborhood. I made friends at work who were a part of the gay community, and I gained an appreciation for the challenges and prejudices that they confronted. I learned that it took a lot of courage to be openly gay in the '90s, even in a big city like Chicago. I drank quite a few beers and shots of bourbon in those rowdy gay bars.

My new gay friends weren't the only relationships I made at The Chicago Diner. Like in most restaurants, the diner's kitchen staff was largely made up of musicians. I made fast friends with a couple of the other line cooks who also played music. One of them had a band called Vambo Marble Eye that played small gigs around the city. We all had different tastes and influences, and we were eager to share them. Dinner shifts were a show-and-tell of our favorite bands. Those guys opened my eyes to the perfection of Television's classic *Marquee Moon* album, and they hipped me to the lo-fi genius of Guided by Voices. I returned the favor, introducing them to Shudder to Think's brilliant *Pony Express* album and the abstract grooviness of my idols in Breadwinner. The Vambo Marble Eye guys had a house on the northside with a full basement. We'd hang out there, drinking whiskey, smoking weed, and jamming in various combinations, improvising and rolling with whatever came out.

My fall semester at Roosevelt went well. I enjoyed my classes and was proud to be a graduate student pursuing a master's degree. I still missed having a band, though. I was jamming with friends, but nothing serious was coming together. I was in touch with Campbell and Chris back in Richmond. They told me that things were progressing with Burn the Priest and that they had built a small audience in town. Abe was working out well on guitar. They were writing some new songs and thinking about getting a singer, though they didn't have anyone lined up.

During the holiday break after my first semester of graduate school, I went back to Virginia for a couple weeks to visit. Coincidentally, Burn the Priest was playing a party in Richmond while I was there, so of course I went. They were amazing. The small brick carriage house they were playing was packed to the gills and pulsating from the power of the riffs that poured out of the band. They were still playing songs that I'd helped to write. It was hard for me to watch. I knew I belonged back in that band.

I soon went back to school for my second semester. The workload was heavy: there was a lot of required reading and long essay assignments that counted heavily toward my final grade. I studied highly specialized topics like post–Cold War nuclear proliferation and the suburbanization of the American electorate. I was diligent about attending lectures, but somehow I always put off my writing assignments until the last minute. I was also drinking a lot, even more than usual. I remember starting several important assignments the night before they were due. I'd sit down to write a twenty-page essay around 9 p.m., crack open a beer, and write all night, making it up as I went along. I'd finish as the sun was coming up, drunk, having killed a twelve pack. I'd shower and drink some coffee, showing up to class bleary eyed and still half drunk. But my grades were good. My grade point average after my second semester was 3.6.

My solution to not having a band was to act like I did. I started putting together riffs and song ideas for Burn the Priest, recording them on cassette so that I wouldn't forget them. I channeled the off-time grooves of Sliang Laos and the crawling, heavy doom dirges of Eyehategod. I knew I had good riffs. If I couldn't use them for anything, at least maybe Burn the Priest could. I told Chris back in Richmond I had some new material that maybe they could use.

"Just come *home*, dude," he told me. "Things are really starting to get cool with the band. It could be even better with you back in."

Chris said that Burn the Priest had made a big step. Randy Blythe had joined the band as the vocalist. I didn't know Randy very well, but I knew of him. Randy was a tall, lanky punk rocker dude who was a fixture on the Richmond scene. He had always struck me as a bit of a loudmouth. He had a booming speaking voice that somehow interrupted you even if you weren't in a conversation with him. He drank a lot and chain-smoked cigarettes. Randy was genuinely punk rock but also had a nerdy quality. He wore thick, black-framed glasses and was practically blind without them. He read voraciously and could talk knowledgeably about the works of Ernest Hemingway and Arthur Miller. He also knew a lot about punk rock music. The first time I ever heard New Orleans sludge masters Eyehategod was when Randy played them on the stereo at a small house party.

I knew Randy had a strong voice. He had been in a band called Furious George along with Burn the Priest's new guitarist Abe Spear. I'd seen them once or twice, but they weren't very good, and I didn't pay much attention. But I *had* noticed Randy a couple of different times when he rather randomly jumped on stage to sing with Hose Got Cable. He had a powerful guttural growl and shredding higher pitched scream. His vocals were blown out and extreme in the vein of Napalm Death's Lee Dorrian and Eyehategod's Mike Williams. I knew without even hearing anything that he was a perfect choice for Burn the Priest.

Randy hit the ground running with the band. The addition of a singer added a lot of momentum. All the songs that had been instrumentals soon got vocals. They were steadily writing new material and had recorded a demo tape and two seven-inches. They were also playing a lot of shows, both in and out of town. I kept in regular contact with the guys and was impressed with their progress.

Back in Chicago, I decided to quit school. I didn't really have a good reason why. My grades were good. I was enjoying my classes. But my heart just wasn't in it. I wasn't as excited about school as I felt like someone at the graduate level should be.

I took a full-time job in the nearby suburb of Skokie working as a picture framer. It paid well, and I liked the people I was working with, but it was monotonous. It was the same thing day after day: framing mass-produced prints of drab watercolor flower arrangements or gaudy glitter-splattered color panels to be hung as hotel room decorations. Fake art.

I had nothing going on musically other than just goofing off with friends. I'd been dating a girl that was serious for a time, but that had recently crashed and burned. I was also still drinking a lot. I was giving a lot of thought to Chris's suggestion that I come back to Richmond and rejoin Burn the Priest. I missed playing with those guys. Even when we had just barely gotten started, I knew it was special. And they'd been building momentum ever since. Chicago was exciting too, but it was huge and loud, crowded and bitter cold. I never felt like I'd settled in there. I missed Virginia. I missed being close to family. I missed the slow pace of Richmond.

The lease on my apartment in Chicago was ending soon. If I was going to keep my place, I'd have to renew it. Two years after moving to Chicago, I packed my life up once more and moved back to Richmond. I was coming home with a renewed excitement to play music, rejoining the band that I had helped to start. I was coming home with a new love for home. In the spring of 1997, I drove back into Richmond from the north, passing slowly under the canopy of trees that arched over on Chamberlayne Avenue with tears in my eyes.

CHAPTER 9

BURN THE PRIEST

"SOMETIMES SALVATION"
THE BLACK CROWES

I first heard the Black Crowes in the spring of 1990 when their debut single "Jealous Again" was getting frequent airplay on MTV. Despite being a full-fledged thrash metalhead at the time, I loved their accurate but respectful homage to the Rolling Stones, Faces, and early Aerosmith-style blues rock. My friends didn't quite understand the appeal, but I bought the Shake Your Moneymaker *album on cassette and played it alongside my Slayer and Testament albums.*

I continued to be a fan through the reign of their sophomore release The Southern Harmony and Musical Companion, *which saw them solidify their lineup and expand their songwriting from that of a retro classic rock act into a legitimate, contemporary Southern rock band. By the time the band released their third album, 1994's* Amorica, *the Black Crowes were easily my favorite rock band.*

When I left Richmond to go to graduate school in the spring of 1995, I couldn't wait to get out of Virginia. I'd never lived anywhere else.

Moving from my tiny hometown to the capital city of Richmond had itself been a huge adjustment. Richmond felt like a massive metropolis. Eventually, over the course of a few years, I got a feel for the city and its lifestyle. In time, it also began to feel small and restrictive. Chicago appealed to me because it was a big city with what I interpreted to be a massive music scene.

But the big city pace of Chicago made me homesick for the lazy rhythm of the life I'd left behind in Virginia. To feel more connected to my roots, I leaned into the Southern culture that I'd previously dismissed as simple and unhip. I started teaching myself to play slide guitar and banjo. I dug into the works of Virginia bluegrass legends the Stanley Brothers and the Del McCoury Band. Even my rock tastes pointed more strongly to the South. I'd always had an affinity for Southern rock, fostered from an early age by my older brother's musical tastes. But in Chicago, my love for Southern blues rock accelerated, and music from the Allman Brothers Band, Gov't Mule, and Lynyrd Skynyrd became mainstays. The irony was that I had to leave my home to discover everything I loved about it. And Southern rock music changed from being a constant hum present in the background my whole life to being a tightly held symbol of the home I was longing to get back to.

On October 6, 1996, I saw the Black Crowes perform the second of two shows at Chicago's Aragon Ballroom. They were loose and disjointed. I was a little disappointed in the set list, which, after the first few up-tempo songs, lulled into long, sleepy ballads and low-energy jams. Missing was one of my favorite Crowes songs, "Sometimes Salvation." Marc Ford's desperate, lurching, fuzz drenched guitar solo in that song is one of my favorites. But despite the shortcomings of the night, the slide guitar solos and groovy Southern blues blasting from the stage felt like a piece of the home that I longed to get back to.

was ecstatic to be back in Richmond after two years away. I was rediscovering the city and appreciating things that I'd taken for granted. The cobblestone streets, the smell of honeysuckle, and the ornate mansions lining Monument Avenue made me grateful to be back home.

My first couple weeks back in town, I slept on a couch in the small apartment that Campbell shared with his girlfriend. I got a job working for a roofing contractor, even though I didn't know very much about roofing. I'd had some experience working on construction crews, framing houses during a couple summers back in college, so I could at least swing a hammer. That was all I needed to get hired. They were willing to train me. And the pay was decent enough to keep up with rent for the one-bedroom apartment I'd found across the street from Campbell's place, on the corner of Franklin and Harrison.

With a decent job and an apartment, I focused on music. I started rehearsing with Burn the Priest almost immediately after arriving back in town. The band had a rented rehearsal space on Belt Boulevard in a sketchy section of Richmond near Southside. We practiced there several nights a week, working to recalibrate the existing songs for two guitar players. Some were songs that I'd helped write in the earliest days of the band. Others were more recent additions that they'd put together after Abe joined. I loved all of it.

Rejoining Burn the Priest was a unique situation. In one sense, I was coming back to a band that I'd helped create. But the band I was coming back to was something completely different than the one I'd left. There were two new members who I barely knew, and their input had grown the band substantially. Abe Spear had joined on guitar when Matt Conner and I had left the band. Abe had a strong presence. He was big, broad shouldered, and muscular, which helped to back up his confident, slightly cocky personality. Abe was a professional photographer and videographer. He lived and worked out of a converted industrial loft space overlooking West Broad Street, complete with a darkroom for developing film.

Abe was a solid player. Good, but maybe not great. He played awkwardly, left-handed with his guitar strapped high up on his chest. His timing was decent, but his tone tended to be a little muddy. Yet whatever Abe lacked in technical prowess, he made up for in creativity and commitment. Abe loved being in Burn the Priest and worked tirelessly toward the overall good of the band. He helped with booking gigs around town and kept the beat-up band van running dependably. He covered the costs for demos when money was short. But most important, he wrote good songs. Abe's musical contributions to Burn the Priest included "Salivation," "Lies of Autumn," and "Suffering Bastard," all of which were integral in helping to define the sound and character of the band. He hadn't been thrilled when Chris and John informed him that I would be returning. He wasn't given any choice. But Abe had been playing several of my Burn the Priest songs for a couple years by that point and knew the band would be stronger and more productive with me in it. Whatever initial discomfort he may have felt about me coming back, he didn't hold against me. I liked Abe, and we respected each other right away.

The other band member that was new to me was our singer Randy Blythe. I had loosely known of Randy just from being around town, but me rejoining the band would mean much closer ties. "I guess we're in a band together now," he said shaking my hand firmly the first time we were officially introduced. We both knew what that meant. It was a brotherhood. It meant we were on each other's side no matter what. It meant that we might sometimes fight against each other, but we would always fight for each other. We understood that intuitively without having to spell it out.

Randy was brash. He had strong opinions on just about everything and usually made sure anyone within earshot was aware of them. He was also resourceful. Even when he was in between shitty kitchen jobs, he always seemed to magically scrape up just enough money for the next cheap six-pack. He'd shamelessly count out dimes, nickels, and pennies at the register of the Fine Food Superette in Oregon Hill and walk out with a six-pack of Black Label beer. It was a survival skill. But he was always generous. If Randy had beer and you needed one, he would share with you until it was all gone.

Randy didn't always show up for band practice, but that wasn't a problem. We had plenty of work to do getting the instrumentals tight. Randy came regularly enough to stay rehearsed and current with what was happening. And things were moving fast.

Burn the Priest had worked steadily while I was away and had established themselves on the Richmond rock club scene. They also started playing out of town quite a bit, in particular making regular trips to Philadelphia. The band had been well received in an underground network of punk rock shows in inner city warehouses and squats there. I was excited to hear that Burn the Priest had been drawing even more people there than they were in Richmond. We had a show coming up in Philadelphia at a warehouse space called Stalag 13. It would be my first show back with the band.

The day of the show, we precisely loaded the gear into our extended, blue 1978 Dodge Tradesman van. Abe had built a loft into the back cargo section of the van that was big enough to contain all our gear, but only if it were packed tightly and without any wasted space. There was still just enough room above the loft for a couple people to lay out on top if they wanted a break from the captain's chairs up front or the tattered love seat in the back passenger section. The van's only ventilation was the two roll down front windows and two back door windows that pushed out slightly on a hinge. Randy and Abe chain-smoked cigarettes. We all smoked, but they smoked all the time. We were a rolling smoke pit. We kept a few empty

Gatorade bottles handy to use as urinals. We'd figured out that the large thirty-two-ounce wide mouth bottles worked best. We knew we would be drinking beer on the way up to the show, and we didn't want to have to stop for piss breaks. With no seatbelts, bald tires, urine-filled Gatorade bottles, and a few six-packs of Black Label beer, we rambled the four hours up I-95 north to Philadelphia for our show at Stalag 13.

Located in the west part of the city, Stalag 13 was a self-sufficient, independently run, homemade punk rock venue in a bleak neighborhood. For blocks in every direction, abandoned buildings stood shoulder to shoulder with slumlord-owned apartments and run-down markets with iron bars on the windows. Homeless people pushed shopping carts full of aluminum cans and scrap metal down the middle of the street. Police and ambulance sirens wailed with predictable regularity.

In the late 1990s, a group of local punk rockers moved into a vacant and neglected commercial building near Thirty-eighth and Lancaster. They pieced together functional plumbing and electricity, turning the bare bones shell into a semi-habitable space. They sectioned off a living area in the back and built a small platform to serve as a makeshift stage in the front of the narrow brick room. They began booking punk rock shows and named the space Stalag 13. It was perfect timing. Philly's punk scene was thriving, and the success of the locally based Relapse Records had put the city's scene on the radar of larger underground touring bands and national acts. Stalag 13's DIY, outlaw vibe was attractive to both bands and fans alike. In little time, the space was considered to be just as relevant a tour stop as some of Philly's more official clubs. There were legendary shows there, early in the careers of bands who went on to much more mainstream notoriety like Cave In, Dillinger Escape Plan, Coalesce, and of course Burn the Priest.

As we pulled up to Stalag to start loading in our gear, I could tell there was already a buzz about our band. A small group of people were hanging around in front, early arrivals, excited for the show. I noticed them paying close attention to us. They'd been watching us from the second we opened our van doors. We were clearly something different. We didn't dress like the Philly crowd. We looked more metal and less punk. We spoke slower and had a different slang. I could feel that we were a spectacle long before we ever turned on our amps.

Everyone hanging around wanted to talk to Randy, who happily obliged. Randy felt at home in Philly and had a lot of friends there. A couple of years earlier, Randy and his friend, Philly native Mikey Brosnan, had been part of a network of punk rock freight train riders. They'd hop trains and ride in the cargo cars, traveling the country like modern-day hobos. Mikey and Randy had ridden freight trains together for most of a summer. Randy returned home to Richmond, where he promptly joined Burn the Priest, and Mikey went back to Philadelphia, where he helped to establish Stalag 13.

The night of my first Stalag show, the room was slam packed by the time we went on. A humid haze of sweat and cigarette smoke hung low and thick. We were drunk, or at least well on our way to it. Mikey lived just up the street, and we were going to crash on his floor that night. There was no need for a designated driver. Even if we needed one, it probably wouldn't have worked out. We were reckless and stupid.

We stepped up onto the rickety platform stage with Stalag's graffiti-splattered front wall as our backdrop. With no formal introductions other than an indiscernible mumble from Randy into the mic saying something about "Burn the Priest from Richmond motherfuckin' Virginia," Chris swung into a quick succession of staggered, stuttering drum accents. The rest of us followed suit, exploding into "Suffering Bastard." The room erupted.

As we leaned into our first song, it occurred to me that I hadn't considered what this new version of Burn the Priest would be like in a live setting. Of course, I understood the nature of our music. I knew the riffs were uncompromisingly heavy and the song structures frenetic. I was aware that our speed and sheer volume induced a visceral response. But the explosion of chaos that I was a part of that first night at Stalag 13 was a shock even to me. The audience lunged forward toward the band and then pulled back away like a strong ocean tide. Slam dancers and moshers swung their limbs violently, some connecting with the heads and faces of those near them. People toward the side of the room climbed onto the tables and file cabinets that lined the walls, hoping for a better view and a refuge from the violence on the floor.

Randy was a typhoon. He shrieked and growled into his microphone with its black cable wrapped tightly around his arm. Pacing the stage, he stared into the eyes of fans in the front row, grabbing the backs of their heads and screaming directly into their faces, nose to nose. He beat the microphone against his forehead, rhythmically to the accents of the music, so intently that by the third song, a steady stream of blood ran down his face. He climbed the low-hanging plumbing pipes, swinging over the heads of the audience, bleeding and snarling.

The rest of us were charged up as well. I stood planted, with my legs spread as widely as possible, low to the ground with my beat-up 1975 Gibson Les Paul slung almost to my knees. I swung my whole body forward and backward to the rhythm of the music, pivoting at the hip, long hair trailing behind. I looked like one of those pump jacks that extract oil from the ground, bobbing furiously, trying to give myself a concussion. Chris was a fury of swinging arms behind his ragged black drum kit. Campbell lunged in time with the music, his blue Guild Pilot bass hanging low. Abe weaved and bobbed, intermittently gritting his teeth and looking mean but then visibly laughing at the lunacy of it all.

Amid all the chaos, Randy staggered over to my side of the stage and made eye contact. He smirked at me and raised his eyebrows excitedly. I grinned right back. We were annihilating this place. And we both knew that we were just getting started.

After the show, we drank. Of course, we'd been drinking before the show, but we amped it up even more after we played. Alcohol was a constant presence in Burn the Priest. Even in the initial jam sessions before I'd moved to Chicago, Burn the Priest felt as much like a drinking club as it did a band. When I returned to rejoin the group, the collective alcohol intake had picked up even more. I'd been drinking a lot more in Chicago myself, so I fell right into the groove. Burn the Priest drank in the van on the way to shows. We drank while we waited to go on stage. We drank while we played. We drank after we played. We drank when we got to wherever we were sleeping that night. We drank until we passed out. It wasn't necessarily all of us all of the time. But it was most of us most of the time.

With our new lineup solidified, Burn the Priest got busy. We continued booking shows at Stalag 13 and played regularly in Richmond to growing audiences. We upgraded our rehearsal space to a huge, second floor room in a commercial building in the Scott's Addition neighborhood of Richmond. The floor was covered in broken, crumbling asbestos tiles, so we covered it with bright green Astroturf, like you'd find on a miniature golf course. It was hideous. Randy had recently broken up with a girlfriend, which left him homeless, so he moved into the practice space for a while. Nobody minded. If anything, it meant he'd be at rehearsals more often. We were all at rehearsals more often.

Our friend in Philadelphia, Mikey Brosnan, had started an independent record label called Legion Records. He'd begun by releasing seven-inch vinyl split singles with a different band on either side. These relatively low-budget releases were popular in the punk and underground scene as an affordable way to have music circulating. Countless underground record labels made names for themselves by releasing singles from up-and-coming bands. Usually run as a hobby or by musicians to create an outlet for their own bands, most of these labels had few resources and humble ambitions. Some, however, grew into legitimate success stories, like Sub Pop and Dischord Records. Mikey was ready to level up and release a full-length CD on his label. He'd scraped together $2,500 of his own money, much of it from a credit card advance, and was putting it all toward funding a Burn the Priest LP.

With Mikey's funding and an album's worth of material, we set out to make our record. Randy had suggested Steve Austin to be the producer and engineer. Steve was the guitarist and front man of an abstract noise metal band called Today Is the Day. Burn the Priest had played a show or two with them. Although I wasn't a huge fan, I appreciated their confrontational performances and avant-garde interpretation of metal and hardcore. Today Is the Day was signed to Relapse Records, a label that we not-so-secretly aspired to sign to ourselves. Steve was a well-known figure in the scene that we were breaking into, *and* he dug our band. He had his own studio and was willing to work on our small budget. It was a great match.

On the ten-hour drive up to Austin Enterprise Recording and Mastering, Steve's studio in Clinton, Massachusetts, the steering on our van went out. We were stuck for a day and a half in Rahway, New Jersey, as we waited for the parts to show. We spent that time piled up in the shittiest motel room imaginable, drinking the shittiest beer imaginable, and grumbling about how our already rushed recording session was now going to be even more rushed. We couldn't extend the studio time. Steve's calendar was booked solid, and most of us had to get back to our day jobs.

We finally arrived at the studio a couple days late. We were concerned about having lost some time and anxious to get started. I hadn't met Steve before. His stage persona in Today Is the Day was dark and brooding; he was menacing with a convincingly deranged vibe. But as we made our official introductions in the parking lot, I found Steve to be warm and genial. He was entirely different from his reputation as the resident lunatic on the Relapse Records roster. It turns out Steve had been born and raised in rural Tennessee. We had similar musical references. We dressed the same way. We laughed at the same jokes.

Austin Enterprise was a small, efficiently arranged studio. There was a tiny lounge in the front entry that opened into a live room with just enough space to set up a full band. The control room was at the back, housing a large mixing board and an array of outboard effects and processing equipment.

We loaded in our gear while Chris set up his drums in the middle of the live room. Steve placed microphones strategically around the kit once it was in place. Our process would be to record isolated drum performances of all the songs first. The band would play together, but the focus of the takes would be solely on the drums. Once we captured good drum takes, we'd record the rest of the instruments and vocals one at a time, ultimately blending all the pieces into a cohesive recording of each song. Layering the pieces together individually would allow for improved isolation of each instrument, which benefited sound quality. It also facilitated more accurate performances: any mistakes were easier to fix since each instrument was being recorded by itself.

The sessions were rushed but productive. Chris was well rehearsed and got his drum takes for all ten songs down by the second day of recording. Once Chris had finished, Abe, John, and I recorded our parts one at a time, with Steve at the mixing board in the control room. That took a couple days as well. I enjoyed the process. Recording tracks one at a time allowed us to assemble solid performances without the pressure of having to play through entire songs mistake free.

After we recorded all the basic instrumental tracks for each song, it was finally Randy's turn. With the clock ticking, Randy unleashed a chain of venomous vocal performances. Channeling genuine rage, he belted out song after song. His lanky frame twisted and contorted as he held out unfathomably long screams, gasping for breath at the end of each take. He screamed himself into disoriented states, losing his place in the song, overcome with the emotions fueling his catharsis.

Any good producer knows how to assess the mindset of the artist they're working with, and Steve Austin recognized lunacy when he saw it. He tapped into Randy's energy, pushing him even harder with confrontational demands and volatile feedback shouted through the playback headphones. At one point Steve threatened to shove a loaded shotgun in Randy's face. It was all a bit unhinged, but it made for some ferocious vocal takes!

Randy recorded the vocals for the entire Burn the Priest album in one long, insane night. By any measure of professional recording standard, that is astonishing. But we had no other choice. There wasn't time or money to consider anything different.

With the album recorded, Steve immediately mixed the ten songs in an all-night marathon session on our last night there. He printed the final mixes as the sun was coming up, and we loaded up our van to make the long drive home to Virginia. The entire album was recorded and mixed in five days and nights.

We still needed cover art, though. Through our Philly connections, we'd become friends with a young illustrator and graphic designer named Ken Adams. His band, Trailer Park Riot, was based in Newark, Delaware, and had played some shows with us. He loved our band, and he was generous with his time and creative contribution to the project.

I hadn't discussed Ken's plans for the artwork. I'd seen some show flyers that he'd done and knew he was skilled, so I figured we were in great hands. When Ken finished with the album cover, he sent it to Chris who unveiled it to the rest of the band. Everyone loved it. Everyone except me. I hated it.

Ken's art was a detailed illustration depicting a group of demon-possessed nuns burning a priest alive at the stake. They held flaming torches and pitchforks in the air, celebrating while the doomed priest clutched rosary beads and prayed to a blackened sky. It was pure blasphemy.

I've never been a follower of any organized religion. My parents were quietly Christian, but they weren't regular churchgoers and thankfully they never forced religion on me or my brother. Even so, I've always had a general, undefined belief that some sort of higher power, "God"-type force exists. As a young man, I didn't spend much time wondering what that power might be or what it had to do with me. I just believed it was there.

But my distaste toward Ken's artwork had very little to do with offending my spiritual notions. My aversion was that it just seemed silly. The band was already named *Burn the Priest*. A literal interpretation of that phrase for the album art was missing an opportunity for a more meaningful representation. We'd put so much of our time and emotion into the writing and recording of the songs; I hated thinking that people's first impression of the project was going to be a cartoon drawing of a bunch of nuns burning a priest. Of course, this is the type of conversation one should have with an artist *before* they spend weeks on an illustration, not after. Ken wasn't about to start over. Besides, everyone else loved the cover, which meant I was the odd man out.

With the album recorded and the cover art done, Mikey pressed a thousand copies of our debut LP for his Legion Records label. The album was placed on some mail order lists and stocked in a handful of independent record stores, mostly in the Northeast. A few copies were sent out for reviews in punk and metal magazines, and the band was given a couple hundred copies to sell at our shows. That was it. That was the release. But as humble as it was, we still felt verified. It was a huge deal to have a full-length CD. We were proud of the songs and how the album sounded. But I never really got used to the cover. I was embarrassed by it. I wanted to show my parents the music project I'd been working so hard on, but it's not the most comfortable thing to show your mom a CD cover of nuns murdering a priest. She was supportive but didn't really understand it. My dad told me that he could tell the music was well played, but suggested we get someone that could "actually sing" to front the band.

Burn the Priest spent the year that followed performing live as often as we could. We played shows at The Caboose bar in Garner, North Carolina, and at Stalag 13 and Fake House, two warehouse spaces in Philadelphia. We booked punk rock bars in Baltimore, Maryland, and Wilmington, North Carolina. We played on campus at James Madison University in Harrisonburg, Virginia, and in a suburban Delaware garage, sharing both of those shows with an early lineup of the band Dillinger Escape Plan. Willie, Chris's younger brother, often rode along with us. Willie was about four years younger than the rest of us and was a talented drummer and guitar player himself. He was always fun to have around and helped us out at shows. Everywhere we played, we'd sell a few copies of our

CD along with some T-shirts we'd had printed to help keep gas in the van.

We were starting to build a name for ourselves and moving up the ranks. And Relapse Records had been noticing. Representatives from the label were often at our shows. They'd chat with us afterward and seemed interested in everything we had going on. We were dying to be on that label and felt like it only made sense that they sign us. Relapse even gave us an unpaid, unadvertised opening slot on their showcase stage at the Milwaukee Metal Fest. We drove straight there from Virginia, arriving a day early and living out of our van. Campbell met some dudes who drove down from Canada to see the festival and had crossed the border with bags of weed shoved up their asses. I didn't smoke any of that. The next evening we played a short but rocket-fueled set that got rave reviews. Following our performance that night, Randy did a stage dive during Brutal Truth's set. He landed headfirst on the floor, splitting his forehead open to the bone. Abe, ever the videographer, went with Randy to the hospital and made a 9mm film of Randy getting stitches and staples in his head. They were both shit-faced drunk. We all were.

We had convinced ourselves that we were a perfect fit for Relapse Records. But they remained hesitant. We'd heard from a few sources close to the label that much of their apprehension toward signing us was that we were just too volatile. From the outside looking in, we must have appeared chaotic and reckless. We were pretty much always drinking. We were aggressive and callous with one another. We were blood and vomit and broken glass. We looked like a band that could break up any minute. But that's just the way we were. Our threshold for confrontation and squalor was so high that what felt normal to us made other people uncomfortable.

Around the same time, another huge show opportunity arose. Our friends in the New York City band Disassociate helped us get added to a bill at the legendary CBGB club in Manhattan. Widely recognized as one of the birthplaces of American punk rock, CBGB was the site of some of the earliest performances by the Ramones, Talking Heads, Television, Patti Smith, and countless other legendary acts. It later became home to New York's groundbreaking hardcore scene, featuring acts like Bad Brains, Beastie Boys, Misfits, and others. CBGB was sacred ground, so we were thrilled at the chance to play such a historic venue.

As more opportunities presented themselves, we began to take our band even more seriously. It may not have been apparent to Relapse Records, but we were becoming more driven. Our goals certainly didn't include world tours or major label record deals. Given the type of music we played, those would be ridiculous aspirations. We simply wanted to write better songs and to elevate our performances. We wanted to dominate the small underground scene that we were a part of.

It was also becoming evident that Abe wasn't nearly as focused as the rest of us. His career in videography had been steadily growing. He was getting bigger and more labor intensive contracts that left him with less time to write and rehearse new material. We all agreed that Randy should speak with him since they had the most musical history together. To everyone's surprise, it was an easy conversation. "Yeah, man. I've totally been slacking," Abe chuckled in agreement. "I've just been slammed with work stuff. Give me a couple months. I'll make music a bigger priority. I'll turn it around."

It was a fair request. And we were relieved that he understood our position. But as we rehearsed for the upcoming show at CBGB, nothing much was changing. Abe was still preoccupied. He seemed agitated and stressed trying to balance his band and work obligations. He hadn't brought in any new riffs, and his playing was still sloppy.

We quietly started thinking about another option. Willie had recently moved to Richmond. He was a killer player and had a ton of riffs. We all liked Willie and were already used to having him in the van on road trips. Willie wasn't pushing to be in the band and he never said a word about taking Abe's spot, but it was easy to see that if the slot were to open up, Willie was ready to jump in.

It was an uncomfortable predicament, but it was clear what we had to do: we were going to have to part ways with Abe. That conversation was more difficult than the first one. We called a band meeting. Together, we explained our position to Abe. We loved him but we felt held back. We didn't want to compete for his time and creative focus. We understood why his career was more important, but we weren't willing to work around it.

Abe handled the situation with class. He was disappointed and hurt, but he knew as well as we did that his focus had shifted. He knew he was no longer keeping up. Abe humbly accepted our decision with one request. "I really don't want to miss that CBGB show," he confessed. "I've always wanted to play there. That place is legendary!"

This was a fair request. Abe had given over three years of his life helping to build Burn the Priest. He'd fixed the van countless times, helped pay for recordings that we couldn't afford, made posters and flyers, built lofts, and remodeled rehearsal spaces. Most important, he'd been a big part of writing some great songs. Abe was an integral component of our early sound and style. We all agreed that he had more than earned the right to play one last special show. A few weeks later, we drove to New York City and performed at CBGB. It was a poorly attended show, but it was still special for us. We'd made it to that historic stage together. It was Abe's last show with us. When we returned home, Abe amicably left Burn the Priest.

Having known in advance that Abe would be departing, Willie was ready to take over his spot. He'd learned all the songs. With a couple rehearsals under our belts, we got right back to booking gigs locally and out of town. One of our first road trips with Willie as an official member was to Indianapolis for a show at the Lincoln Theater with Zao and Soilent Green. Willie was phenomenal. We'd never sounded so tight.

We also immediately started writing new material. Willie had brought in an excited energy with lots of new riffs and song ideas to contribute. He and I quickly got into a songwriting groove, compiling riffs that, as a band, we turned into songs.

A new album was becoming possible. Though we hadn't sold huge numbers of our first album, we had gotten some visibility and positive press. Our drummer Chris worked as technician in charge of a network of computers in a research lab at VCU. His extensive computer knowledge and early fluency on the internet was a big advantage. Chris had posted some MP3s of our music on a file sharing site. The name *Burn the Priest* attracted a lot of attention, and our music saw significant traffic there. Our fiery appearance at Milwaukee Metal Fest had also caught the eyes of a national music magazine that gave us a positive review and identified us as an up-and-coming band. And that message had been received: record labels were reaching out to express interest.

The first was a fairly well-known European-based metal label with a small American office who sent a scout out to meet with us. The young A&R representative was awkward and nervous when he showed up for our band practice showcase, but he tried his best to put on an attitude of hip, music business wisdom. After we assaulted him with an hour-long Burn the Priest rehearsal in a sweltering cinderblock room at about 115 decibels, Chris and I took our new friend out to a shitty strip club in South Richmond where we spent the next few hours drinking heavily and talking all things metal. By the time we dropped him off at his hotel at the end of the night, the poor dude was stumbling and slurring his words. He appeared to be having fun, but he was a mess. He was in over his head. Chris and I had a laugh together, wondering if the dude would even make his flight in the morning. A couple weeks later we received a shitty contract offer from that label. It was essentially an agreement for them to put out our records in exchange for us giving up ownership of everything, including our merchandising rights. Not a fucking chance. Pass.

The only other label interested in Burn the Priest was a new label started by EJ Johantgen and Dan Fitzgerald. EJ and Dan were high-level staffers at Metal Blade Records, one of the world's largest heavy metal record companies. Metal Blade was legendary, helping launch the careers of acts like Slayer, Cannibal Corpse, Armored Saint, and countless others. Their new label was called Prosthetic Records.

We were initially skeptical of Prosthetic. They had only put out a few releases, none of which were all that successful. Additionally, unlike Relapse, who we'd long been hoping to sign with, Prosthetic didn't have an established roster of bands. They weren't a community, and they were unproven in terms of their ability to sell a lot of records.

Despite these drawbacks, Prosthetic did have a couple things going for them that intrigued us. They had access to all the marketing and distribution infrastructure of their parent label, Metal Blade. This meant that Prosthetic releases were primarily handled by the same teams of people who worked on official Metal Blade releases.

The other asset we saw with a small label like Prosthetic was that we wouldn't be competing with a lot of other bands for support and resources. A large established label gives a band the benefits of an existing infrastructure and promotional machine. But new bands often take a back seat to the established, moneymaking artists on the label. Prosthetic Records was unique in that it would present the best of both worlds: a small and dedicated team with access to a large-scale label machine. We saw promise.

And they saw promise in us. EJ and Dan soon made the long trip from Los Angeles to Richmond to see us perform. We scheduled a show at a tiny bar called Hole in the Wall to coincide with their visit. The show was lackluster. It was a lightly attended, weeknight show. The club didn't even have a proper stage or sound system. But none of us cared much about those details. We all knew that we were really only performing for EJ and Dan. That night we played as if it were a packed house in the biggest venue we'd ever set up in.

After the show, we hung out with the two of them. They were cool and casual regular dudes. We discussed their philosophy as a label. They only cared to put out music that they liked. They had to believe in a band creatively to be willing to invest in them. We talked about different touring strategies and the various music scenes that a band like Burn the Priest could link in with. They liked what they saw in us and could tell we were dedicated. And nobody got shit-faced drunk that night.

Soon after EJ and Dan returned to the West Coast, they sent a deal offer to us, which we forwarded to a trusted attorney we'd started working with. With the help of our lawyer, we discussed the ins and outs of the contract. The deal provided us with a decent enough budget to comfortably make another album without giving up ownership of our band and merchandise. Prosthetic Records would have the option to keep us on their label for several records if they chose, and the recording advances would grow a bit with each successive album. The royalties and recoupment terms leaned heavily in favor of the label, but we didn't have much leverage because we hadn't sold many records. They were the ones taking the financial risk by investing in us, so we understood why they would want such favorable returns.

Even so, we understood that nobody was getting rich from this. It was an introductory deal for an introductory band.

Like everyone else, I understood that Prosthetic's modest deal offer was fair considering where we were as a band. But I did have a dilemma. I was still uncomfortable with our band name. My distaste had only gotten worse as bigger opportunities arose for us. I knew that if we signed a real recording contract, we would forever be locked into the name Burn the Priest. I couldn't reconcile working so hard at something, putting so much creative energy into it, then representing it with a band name as silly and absurd as Burn the Priest.

I lobbied my case to my bandmates. They all knew how I felt, but for me to be pushing so hard to change the name just as we were getting real label interest was difficult for them to swallow.

Campbell loved the name Burn the Priest. He thought I was overthinking the whole thing. "I don't see the big deal," he reasoned. "Let's face it, the music we play is pretty extreme and kind of ridiculous. And so is the name. It makes sense. Plus, it's cool and people remember it." He wasn't wrong. And maybe I was being unnecessarily dramatic about it. But I couldn't get past my apprehensions.

Chris wasn't thrilled about changing the name either. His resistance was based on a more practical mindset. "We're about to get signed based on the buzz we've created as Burn the Priest," he pointed out. "Changing the name means starting over and rebuilding. The label may not be interested in that." Chris had a solid point. It was risky enough for Prosthetic to invest in a relatively unknown band. That risk got even more severe if we changed the name. We'd be starting from zero.

Randy and Willie were on the fence. They both understood my point that our name was a potential liability. They agreed that it could limit our options from a marketing standpoint and could dictate how audiences would receive the band. But they also saw Chris and John's points about the value of the name we'd built for ourselves as Burn the Priest. It was a lot to consider.

Over the weeks that all this debate was going on, we continued to write and rehearse. Willie and I locked into a productive songwriting rhythm, churning out streams of groove-heavy riffs that the band would then collectively mold into songs. Songs like "Pariah," "The Subtle Arts of Murder and Persuasion," and "In the Absence of the Sacred" flowed through our hands, feeling almost divinely inspired. We were flooded with ideas, sometimes so intensely it was difficult to keep up.

During our creative surge, I thought about how deeply committed we were to our music and how intense the writing process was for us. To me, it felt spiritual in nature, almost like a religious experience. I'd earlier stuck an American flag sticker on the 1975 Les Paul that I used as my main guitar. I liked the juxtaposition of feeling like we were counterculture and punk rock but still flying the flag. A loud and proud punk rock patriot. Those concepts coalesced for me into the phrase "New American Gospel." I liked it so much, I suggested we use it as the new name for the band.

"I don't know man," Chris said. "It's definitely cool, but it feels more like an album title than a band name." I knew he was right. So now we had a great name for an album, but we still had a shitty band name. Fortunately, Chris was open to suggestions for a new band name. It was an idea that had been hiding in plain view. "If we're really going to change our name, why don't we use the name of that other band that you played in for like two seconds back when we started?" he asked.

Several years before, just as Chris, John, Matt, and I had first begun jamming together as Burn the Priest, I was also playing with a couple other people. It was similar type of project, consisting of me on guitar and my friends Elisa Nader on bass and Chris Gallo on drums. True to Richmond tradition, we played heavy, original, instrumental songs. We sounded a little more math rock and slightly less thrash metal than Burn the Priest. We only lasted long enough to write a few songs and play a party or two, but we did have a band name. We had called ourselves Lamb of God.

Chris continued his pitch. "That's a pretty great name for a metal band. Only a handful of people ever saw that band. It's not like anyone would know. Do you think Chris and Elisa would care if we used it?"

I loved it. Truth is, I probably would've loved just about anything in place of Burn the Priest. But Chris was right that Lamb of God was an awesome name for a metal band. It carried on a classic tradition of using religious iconography in a heavy metal context. Metal legends Black Sabbath and Judas Priest had juxtaposed religious concepts with dark, doomsday aesthetics to create heavy, foreboding backdrops for their music. The name Lamb of God served the same end by pairing a Christian reference to the messiah with our extreme metal music and self-destructive, apocalyptic lyrics. I loved everything about it. After a few discussions and a couple days of thinking it over, we were all in. I felt incredibly supported. Even though not everyone in the band had initially been in favor of the idea, they all knew how strongly I'd felt about it and were willing to consider it.

I nervously made a call to my friends in the "first" version of Lamb of God, just to make sure they were cool with us using the name. I'm not sure what I would've done if they hadn't been okay with it, but fortunately both Chris and Elisa had no problems with us adopting it. And with that, it was official. Burn the Priest would become Lamb of God.

There was, however, one final detail left in our name change saga: our recording contract. Our deal with Prosthetic Records had been moving forward. Our attorney had smoothed over a couple small points we wanted changed, and everything was just about in place. All that was left to do was for us to sign the deal. But the label was signing Burn the Priest. We still needed to find out if they were willing to sign Lamb of God.

We all met at Chris's house to call EJ and Dan as a group and tell them the news. We were optimistic that they'd be willing to move forward, even though changing the band name was a big deal. We were confident and committed to our decision. "What's up, guys!" Chris cheered into the phone, trying to mask any anxiety that EJ might notice. "We're all here together. The contract looks cool. Our attorney has given us the go ahead to sign it and we're all super excited to be a part of Prosthetic Records."

"Great! We're thrilled to get going," said EJ.

"There's just one thing," Chris continued.

"Yeah, what's that?"

"We've decided to change the band name!" Chris blurted out as enthusiastically as possible.

There was silence on the other end. After a pregnant pause, EJ replied as calmly as he could. "I don't know if that's a good idea. You've done a whole lot of groundwork as Burn the Priest. Why would you want to erase all of that and start from scratch?"

"We just want the focus to be on the music," Chris explained. "We don't want to have some silly, childish band name pigeonholing us forever."

"I don't like this idea at all," EJ protested. "You're pulling the rug out from under us before we even get started. It could derail the whole plan. But just out of curiosity, what's the new band name?"

"Lamb of God."

There was another long pause. We all held our breath, waiting to hear some kind of response. Finally, it came. "I fucking love it! It's perfect! Man, you guys scared the shit out of me. But this is going to be great."

Relief and excitement swept over us. We'd done it. We'd changed our name to something that wouldn't narrow our possibilities. And we'd signed our first real record contract.

CHAPTER 10

NEW AMERICAN GOSPEL

"ONE WAY OUT"
THE ALLMAN BROTHERS BAND

The Allman Brothers Band are one of the most perfectly assembled musical mosaics in the history of rock, though the uninitiated may easily overlook them. Their most widely known song, 1973's "Ramblin Man," is a jangly, country twinged pop song that reached number two on the Billboard charts. It was kept out of the number one position by Gregg Allman's future wife Cher. Guitarist Dickey Betts wrote the song after his bandmate and guitar partner Duane Allman died. "Ramblin Man" was a product of the band's search for new footing after losing a key member. It is a well-written song, a rock classic, but its sweet guitar harmonies and catchy chorus hooks steer clear of the deep blues and R & B roots where the band finds its true soul. No amount of studio production or pop sensibility can compete with the majesty of Berry Oakley, Jai Johanson, and

Butch Trucks locking into a hypnotic groove while Dickey Betts, Gregg Allman, and Duane Allman decorate it with tear-jerking blues solos and tortured vocals delivered with Gregg's signature rasp.

The band's At Fillmore East LP has long been my favorite showcase of their genre-bending alchemy. Assembled from a two-night stand at promoter Bill Graham's legendary venue, it features live, stretched out versions of both original songs and covers of classic blues numbers. The solo sections are often improvised, which facilitated freestyle, stream of consciousness guitar leads highlighting Duane Allman's virtuosity.

For decades I've used it as my own personal guitar lesson. Duane Allman died before I was born, but dropping the needle of my turntable on my well-worn copy of the double album allows me to jam along with the band almost as if I were standing there with them playing along to "One Way Out" or "You Don't Love Me," two of my favorite performances on the album. I've never stopped learning from it: I always seem to find a new chord voicing or note pattern that I hadn't keyed into before, while previous sections further ingrain themselves into my guitar vocabulary. Duane even repeats lines several times in places, almost as if to reinforce them for me as I'm trying to figure them out.

Playing guitar is a constant state of learning. I've never considered myself to be a very accomplished player. I've struggled at times with imposter syndrome regarding Lamb of God's eventual success. I'm not that knowledgeable about music theory and I'm not the fastest or most accurate player, but I do have good groove and a good touch. I frequently stumble onto great riffs and seem to have a unique voice on the instrument. Those things are difficult to quantify. It's just a feel thing, and I'm grateful to accept it as a gift from the universe. But guitar lessons from Duane Allman probably help too.

Bolstered by the creative partnership between Willie and me, and freed from the psychological annoyance of our former band name, Lamb of God was riding a wave of creativity. We built on the Burn the Priest sound and fused thrash, doom, death metal, and hardcore with our native Richmond math metal into a combustible mixture that didn't sound like anyone else. Songs like "A Warning," "The Subtle Arts of Murder and Persuasion," and "Pariah" fell from our collective hands as if they'd already existed and we were just the antenna receiving the audio transmission. And one of the last songs we wrote for the new album became one of its most important.

Our deal with Prosthetic Records meant we'd have a slightly better budget to record our new album, but it was still modest. We again brought in Steve Austin to produce, engineer, and mix the project since we were happy with the Burn the Priest album we'd done with him. Steve came from the same low-budget, underground scene that we did, so he was willing to work with what we had.

About a week before we left for the studio, Willie came to rehearsal with a menacing riff to jam on. At first I was annoyed with the idea of working out another new song so close to our studio time. But Chris was particularly excited by Willie's riff, and I couldn't deny that there was something special about it. Willie played his dark, rolling, top string riff over and over while Chris worked out a simple cadence of accents on the drums for the intro. John and I locked into Chris's drum pattern for the first few measures, then the whole band exploded, fleshing out Willie's winding guitar line. For the second section of the song, I improvised a bluesy turnaround that quickly shifted into a descending chromatic scale pattern. Willie and I often write that way. It's an intuitive creative connection: one of us plays a riff and the other freestyles the next change because the idea that pops up out of nowhere is often the perfect part. Chris added to our new composition, directing a bridge section in which we all synced up to his off-kilter kick drum rhythm. This bridge idea borrowed heavily from Swedish math metal wizards Meshuggah and added an interesting dynamic.

We knew we'd come up with one of the most exciting pieces of music in the new batch of songs. We were so thrilled with it that we decided it would be the first song on the album. Never mind that it had no lyrics or vocal patterns. This meant that Randy would have less than a week to get familiar with a new song that was going to be the lead track for our new album and then come up with the lyrics—with no rehearsal. No pressure. To honor our favorite cheap beer, we gave the song the working title "Black Label."

In the spring of 2000, we headed back up to the Austin Enterprise studio to record our first album as Lamb of God. This time we had enough money to book a single hotel room for the entire week that we'd be there. It was a step up from our previous trip when the whole band slept in the studio. When we arrived to load in the first day, we found that Austin Enterprise had some new members. Steve had recently signed a new bass player and drummer in his band Today Is the Day. They'd left their band Lethargy and their hometown of Rochester, New York, to move to Massachusetts and live in Steve's studio while they wrote and recorded their album. Their names were Brann Dailor and Bill Kelliher. We all became fast friends.

Our recording schedule was tight, which meant we had to start working early each day. While we warmed up in the morning and rehearsed the songs that we'd be recording that day, Brann and Bill slept in the lounge, oblivious to the speed metal band blasting just a few feet away. As seasoned veterans, they were immune to the noise. A few years later, the pair gained worldwide success as founding members of Mastodon.

Our recording process for *New American Gospel* was similar to the way we'd tracked the Burn the Priest album. Willie played along with

Chris to get solid performances of each song on drums, then we layered all the instruments individually on top of the drum takes. We'd predetermined the order of the album's song sequence, and Chris got it in his head that he wanted to record the songs in the same order that they would appear on the finished album. I never understood why this mattered so much to him. It didn't matter to me. We could've recorded the songs in whatever order we wanted and then sequenced them when the album was mixed and mastered. That's most often the approach. But like many creative people, Chris sometimes had idiosyncratic ways of doing things that made him feel more comfortable. That's not meant to be a knock against him because I'm sometimes the same way.

Another idiosyncrasy in our drum takes was Chris's use of metal plates on his kick drums. Each of his bass drum heads and kick drum beaters had a small round, metal disk fastened to them. When the beater hit the drum, the disks impacted, forming a high-pitched sound on top of the lower boom created by the bass drum head. This was supposed to give the drums a sharper, more audible attack like the triggered, sampled kick drum sounds common on many modern metal recordings of the time. I guess it's a matter of taste, but I always thought they sounded obnoxious, like an antique typewriter or a toy drum set. But I figured we could make it sound heavy in the mix, and besides, I wasn't the drummer. I wouldn't have been receptive to Chris telling me how to dial in my amplifier, so if he wanted silver dollars taped to his drum pedals, who was I to disagree? Steve Austin very likely saw trouble on the horizon when he saw the strange metal kick pads, but it wasn't the kind of session where the producer mandated the drummer change his kick pedals, so we moved forward. Odd kick drum sounds aside, Chris's performances were spectacular.

With the drums laid down, guitars and bass were next. Though we had recorded a few demos in preparation for the album, the *New*

American Gospel sessions were the first time Willie and I worked together in a proper studio. Isolating each other's instruments during recording magnified how well our individual playing styles complement each other. Willie's playing is unique. He has an oddly stiff picking hand, holding his right arm locked parallel to the guitar. He plays with a very light attack, which helps facilitate his stunning rhythm speed and accuracy. Willie is largely unfamiliar with traditional music theory: scale patterns, modes, and sophisticated chord voicings aren't a language he speaks since he's self-taught and learns by ear. He's focused on the heavy riffing in his favorite bands growing up, like Sepultura and Kreator. This detachment from the standard rules of music has always been an asset to the band. Willie often makes irregular note choices in his riffs, intuitively rejecting the "correct" scale pattern. His abstract genius has become a core component of the Lamb of God sound and provides a valuable balance to my playing style.

My playing style is far more conventional. The lessons I took when I began playing gave me a basic understanding of music theory. My earliest guitar heroes were legendary guitarists like Eddie Van Halen, Jimi Hendrix, and Jimmy Page, all of whom had deep musical knowledge. I also spent a lot of time learning songs by ear, and the classic rock songs I was figuring out helped reinforce my rudimentary understanding of music theory. My picking hand is also different from Wille's. Where he has a light touch, I'm heavy handed, digging the pick hard into the strings. This creates a different texture: Willie's sound is accurate and concise, while mine is heavier and more expansive.

Our timing also has minute differences. Willie's picking lines up directly on top of each beat, but I innately play just behind the count. It's not that my timing or meter is bad; on the contrary, it's actually quite good. It's just that mine is more of a style nuance based in a bluesier, old-school feel that comes natural in my playing. The result of our different playing styles is an ideal balance of modern metal accuracy and throwback bluesy swagger. And that balance became the musical cornerstone of the Lamb of God sound, beginning with the material we wrote together for *New American Gospel* and continuing today.

We laid down our guitar tracks in fast time. It was exciting to hear the new songs coming to life. John followed up with powerful bass performances delivered with the efficiency that was becoming his hallmark style. John's playing is sometimes overlooked in the band, upstaged by Randy's outrageous energy and by the acrobatic drum and guitar parts flying around. But John's ability to fold into intricate riff patterns is top tier. He's also remarkably adept at transposing complicated guitar parts into smartly arranged bass lines, accentuating the core components of the riff. This solid anchor allows the rest of us to go apeshit without the whole thing falling apart.

But we had a problem. By the time we had recorded all the music for *New American Gospel*, Randy had hardly any time left to track his vocals. It was the same predicament he'd faced in the Burn the Priest sessions. In the early days, there was a flippant attitude among most of us regarding the importance of Randy's vocals compared to the rest of the music. Willie, John, Chris, and I considered them to be somewhat incidental. We were so focused on the details of the music and putting the instrumentals together that we overlooked the importance of Randy's role. It's an incredibly amateur way of seeing things because, if anything, people pay more attention to the vocals than they do to the minute details of the guitar or drum patterns. But we all had to learn that over time.

During the making of those first few albums, Randy often felt like an outsider in his own band. He didn't play an instrument. He didn't always understand the vernacular the rest of us used when we

139

composed music. He operated outside of the fraternity of the "musicians" in the band, unfairly relegated to second-class citizenship in the songwriting process. By the time we presented the songs to Randy for vocals, the rest of us had already had our say with them. We liked to consider ourselves a "democracy" when it came to writing music, but Randy didn't get much of a say until the music for the songs was already in place. When he did have suggestions, the rest of the band didn't take them too seriously.

Our band's early dysfunction in this "democracy" is revealed in the song "Black Label." We all agreed that the song had spectacular energy. It felt like the perfect way to start the album. But since Chris insisted that we record the songs in the order of our predetermined track listing, this meant Randy would be starting his vocal sessions with a song that he'd had very little time with. The rest of us didn't put up any resistance to recording the songs in any particular order because we simply didn't care. We'd already had enough time to learn and confidently perform our parts. Randy was the only band member affected by this process, and his argument for a more reasonable approach went overlooked. "Just take whatever you want the lyrics to be and scream them over the song" was the general attitude from the rest of us. And that's exactly what he did.

What resulted is one of the most caustic, incendiary vocal performances that Randy has ever laid down. The vitriol in his vocals on "Black Label" is genuine and rooted in his total disdain for being expected to commit a vocal to the album's opening track without having appropriate time to work it out. Sections of Randy's seething vocal are unintelligible, with very little connection to the actual lyrics. But in the same the way the instrumental had a magical energy, Randy's cyclone of contempt was undeniable.

The "Black Label" detour aside, Randy wrote fantastic lyrics for *New American Gospel*. "In the Absence of the Sacred" is a scathing critique of civilization's dependence on technology, and "The Black Dahlia" rants against growing nihilistic social attitudes. The personal accounts of police brutality in "O.D.H.G.A.B.F.E." added depth and meaning to the landscapes of unrelenting riffing that we had created.

Randy's writing inspired me to contribute to the lyrics too. "Confessional" was inspired by a recurring, anxiety-fueled dream of infinitely long steel rods falling from the sky as the ground beneath me collapsed into a free fall. Randy sat with me, thoughtfully reading over my lyric ideas and filling in spaces with his own contributions. It was the first of our many lyrical collaborations.

Once again, just as he had done on *Burn the Priest*, Randy belted out all the vocals for the *New American Gospel* album in a little over one day. Steve Austin mixed it on the fly as we packed up our gear to make the trip back to Richmond.

I had conflicted emotions about the album once we finished. I loved the songs and knew that everyone's performances were stellar. There was something magical about the energy we captured. But the overall sound quality was poor. The kick drums sounded bizarre, like we'd mic'd up Tupperware containers instead of bass drums. To make things worse, the weird click pad sounds had been picked up in the overhead mics as well, which meant that the cymbals couldn't be adjusted in the mix without having to work around the incessant metal tapping of the kick beaters. Steve Austin was left with the unenviable position of working around the mess created by the metal tapping all through the drum tracks. It would've been challenging for any engineer to mix around, but Steve had only a couple of hours. It's easy to see why the results fell short of expectations. Nonetheless, despite its sonic shortcomings, we knew the songs were great.

With the album recorded and mixed as good it was going to get, we worked on the cover art and CD booklet design. We again recruited Ken Adams to do the album artwork in keeping with the theme of seamless transition from the Burn the Priest release. I learned from my previous mistakes and was very engaged with Ken this time. But I didn't have a huge influence on the actual art because it wasn't necessary: a crown of thorns created from discarded industrial scraps was the perfect image to tie in Randy's dark, dystopian lyrical themes and the religious iconography of the band name. Ken, always going above and beyond, didn't simply illustrate the cover image. He actually created the crown of thorns and then photographed it. The matte brown and beige tones along with the rough, card stock paper of the original CD booklets gave the album a different aesthetic from the largely glossy, vibrant album covers popular with our peers.

Keeping things in the family, our old guitarist and talented photographer Abe Spear took the band photo that appears on the album art. The short haircut I'm sporting in the photo is evidence of my struggle to commit to a life path around this time. The journey of Burn the Priest and Lamb of God up to that point had taken a great deal of effort and sacrifice. We spent a lot of weekends out of town playing shows. We'd often leave after work on a Thursday or Friday and wouldn't return until late Sunday night, just in time to catch a few hours of sleep before going back to my roofing job early Monday morning. I was fortunate to have a trade job that allowed me to take time off work when I needed it, but time off work also meant not getting paid. This could be a problem because I had recently scraped together just enough money through my day job to buy a tiny house down an old forgotten street just east of downtown Richmond. I was working toward establishing stability in my life. Still, while the band was beginning to make a little money here and there, most of that was going toward gas, van maintenance, and rent for our practice space. So even with our growing success, the band didn't feel like a viable career path. Our music was too extreme to have any real hope of making it to a level that would allow us each a comfortable long-term living. This was a dilemma I'd been wrestling with ever since I'd rejoined the band a couple of years before.

A short time before we recorded the Burn the Priest album, I responded to a job posting by the Chesterfield County Fire Department for new firefighter recruits. Chesterfield is a large suburban county just south of Richmond. My older brother was a career firefighter, so I had spent plenty of time in fire stations. I understood the lifestyle and culture around fire service, and I also understood that it provided a stable living and great career opportunities.

A career as a firefighter was a terrifying prospect. I knew it would mean giving up my dream of playing music full time. I couldn't see a scenario that would allow me to balance both music and firefighting, but job security and financial stability was appealing. There was one problem, though: having long hair down past my shoulders was not going to make me an attractive job candidate, so before my first firefighter test, I walked into a barber shop on Broad Street.

"Can I get a haircut this morning?" I asked.

The barber, who also owned the shop, was an old man in his seventies. He looked me up and down and smiled wryly at my request. "It'll be my pleasure. Take it all off?"

"Yes sir. But leave me some on top, please. I don't want to look like a Marine."

"No danger of that," he mumbled. "Have a seat, son."

The old man quickly wrapped a cape around my shoulders, pulled out his electric clippers, and went to work. I watched my hair collect on the floor. He brushed me off, and I looked in the mirror. This was a good haircut.

"Looks much better," the old man said.

I smiled and thanked him as I paid. But even though it was a good haircut, I still hated it.

A few days later, I reported for the first stage of the firefighter application process, which covered background information, education status, and why I wanted to be a firefighter. After completing the written questions, I met some firefighters in charge of recruitment. They were chatty and engaging. The whole environment felt familiar to me since I'd spent all that time around fire stations hanging out with my brother during his shifts. Having a college degree and a brother who was already a firefighter would also help my chances. I was beginning to feel like this job could become a reality.

The second test was to be held on a Saturday morning in a few weeks. It was a physical test focusing on strength, agility, and endurance. I felt good about my chances. I was twenty-seven years old and had been a slate and copper roofer for a couple of years. I carried piles of heavy slates on my shoulders up forty-foot ladders daily. I'd worked eight-hour days, five days a week on a roof in sweltering hot Virginia summers. I was in the best shape of my life. There was no way I would fail this test.

Yet as appealing as this career move looked, I had a few reservations. The more the firefighting job grew from a dream to a reality, the more I felt the impact of what I'd be sacrificing. Cutting off my hair was one thing, but accepting a job with a defined, demanding schedule meant music would take a permanent back seat. Sure, I could still play guitar and maybe even have a band as a hobby. But my days of taking off work to go play shows would be over.

My plan had always been to perform the physical test to the best of my ability. But when I woke up the morning of the test, I looked at myself in the mirror as I brushed my teeth, and one thing became clear: I did not want to give up on this music path. No part of me believed at that moment that Lamb of God would ever provide me long-term financial stability. I didn't care. Music had been the most consistent source of joy in my life, my driving force. I couldn't let it go. And I was willing to accept whatever consequences came with that.

The time to report for my second firefighter application test came and went. That morning, the sun shone through my living room window. Duane Allman's Les Paul sung out a stream of soaring licks through my turntable and speakers. I was free. I'd let go of any expectation that I'd ever be financially stable and surrendered to my dream of pursuing music—wherever it might take me.

CHAPTER 11

DRUNK

"ONE HEADLIGHT"
THE WALLFLOWERS

I've long believed that one of Lamb of God's primary strengths is that we have always sounded different from our peers. Even when we were lumped into scenes or music trends like metal core or the New Wave of American Heavy Metal, we were always set apart from the rest of the pack. Any unique sound a band might have is usually rooted in the musical influences of its members, and our influences were diverse. Nowhere was that more apparent than in our van on road trips.

The rule in the Lamb of God van was that if you were driving you got to pick the music. The driver could allow a guest DJ, but control of the stereo could be reclaimed at any point. This would've been an equitable distribution of musical airtime if the driving duties had been evenly split. But that was never the case. While we all drank a lot, Randy tended to start drinking too early in the day to be a driver. It was a role he was happy to forfeit. Chris's classification was a bit more of a gray area, but when he did drive, the rest of us ended up terrified. So he was usually ruled out. This left almost all of the driving to Campbell, Willie, and me.

Willie was laissez-faire with the stereo. He grabbed whatever CDs were within easy reach in the front console. One of his go-to picks was the avant rap project Dr. Octagon, which featured pseudo psychedelic, retro futuristic beats from producer Dan the Automator, paired with Kool Keith's bizarre raps about being an extraterrestrial, time traveling surgeon. It was a band favorite. We'd howl with laughter, reciting as many of Kool Keith's absurd lines as we could remember. I can't say that the Dr. Octagon album directly shaped our sound, but rap has always been a reference point in our quest for heavy grooves and vocal patterns that sit rhythmically over the riffs.

Campbell's driving music reflected his deep love for music native to Richmond. The hometown indie punk rock trio Kepone was a consistent pick. Their 1994 album blended traditional punk rock energy with off-center rhythms that were Richmond music scene hallmarks. It was top-tier technical ability incorporated into memorable well-written song structures.

I was likely the most obnoxious van DJ. I was certainly a fan of metal, rap, and punk, but those elements of my musical taste were balanced out by my love for more conventional songwriters like Steve Earle and Jakob Dylan. The Wallflowers' LP was heavy in my rotation, which probably annoyed some of my bandmates. Though not as energetic as some of our other stereo regulars, that album was a lesson in modern rock songwriting, production, and arrangement. Smart song structures and super classy guitar tones swirled around Dylan's smoky vocal. Lead guitarist Michael Ward's performances expertly rise and fall with the dynamics of each tune, popping up to adorn sections when appropriate but just as readily laying back to create space where it's needed. T Bone Burnett's production is impeccable, and Bringing Down the Horse, along with Tom Petty's Wildflowers, is one of the first albums that made me aware of the value of minimalist, *classic, and sparkling production. It might not be the easiest thing to identify in Lamb of God's music, but Jakob Dylan's efficiently structured songs did help teach me how to trim the unnecessary extras and stick to the essence of a song.*

Lamb of God's debut album *New American Gospel* was released on September 26, 2000. The reviews were largely positive, with many noting our unique blend of heavy groove and technicality. But sales were slow. Since we were essentially a new band, we expected that. Still, it was encouraging to see the album so well received by critics and music publications.

Before the album release, we filmed a low-budget music video for the opening track, "Black Label." Randy's untethered, indecipherable vocal performance had an undeniable fury, and the track's up-tempo groove was a fantastic representation of the band. We thought it would make for a great introduction to the world. We enlisted a local friend of the band, Will Carsola, to create the video. Will later worked on big-budget television productions for Cartoon Network's *Adult Swim*, but when he took on the "Black Label" video, he was simply an ambitious and talented local videographer with a creative vision. Will combined some recent live performance footage with conceptual shots of our friend Matt acting out some sort of abstract hallucinatory experience. We threw some shots of Matt running through the Evergreen Cemetery in the East End neighborhood of Richmond to create an eerie vibe. It was all a bit haphazard, but to Will's credit, once the video was edited and visual effects were added, it looked cool. And it was cheap.

Fortunately, around this time MTV was working to get momentum for their spinoff network MTV2. It played only videos just like the original MTV, and it was designed to offset the parent network's shift toward reality television programming. The program directors at MTV2 were open minded about playing a diverse range of new acts. They had proactively petitioned Prosthetic Records for video submissions, so we gave them our dark and artsy "Black Label" video, which they loved. Our video went straight into rotation on MTV2, and the timing coincided perfectly with our album rollout. We needed all the help we could get to gain exposure for our rebranded band.

With a new album and a cool music video getting some airplay, we prepared to set out on our first professionally promoted, national tour. Our friends in Gwar, a successful theatrical metal band from Richmond, had been big supporters of the band from the beginning. They'd given us a coveted slot early in our career at their annual Gwar-B-Q concert. It wasn't a game changer, but it was a nod to our growing momentum and a morale boost for us to be acknowledged by our local heroes. Their front man and conceptual mastermind Dave Brockie was always a big help, sharing his experience and insight about the record industry.

In a stroke of luck, our album was released just a few weeks before Gwar was supposed to start their annual fall tour. They deliberately scheduled their shows around Halloween to mesh with their over-the-top, horror theater motif. Gwar offered us the opening slot on the tour, which also featured a new band called Amen that was championed by hotshot producer Ross Robinson. It was a huge opportunity and one we gratefully accepted. Unlike our previous tours, which we had handled ourselves, this tour was booked and promoted through professional channels. When we signed to Prosthetic, we'd joined up with a booking agent who helped work out the many logistics involved in filling the tour slot. Things like payment, travel coordination,

My second birthday
Mark Morton

Christmas 1976
Mark Morton

1978 *Mark Morton*

Riding trails next to our house *Mark Morton*

Early '80s with my dad and my dog *Mark Morton*

Axis *Photo courtesy of Michelle Spalding*

Playing at Stockwood
with Axis *Mark Morton*

Germany with Mom *Mark Morton*

Killing Cycle recording our first demo *Photo courtesy of Joey Huertas*

In front of Fresh Tracks Recording Studio in Williamsburg *Photo courtesy of Joey Huertas*

Killing Cycle live *Photo courtesy of Joey Huertas*

FIRST PARTY OF THE 90's

"Cornfield Party"
12/1/90

The band, Killing Cycles, will perform in King William on Route 625. There will be 1 Keg and lots of fun. It will happen around 7:00 pm Friday, Feb. 2. Party is given by Lisa, Amy, Shannon, and Tina. c/o Bobby Dawson

school bu
yelbw
green
white
X X X X X
ORCC
about 5 mi.
yellow house
RT 625
field the party spot
RT. 33
BRIGDE
1/2 mile
STOPLIGHT
RT 625
Blue Building
B&B auto
TRIBLES QUICK STOP
about 5 miles
STOPLIGH
RT. 30
Rite AID

Directions = ENTER WEST POINT ON RT. 33
TURN AT THE RED LIGHT BY Rite Aid and
Tribles Quick Stop onto Rt. 30. Continue
onto Rt. 30 for about 5 miles. You
should see Cheaspeake on the left.
When you get to the police station
you should slow down. There will
be a curve coming up. In the middle of the curve, you need to bear to the
right onto Rt. 625. On the corner of Rt. 625, there is a blue building
called B&B Auto. You go down about a 1/2 mile and the road ends
(there will be a yellow house on the hill) You should go to the right. This is still
Rt. 625. You should go about 3 miles and you will go over a little
bridge like-structure. You then go about another 3 miles and you
should be there. There is a white house, green house, and yellow house
The party is in the field behind them. Try to go into field in front of 1st house.

Flyer with directions to a Killing Cycle show *Photo courtesy of Joey Huertas*

Drunk in Williamsburg *Photo courtesy of Jeff Seibert*

Hgual at Bunratty's in Boston *Mark Morton*

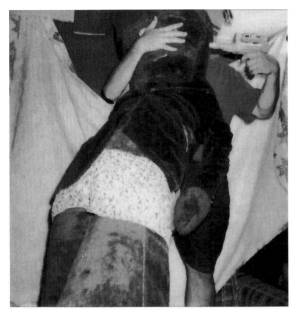

Gumby held hostage *Photo courtesy of John Partin*

Me, Randy, and Mikey Brosnan...broken down in New Jersey *Photo courtesy of Abe Spear*

Corntooth in New York City *Photo courtesy of Denise Korycki*

Writing songs for *As the Palaces Burn* in Brooklyn *Photo courtesy of Denise Korycki*

New American Gospel era
Photo courtesy of Denise Korycki

Midsong hug with Randy, Las Vegas 2015 *Photo courtesy of Strati Hovartos*

Somewhere on tour…2023 *Photo courtesy of Steve Rose*

Me and Brittany *Mark Morton*

parking, merchandising parameters, food and alcohol riders, and access to sound equipment all must be arranged in advance. It was a big—and necessary—step to sign with a booking agent.

Unfortunately, not even a booking agent could solve all our issues. The budget for the tour was meager. Gwar was the head-liner, and it cost them a lot to put on their show. They made their living doing this, so they had to make sure their financial needs were met. There simply wasn't much money left over to pay sup-port bands. Being the lowest band on the bill meant $100 per show. Total. That was hardly enough to keep beer in the cooler and gas in the van. It certainly wasn't enough to pay for hotel rooms or for us to come back with any money to pay ourselves. Knowing how chal-lenging it would be for us to make it through on a budget of $100 a night, Brockie paid us an extra $50 a night out of his own personal money. That's the kind of dude Dave was. That extra $50 a night wasn't much, but it made a big difference in our ability to accept the tour. MTV wrote, "Fans of fake blood and latex phalli rejoice. Gwar has lined up another round of touring." Brockie's stage character Oderus Urungus said in the press release, "We fart loudly at the approach of our warty comrades and can't wait to get out there and kill you."

Thus was our entrance into our career as a professional touring band.

The tour began at the legendary venue Birch Hill in Old Bridge, New Jersey. Our tour van was a faded maroon 1989 Ford Econoline. It was a big step up from our earlier vans, furnished inside with cap-tains' chairs and a bench seat in the back that folded out into a bed. The seating in the back was very important because if we couldn't find friends or fans to put us up for the night, that's where we'd be sleep-ing. We had saved up enough for a small trailer for our equipment and a few boxes of T-shirts to sell at the shows.

We drove up from Virginia and arrived early in the day at the venue, parking our weathered van and trailer next to the massive, shiny Gwar and Amen tour buses. Gwar generously gave us a brief soundcheck. Knowing all was in order before the show helped our confidence. I sat out by our van just before doors opened, watching the excited Gwar fans line up. Their fans have always been notoriously intolerant of opening acts. To thwart any potential jeers from what would likely be a hostile audience, we agreed to blast through our songs back to back, with little to no break in between them. After every song, the plan was to ring out loudly and wait for the count off into the next one so that any boos or insults would be masked by our feedback. It was a good plan. Nonetheless, I knew to expect some heckling from the rowdy crowd. As usual, I started drinking before the show to take the edge off my nerves.

My anxiety had retreated by showtime, flooded into a state of temporary dormancy with alcohol. We took the stage to a full room and tore into our first song. Our set list consisted of every song from our new album, slightly rearranged for optimal flow for a live setting. We opened with the up-tempo pounding of "In the Absence of the Sacred," and much to my surprise the rowdy Gwar audience seemed to like us, bobbing their heads and moshing to our heavy riffing. Randy, of course, was a lunatic. Pacing back and forth, flailing his arms and lunging into the front rows, he shrieked and roared his way through the set. He was the perfect balance of confrontational and captivating: just unhinged and unpredictable enough to elicit a feeling of chaos and danger, but charismatic and confident enough to still be cool. By the time we closed our set with our album opener, "Black Label," we had won over the Jersey crowd.

We packed up our gear and celebrated a great first show of the tour. We quickly drank through the alcohol provided on our tour rider, but there was no shortage of excited fans willing to buy a shot and a beer for members of the band they'd just seen open the show. We had played enough out of town shows to know how to work a room for booze and whatever else we might be looking for. Everyone got shit-faced.

But in getting ourselves good and drunk, we either overlooked or simply failed to secure ourselves a place to stay for the night. We weren't too concerned about this. We had spent plenty of nights in our van, so we figured we'd be doing the same thing on this tour. Knowing we were staying put for the night meant that we could keep partying without anyone having to figure out driving.

After the show, the party moved to Amen's tour bus. With their highly publicized album *We Have Come for Your Parents* just days away from release, Amen was enjoying full backing and financial tour support from their label, Roadrunner Records. This afforded them a gorgeous bus. Naturally, we partied like dirtbags in their luxury accommodations as if it were ours, downing their liquor and taking over the stereo. As the late night wound down, Willie followed someone exiting the bus through the side door and skipped the three tall steps leading off the bus. He fell about six feet to the ground, landing on his face in the gravel parking lot. He staggered his way back to our van. While everyone else bedded down for the night on their heated tour buses, we crawled into our shabby van and passed out drunk wherever we could claim a space.

Later that night, as I lay bunched up in a ball in the front passenger seat, I awoke to a loud commotion inside the van. Randy was behind me and attacking Willie. Without thinking, I lunged at Randy to defend my riff partner. "Get the fuck off of him!" I shouted. I grabbed Randy by his shoulders as he wrestled Willie into the back of the van.

"Fuck you. Get off me!" Randy roared, throwing elbows into my ribs while still tussling with a very drunk Willie. As our melee escalated, John and Chris woke up to the chaos, apparently believing that Randy and I were both attacking Willie.

"What the fuck is going on? Stop!" Campbell yelled as he and Chris dove in to untangle us. In a matter of a minute, our sad scene of five extremely drunk bandmates, passed out in various contorted positions an arm's length away from each other, had erupted into a sloppy, drunken brawl in our shitty, cramped Ford Econoline. This van could barely accommodate five sleeping bandmates. It certainly couldn't hold five fighting bandmates all at blows with each other.

Randy swung his long arms wildly, backing all of us up to avoid his flailing haymakers. "Back the fuck up!" he barked. "He fucking pissed on me, dude!" The van fell silent. "This drunk motherfucker pissed on my fucking head!"

Willie mumbled incoherently, calmly curling up behind the back seat and falling back to sleep as if nothing had happened. Randy had been sleeping on the floor and was startled awake by a blacked-out Willie, standing over him pissing on his head. Randy reacted by jumping up and trying to throw Willie into the very back of the van. And the dominos fell from there.

Once we all understood what had happened, there wasn't much left to do. Randy grabbed a towel and some bottled water and cleaned himself up. Willie was already back to snoring. The rest of us returned to our corners and passed back out. Our van went from smelling like cigarette butts and dirty socks to smelling like a truck stop bathroom.

I'd like to say that this was an isolated incident. I'd like to say that Willie was the only one of us in the band's history that was guilty of a nighttime urinary assault. But unfortunately, that's not true. More on that later.

With an event-filled first night of tour out of the way, we carried on to the next shows in Worcester, Massachusetts, and New Haven, Connecticut. Even for seasoned partiers like us, that first night had been a bit over the top, so the next couple of days were calm by comparison. We licked our wounds and focused on playing, and we continued to be well received. We slept in our van parked outside of the venues. Late October nights in New England are cold, so I'd often wake up as soon as the sunlight hit the front window, shivering in my sleeping bag and painfully hung over. Because I was always the first one awake, I usually took the morning driving shifts.

By the time we rolled into Columbus, Ohio, for a show at the Newport Music Hall, we were getting into a groove. The shows were going even better than we'd anticipated, and the driving distances in between venues were reasonable. Our biggest challenge was not having anywhere to stay. Though we'd already had experience with it, living out of our van wasn't getting any easier. We'd had no success in securing places to crash after the shows, but that night in Columbus, our luck changed.

After our set, Campbell weaved his way through the audience like he usually did. He chatted with fans, posed for pictures, and signed a few autographs while working the crowd for charity beers and the inevitable invitation to smoke a joint. In the course of his hustle, Campbell met a concertgoer who lived just up the street from the gig and was having an after show party. The kind young man not only invited us to the party but said that we were more than welcome to crash at the house. We were out of the van for a night. It was good timing for me because I was quickly coming down with the flu. This has been a pattern throughout the band's history: I'm always the first to get sick on tour.

After the show let out, we walked over to the crash pad. The party was already in full swing. By this time, I was definitely sick. I felt so shitty that I'd barely had anything to drink. I found a quiet spot to roll out my sleeping bag under a table in an upstairs bedroom. I chased a couple of gulps of NyQuil down with the last few swallows of a beer and fell asleep. Later, as the party wound down, Randy committed the cardinal sin of passing out with his shoes still on. We had previously agreed that anyone who fell asleep like this would, as punishment, get their faces drawn on with Sharpie markers. In this case, Randy became the unconscious recipient of an impressive collection of penis drawings on his cheeks and forehead.

Sometime very early that morning, while I was still knocked out and sweating through dextromethorphan hallucinations and fever dreams, Randy woke up from an extremely intoxicated sleep to take a piss. The first suitable place he found was a flat roof accessible through the second story bedroom where I was sleeping. The roof covered a downstairs porch adjacent to the house. As it turned out, Randy would've been much better off pissing on my head. Teetering on the edge of the roof, wasted drunk and watering the overgrown shrubs twelve feet below, Randy lost his footing and fell. He extended his arms on the way down to break his fall, snapping his left wrist as he hit the ground. Someone in the house woke up to Randy's groaning as he lay on the ground. Campbell and Chris scooped him up and took him to the hospital. He was prepped for surgery with dicks still drawn all over his face. I slept through all of it.

Later that morning with Randy at the hospital, the rest of us gathered at the roof's edge to survey the scene of Randy's fall. In the daylight, we could see that he had miraculously landed between several small, broken off trees. Had he fallen a foot to either side, he would have been impaled on at least one of the stalks. The reality of how badly things could've turned out made us rethink how we would travel: we agreed that we would get a hotel room every night from that point on. We couldn't really afford it, but our T-shirts had been selling a bit better than we'd anticipated. The plan was to put any merch money we made toward getting a hotel and hope it all worked out.

We opened for Gwar that night at the Empire Club in Hunting-
ton, West Virginia, without our singer. It never occurred to us to
cancel. Our roots as an instrumental band kicked in, and we played
a blistering set to a rowdy room. Oddly, we sold more T-shirts that
night than we did at any other show on the tour, a fact that I periodically reminded Randy about for a year or two after.

We picked up Randy from the hospital the next day. He climbed
into our shitty van with a huge cast covering his left arm and a bottle
of painkillers almost as big. We continued on to a couple more shows
back in Ohio, including one in Cincinnati that was easily our worst
show of the tour. It was there that we finally came across a hostile
Gwar crowd. Even with our songs paced back to back, the sneering
audience showed their distaste with middle fingers and audible jeers.
Randy is usually remarkably adept at handling a heckler, but he was
a little extra loaded on painkillers and booze, which dulled his front
man reflexes. But it wasn't his fault. It was just a shitty Gwar crowd.
And we couldn't get off stage fast enough.

We rolled on through Chicago, where after a show at the Vic
Theatre, members from all three bands on the tour descended onto
a neighborhood bar. Gwar's Dave Brockie, always the master of cer-
emonies, generously doled out expensive shots of liquor, so I happily
took full advantage of his generosity. That night we all crashed on the
floor of our friend Cathy's apartment. This time it was my turn to
be the asshole. At some point in the night, still blacked out drunk, I
stood up in my sleep, staggered a few steps away from where I'd been
sleeping, and pissed on Campbell's head. Lucky for me, it was so dark
in the room that he wasn't sure who had done it. He blamed Randy.
I don't remember anything of what happened, but we later pieced
together that it was me.

After Chicago, the tour wound down with a few shows back on
the East Coast, ending on November 4 in Poughkeepsie, New York,

at the concert hall The Chance. We made our way home to recuperate and, in Randy's case, heal. We had successfully completed our first national tour. We were proud that we had held our own with Gwar's contentious fans and felt like we'd converted many of them into Lamb of God fans. We'd also pushed the limits of our own alcohol-fueled recklessness. But in the moment, all our chaos felt very rock 'n' roll. As if that were exactly how it's supposed to be done.

CHAPTER 12

CORNTOOTH

"WINDFALL"
SON VOLT

I have a complicated relationship with heavy metal. Like so many of its fans, I discovered my love for it when I was a kid. The overdriven, extreme energy and power of the music was compelling, while the dark, taboo imagery in many of its lyrics captivated my imagination. Metal felt rebellious and offered me an entire world I could be a part of.

By the time I'd started learning to play guitar, metal was a teacher. The playing was skilled, emphasizing technique and accuracy. As an ambitious young guitarist, I had an endless line of guitar heroes to learn from.

But there were times when I felt disconnected from heavy metal. During the grunge and alternative explosion of the early and mid-1990s, the loose, abstract, and sometimes downright noisy playing styles of the era's popular bands made heavy metal's acrobatic riffs and show-off solos feel dated and corny. As trends changed, I gained a different perspective, absorbing all I could from the popular guitarists of the day. I began to explore other genres, seeking out different approaches to playing guitar and weaving it all into what would hopefully become a voice of my own on the instrument.

In the early 2000s, as Lamb of God was just beginning to tour professionally, I was also engaged with an Americana-style band called Corntooth. Lamb of God was much further along when it came to getting bigger gigs and releasing music. But for a few years I was equally com-mitted to both bands, and I wasn't sure which one I had the most faith in. Lamb of God was better at what Lamb of God was doing than Corntooth was at what Corntooth was doing, and I was aware of that. But it also seemed like there would be a limit as to how successful a metal band like Lamb of God could get. We weren't shooting for the stars as a band, and our ambitions stayed very much in the moment. But I was starting to consider where my future as a player would be. The organic sonic tex-tures, introspective lyrics, and timeless playing of Americana music was as intriguing to me as metal had ever been. Once again, I had so much to learn and there was an endless array of great teachers.

Son Volt's Trace *is the perfect modern Americana album, setting the standard for so many of the great releases that would follow in the genre. Jay Farrar's rich, crooning vocals fit perfectly into the band's spacious but confident compositions. His lyrics paint faded pictures of small-town scenes. It's what a beautifully painted watercolor landscape would sound like.*

I was first exposed to Trace *shortly after its release in 1995. The single "Drown" was getting airplay on a Chicago radio station during my time there, and the alt-country scene was getting a lot of attention everywhere. When I came back to Richmond to rejoin Lamb of God, I was a surprised to find that Randy was also a huge Son Volt fan. It's one of the first musical bonds we shared. It helped me trust his judgement. I figured that if he was into Son Volt, then he must be alright.*

eturning home from our two-week tour with Gwar, we slowed down for a few months and returned to our versions of home life. I had been bouncing around between jobs, from roofing to working in a cabinet shop and back to roofing. My employers tended to grow tired of my touring commitments, which kept me away from work. The band was my priority, so jobs came and went. Fortunately, I'd gathered some decent skills and never had much trouble picking up work in between tours.

But even though Lamb of God had slowed down for a bit, I played music as much as possible. My friend Matt Conner and I were working on some of his original material whenever I had time. Matt, who had been part of the earliest instrumental incarnation of Burn the Priest, had since evolved into an ambitious and talented lyricist and songwriter. His songs were a blend of folk, country, and Americana, heavily influenced by John Prine, Jerry Jeff Walker, and Townes Van Zandt. His lyrics were clever, his voice smooth and rich, and his songs were good. Combined with my simple but honest slide playing and bluesy lead guitar work, we created an indie rock, folk, Americana style that fell in line with a lot of the alt-country bands of the era. As we progressed, we added Kepone guitarist Tim Harriss on bass, as well as Ed Trask from Holy Rollers, Kepone, and Avail on drums. We were joined by an additional singer named Janey Bise and pedal steel guitar player Phil Murphy, who was easily the most skilled player out of all of us. We searched for a band name for weeks and somehow decided that Corntooth was good enough. We probably should've searched a little longer.

With a complete band and full set worth of originals and covers, Corntooth started booking gigs. It didn't take long for us to build a loyal following around Richmond. We played regularly at the hip Richmond bars Hole in the Wall and Sweetwater. We performed live on the radio show of Big John Trimble, the legendary AM country

DJ. We played Richmond's Capital City Barn Dance, organized by local scene kingpin Wes Freed, who had condescendingly referred to us as "upstarts" but who supported us anyway. To be fair, Wes was probably right.

Corntooth also got requests to open up for touring bands. We played shows with the Drive-By Truckers, who came through town frequently. We also opened for Hank Williams III at a packed show in Richmond's Alley Katz club. After our set that night as I drunkenly meandered my way through the shoulder-to-shoulder crowd, I must've been too aggressive with my meandering. Some skinhead-looking dude took offense and started jamming his bony elbow into my ribs. He turned and faced me with his best menacing scowl and shouted some shit that I couldn't make out over the band blasting from the nearby stage. I responded by extinguishing my cigarette directly in the middle of his pale, sweaty forehead. His jaw dropped in disbelief. I was kind of surprised by what I'd done too, but there was no time to unpack it. We lunged at each other's necks. As luck would have it, when I'd sloppily grasped at his head, the middle and ring fingers of my right hand had miraculously wedged inside of his mouth, between his left cheek and his jaw. He was hooked like a catfish.

I was scared by this point. I was pretty sure I could get the better of him in a fight. But a couple of my fingers were jammed into his mouth, and he was understandably pissed off about it. The last thing I needed was for this asshole to start biting my digits off. I had more gigs coming up and I needed those fingers. I yanked him by his face as hard as I could, pulling him off balance and sending the crowd around us jostling and swaying. It must've been visible from the stage, because, as it was happening, I glanced up and saw Hank III grinning at us as we grappled. "Uh-oh!" Hank yelled into the microphone with a laugh, acknowledging our tussle.

I started pulling my unlucky opponent toward the side wall of the club where the crowd thinned out a little. At least there we'd have room for a regular fight. And I was pretty anxious to get my fingers out of his mouth. He was probably looking forward to that even more than I was.

Just as my new friend and I managed to stagger to the side of the room, a massive bouncer grabbed us by the back of our necks and threw us both out of the side door of the club into the adjacent alley. In a flash, we'd gone from grappling in a packed club with the music blaring so loud we couldn't hear each other shout to standing face to face in an empty alley, the brick walls next to us rumbling from the muffled din of the show inside.

"What the fuck's the matter with you?" the skinhead dude shouted. He was clearly furious but was keeping his distance. There was a bright red cigarette-sized dot dead center on his forehead. "You put a fucking cigarette out on my head!"

"You damn near broke my ribs!" I shouted, trying to justify what I'd done.

I felt bad for him. The whole cigarette thing was probably too much. We stood there awkwardly for a few seconds until it was clear that neither of us felt like finishing our fight. He slid off down the alley mumbling some "fuck yous" and I pounded on the thick, metal door of the club, pleading my case to be let back in. I still had guitars and amps in there.

I do hope the dude's red dot burn scar went away. I would never have done that if I hadn't been shit-faced drunk. But alcohol fucks up people's judgement and changes their character. In my case, I mistook my drunken asshole aggressive behavior for confidence and fearlessness. We had played a great show to a packed house. I wish I'd have just left it at that.

Back in the band, Corntooth's opportunities were expanding. We started playing out-of-town shows. We become friendly with Colorado-based alt-country band Drag the River after playing a show together in Richmond, and they invited us to open for them at Siberia, a small but cool club in New York City. Drive-By Truckers invited us down to Atlanta to play with them at the annual Bubbapalooza, a weekend-long tribute to Georgia musician Gregory Dean Smalley, who had died of AIDS-related illness several years before.

With so many shows happening, Corntooth decided to make a proper studio recording to help showcase our band and possibly generate some label interest. We booked a couple nights at Sound of Music in downtown Richmond. The studio was owned by David Lowery from the bands Camper Van Beethoven and Cracker, the latter of which had scored a massive hit in 1993 with their song "Low." But what really excited me about the place was that the producer-engineer we'd be recording with was Brian Paulson.

Paulson had come out of the Midwest independent music scene and had transitioned from playing in touring bands to recording other bands. He had produced and engineered some of my favorite albums, including Superchunk's *Foolish*, Slint's *Spiderland*, and Son Volt's alt-country masterpiece *Trace*. When David Lowery opened up Sound of Music in his adopted home of Richmond, he wisely asked Paulson to take up residency at the studio, knowing it would attract clients. I knew I'd have to try to contain my enthusiasm in the sessions. I didn't want to come off as obnoxious or overly giddy to be working with someone who was in my eyes a legendary producer.

Corntooth had been playing a lot of shows, so we were tight. We set up all the instruments in the studio's spacious live room on the first night. Brian mic'd everything up, and after spending a little time dialing in tones, levels, and headphone mixes, we started playing the songs. We played each song instrumentally a few times until we'd get a take that had a good feel and no mistakes. Then we'd move on to the next song and repeat the process. It was fun. Everyone in Corntooth had recording studio experience, so we were comfortable with the environment. I was thrilled to be back in the studio working on a project that couldn't be any further away stylistically from Lamb of God.

The following night, with the basic tracks recorded, we returned to the studio to add the vocals and guitar solos, after which Brian would mix the four completed songs. I laid down my solos and overdubs quickly and was happy with how they turned out. I spent the next few hours drinking the two bottles of red wine I'd brought with me and listening to our two singers lay down their parts. By the time they were finished, I was flat out drunk and looking for some spare beers so that I could keep drinking.

Being drunk wasn't out of the ordinary for me. Had I simply gone home like the rest of the band, it wouldn't have been an issue. But I decided to stay. Brian Paulson was going to be mixing our recording late into the night, and in my drunken, self-aggrandizing fantasy, I decided that it was my responsibility to pull up a chair and "oversee" the mix. It's still embarrassing to think about the audacity it took for me to post up next to the man that produced Son Volt's *Trace* and to direct his mix. Telling Brian Paulson to turn down the pedal steel guitar and put more attack on the kick drum makes about as much sense as me telling LeBron James he should work on his passing accuracy. But there I was, thinking I was running the show. To his credit, Brian was professional and tolerated my obnoxiousness. And despite my nonsensical suggestions, the demo came out sounding good.

Like so often happens, after sobering up the next day it occurred to me how stupid I'd been. I had an opportunity to work with someone I'd greatly admired, and it was all going cool until I'd gotten shit-faced and made an ass out of myself. Sometime later, my friends in the band Avail asked me to play slide guitar on the intro for their song "West Wye." I showed up for the session at Sound of Music, and Brian Paulson was working on it as well. We all had fun tracking the part. I should've taken that opportunity to apologize for my drunken idiocy, but I was too embarrassed to bring it up.

But while Corntooth was getting busy, Lamb of God was even busier. After a short break following the Gwar tour, we set out on a monthlong run opening a bill that featured death metal veterans Cannibal Corpse, Norwegian black metal band Dimmu Borgir, and the Swedish melodic death metal band the Haunted, which had risen from the remnants of the legendary band At the Gates. We were still nobodies looking for exposure and weren't getting paid much at all, though we did have access to a small amount of tour support from our record label. The Haunted were doing well but were still working to gain traction in the United States, so to save money, Lamb of God and the Haunted agreed to share a tour bus and employ a skeleton crew that would work for both bands. It was our first time touring on a bus, and I'm sure the Haunted regretted their decision by the second day.

Being the first band on a four-band bill doesn't come with a lot of benefits. You get the remaining crumbs, and on this underground metal tour there wasn't much bread to begin with. We didn't get a dressing room or a soundcheck most nights. We regularly had to set up with our drum kit set off to the side because we weren't left with enough room to place it in the center of the stage. The band members were all cool, but the tour manager and crew from the Cannibal Corpse and Dimmu Borgir camps treated us like unwelcome, second-class citizens who were constantly in their way. We all took it personally.

We released our frustrations on the stage. Our sets were scalding, amped up with fire-spitting aggression and fueled by our collective frustration. It made for great shows. My competitive nature kicked in: I wanted to blow every band away, every night. I enjoyed that feeling of rage and resentment. And I dumped gallon after gallon of alcohol on top of it.

One night, I rose from being passed out in my bunk and staggered into the front sitting area of our shared bus, where several members from both bands were still up drinking and hanging out. Flinging the door of the small refrigerator open as I walked past it, I squared up and started pissing toward the general direction of the kitchen sink. I was blacked out drunk, so my aim was poor, which meant the Haunted's guitarist Patrik Jensen was getting hit by piss about as much as the sink was. The reflexes of my tour mates were pretty quick when they saw me starting to piss all over our front lounge. They grabbed me, spun me around, and threw me into the bathroom to figure it out in there. The next day I at least had the decency to apologize to Patrik. He laughed it all off as no big deal because that's the kind of compassionate dude he is.

A week later, after a rowdy performance at Harpos, the infamous metal club in Detroit, we crossed the border into Canada for a show the following night at Toronto's Opera House. Blacked out drunk once again, I became incensed that the Canadian border patrol made us get off the bus so that they could search it for contraband, which I have since learned is common practice. But being the drunken asshole version of myself that I was that night, I took it as a personal attack. Randy practically tackled me as I walked past the border guards, whistling "The Star-Spangled Banner" as loud as I could and flipping off the Canadian flag. We made it across the border without much trouble, but no thanks to me. The following morning as we pulled into Toronto, I was on my knees in the bathroom of the bus vomiting into a trash bag. Once we parked, it was still hours before the venue would open. I stumbled off the bus and laid down next to a bench on a quiet side street near the venue, where I spent the rest of the morning dry heaving.

By the time the tour finished at the New York club Limelight on May 7, 2001, we had used up whatever little bit of tolerance the headlining band's crews had for us. As we broke down our gear during the changeover between bands, the tour manager shared by Cannibal Corpse and Dimmu Borgir started kicking our drums off the stage onto the floor, grumbling about us taking too long to break down. Years later, after we had come up through the ranks, he sent word that he would like to work for us. Fuck that dude.

The tour bus had picked us up in Richmond at the start of the tour, but we had to arrange a ride back home. Some friends of ours had driven up to New York with an empty van to carry us and our gear home, but by the time it was all loaded up, there was barely anywhere to sit. I didn't want to ride six hours back to Richmond hunched over and bouncing around on top of a speaker cabinet the whole way, so I opted out.

Earlier that night, I'd talked with Amanda, a girl I knew from Richmond. She was traveling around the Northeast visiting friends on a break from her job as a waitress and had come through New York City to see our show before making her way back home. She mentioned that she was going to catch a bus back to Richmond and I suggested, half joking, that I might go with her. She didn't seem opposed.

Amanda and I didn't have much of a plan as we stood on the sidewalk of Sixth Avenue watching the rest of my band drive away. I had no money. We wouldn't see whatever pay we were getting from the tour for a couple weeks, and I'd left just enough money in my bank account to cover the bills that would be due when I got home. Amanda had enough money for her bus ticket, but only a few bucks left over to put toward mine. Amanda was pretty. She was short and curvy, with cropped blond hair, big bright eyes, and a sweet smile. I, on the other hand, looked homeless and hungover. We walked to Penn Station, and along the way she bummed money from strangers on the street to cover the rest of my ticket. We got to our seats on the Greyhound bus bound for Richmond, but I smelled so bad that Amanda gently asked me to sit across the aisle from her. When we finally got to her apartment, I took a shower and slept for an entire day before I even went home.

I soon jumped back into work. I stayed busy picking up freelance roofing jobs through some local contractors I'd worked for. Looking for a break from roofing in the summer heat, I took a job as a carpenter, building scenery and set designs for an annual Halloween production at Busch Gardens Williamsburg, a popular theme park near where I'd grown up. The jobsite was a forty-five-minute drive from where I lived, but I had a couple of friends on the crew, so we carpooled to split it up.

One beautiful Tuesday morning late in the summer, I rode into work with my friend Chris, a painter on the set crew. We showed up on time and started our shift at 8 a.m. While we worked, our boss, who was the lead carpenter and project manager, liked to listen to one of those regionally syndicated morning radio shows that were popular at the time. I don't remember the name of the show, but it featured a silly duo in the show name, like "Jimbo and the Rocket Man" or something like that. The hosts spent most of the time gabbing about the news, sports, and any other interesting events of the day.

Early in our shift, the radio hosts broke the news of a commercial passenger plane hitting one of the World Trade Center towers in New York City. We were stunned. We continued to work, now listening much more intently to the radio show hosts reporting in real time as details unfolded about what seemed to be a horrible accident. Sixteen minutes later, when the shocked radio personalities reported a second plane hitting the Twin Towers, we stopped working and stared in disbelief at the small silver radio plugged into a long orange extension cord in the center of our workspace.

Unlike so many people's experience on September 11, 2001, I spent most of that day without any imagery of the attack. Our carpentry crew continued working through a full work day, with only our radio to tell us what was happening in New York, Pennsylvania, and at the Pentagon. I didn't see any of the video images until I got home much later that evening. I'm not sure exactly how that made things any different. But it was an eerie feeling jigsawing counters into shelving boards to be used for scenery props while not knowing if World War III was playing out through the speaker of a small jobsite radio.

Lamb of God had dates booked for a monthlong North American tour opening for Six Feet Under. The tour was to start on September 26, 2001, just two weeks after the 9/11 attacks. There was initially some question whether it would be canceled, but it was not. Again we shared a tour bus with another band, this time with our good friends in God Forbid. Those guys partied just about as hard as we did, and we all knew what to expect from each other. We'd been playing shows with God Forbid since our Burn the Priest days and have always considered them to be family.

The tour was a success. Despite the horrifying world events, we played great shows to full venues and brought fans a bit of joy and distraction from the heavy times. God Forbid and Lamb of God did a whole lot of partying on that bus. And I didn't piss on one single person.

CHAPTER 13

WE'LL DANCE AS THE PALACES BURN

"THE REGULATOR"
CLUTCH

A good producer can be an asset when you're making a record. But what you expect them to do and what they actually do are two different things. At a minimum, a producer is usually the administrative manager for a recording project. A big part of their job is to oversee the scheduling of the sessions and to manage the organizational tasks. But there's usually much more to it.

Some producers are technically focused and hands on with the audio engineering, tones, and mix. Others will hire additional sound engineers for those things. And then there are producers who stay primarily concerned with creative decision-making, songwriting, song structures, instrumentation, and performances. Some of these types can be heavy handed in their approach and consider themselves to be the final word on what makes the record and what doesn't. There are count-less stories of well-known musicians getting kicked off their own band's albums, replaced by studio musicians the producer keeps on call.

From an artist's perspective, it can be difficult to trust a producer enough to give them access to your creative process. It's an odd relation-ship: you work as an artist or a band for months or even years writing and rehearsing material for what will eventually become your album. Then one day, a stranger starts telling you what they don't like about your songs and how they expect you to change them and make them better. It can be hard not to take that kind of criticism personally. I've been on both sides of that dynamic, many times as an artist and a few times as the producer. It can make for some very uncomfortable, some-times heated conversations.

When Lamb of God signed to Epic Records, our A&R representative, Kaz Utsunomiya, already had a producer in mind for our first project on the label. Kaz had done enough research into our band to know what kind of insight and motivation would elevate our work and get the most out of us. And he knew that Gene "Machine" Freeman was the man to do it.

Kaz had years of experience working with bands, and he knew that accepting a new creative partner into our process would be diffi-cult. He encouraged me to listen closely to Machine's out of this world production on Clutch's masterpiece Blast Tyrant *LP. I fell in love with the album on first listen and kept it on constant repeat. From top to bottom, the album is filled with perfectly fuzzed-out guitar tones and soulful, authentic blues-driven leads from guitarist Tim Sult. The rhythm section of drummer Jean-Paul Gaster and bassist Dan Maines held down heavy, locked-in grooves that stayed interesting without ever upstaging the song itself. Sneaky vocal overdubs popped in and out of the tracks, some sliding by without notice and others jumping out of a hard-panned stereo field, accentuating and ad-libbing with Neil Fallon's preacher-esque lead vocal delivery. And all of it was framed in Machine's quirky, space-age funky production style that made it feel like the soundtrack to the best party you've ever been to.*

But Blast Tyrant *is not just an example of a great production. It helped me understand what I think great production should be: a capture of a band or an artist at peak performance, with an additional focus on audio treatment and sound manipulation to create an exciting and dynamic experience for the listener, one that continues to reveal itself over repeated listens.*

L amb of God's hard work was paying off. In just two years, we'd gone from renaming ourselves and essentially starting over as a new band to releasing a critically acclaimed debut album. We'd made a music video that was getting airplay and completed multiple national tours as an opening act. Our booking agent kept tour opportunities flowing in, and even though money was still tight, the band was generating enough income for me to accept tour offers without worrying about covering my bills while I was on the road.

We followed up our post-9/11 run with a strange tour in early 2002 opening for the theatrical metal band Mushroomhead. Once again we shared a bus with another band on the bill, a new Roadrunner Records act called Five Pointe O. Nobody got pissed on, but they still quickly grew to hate us. We drank constantly and chain-smoked cigarettes inside the bus with no windows to open. We were loud and rowdy, partying well before the show and long into the night. We brought strangers and fans on the bus to party with us. We had no respect for our bus mates and no personal boundaries.

Just a week into the tour, Five Pointe O's young singer and guitar player were already keeping themselves sequestered in their coffin-sized bunks, shocked by our drunken chaos and trying to breathe any unpolluted air in the middle of our rolling smoke pit. The Mushroomhead band and crew were nice, but they were having a moment of relative success that seemed to be getting to their heads just a little bit. It was this slight touch of rock star vibe that collectively kept us annoyed just enough to be a motivator. As was becoming our normal mindset, Lamb of God's intention was to put on a frenetic performance each night with the goal of stealing the show from the headliner.

Adding to the chaos of the Mushroomhead tour experience was our sad, dilapidated bus. Given our limited budget, the only bus we could afford for the tour was a ramshackle, outdated, manual shift Eagle coach. It was probably a decent bus in the mid-1980s, but by this point, it was well past its expiration date. Despite being canary yellow, we named it the Black Lodge in honor of the steady flow of thick diesel exhaust that poured into the bunk area and choked us while we slept. Piloting the Black Lodge was an older Croatian man named Mario, whom we adored. We nicknamed him the "Croatian Sensation." One night as I lay in my bunk while we drove through an Oklahoma snowstorm, I felt the entire bus slide sideways and then straighten back out. Terrified, I crawled out of bed and walked up front to see what was going on. When I stuck my head through the curtain into the driver's area, Mario was cursing loudly and flailing his arms. With no working defrost and only one windshield wiper that functioned intermittently, he leaned forward in his seat, wiping the condensation off the windshield with a towel so he could see the road through the blinding snowstorm. Steering with his knee and downshifting the bus to slow for cars pulling over, he looked like a circus performer spinning plates. "I cannot drive dis piece of shiiit!" he shouted angrily. "I am not a focking octo-puss!"

Many years later, after losing touch, we found out that Mario was a contestant on a Croatian reality dating show called *Love Is in the Village*. He proudly spoke of his time with us on the show, even mentioning the nickname we'd given him. Of course, he went on to win the show.

With solid momentum building from touring on the *New American Gospel* release, Prosthetic Records was ready for us to make another album. Willie and I had been steadily piling up riffs and song ideas, and we were ready to start fleshing them out into songs with the rest of the band. We took on a handful of shows after the Mushroomhead tour, including another appearance at CBGB in New York. But we spent much of 2002 writing and demoing new material.

During our tour with Six Feet Under in late 2001, a friend introduced me to a woman named Denise at our show in New York City. Denise was a freelance television producer, mostly on programming for MTV and VH1. Denise was young and successful, with a vast knowledge of the entertainment industry and a passion for all types of music. Most of the industry people I worked with knew and respected her on a personal and professional level. Soon after we met, Denise and I started talking by phone almost daily, and after my tour was over I began making trips up to New York City to stay with her in her two-bedroom apartment in Brooklyn's Williamsburg neighborhood.

Each morning, Denise headed to her office in the towering Viacom building in Times Square. I'd sleep in, then spend the day playing guitar in her apartment, working out new riffs and scribbling lyrics into my notebook. In between writing, I'd stroll around her neighborhood, sometimes taking the train into Manhattan to meet her later in the day. I felt inspired. I was dating a cool New York City girl with a cool music industry job. She was sweet to me, and being adjacent to her success made me feel good about myself.

I wrote a fair amount of my contributions to *As the Palaces Burn* in Denise's Brooklyn apartment. I had enjoyed contributing lyrics for the song "Confessional" on our debut album, so I leaned heavier into writing words and vocal patterns for my song ideas on the new album. Writing lyrics felt therapeutic. The song "Ruin" explores my guarded awkwardness in personal relationships. The lyrics lamented my own inability to fully give my trust, which sabotaged close connections to those around me, especially with women. Incidental arguments with Denise, or whomever I was seeing at any given time, were often catalysts for negative, self-centered, and self-loathing introspection. But these experiences made for some pretty good heavy metal lyrics.

> *The knowledge that seeking the favor of another means the murder of self.*
> *This is the resolution. The end of all progress. The death of evolution.*
> *It bleeds all life away.*

The song "As the Palaces Burn" addresses the growing conflict in Iraq that dominated the news headlines. Laid over a riff sequence that was heavily influenced by our former tour mates in the Haunted, the chorus lyrics took a cue from Washington, DC, post-hardcore pioneers the Nation of Ulysses, whom I'd been a fan of since my college days. In their 1992 song "The Sound of Jazz to Come," lead vocalist Ian Svenonius shouts, "We dance on your grave every night!" I've always thought that this is such a powerfully disrespectful image. I repurposed it, weaving it into a political doomsday context suggesting that the potential fall of civilization might actually be a positive event.

As the seeds you've cast away take hold, war will be born.
Rejoice, the age of the fall has begun.
We'll dance as the palaces burn.

I also incorporated other influences from more current sources. The song "Vigil" is a soliloquy of self-empowerment that rejects the widespread hypocrisy and corruption in religion and government. Early in 2002, an investigation into the Archdiocese of Boston had uncovered widespread sexual abuse in the Catholic church. It was a huge news story, and it was disgusting to learn that what so many had feared had now proven to be true. Meanwhile, the Bush administration was justifying its invasion of Iraq, which seemed like a knee-jerk reaction to 9/11 with nefarious underpinnings. It all weighed heavy on my mind.

The LA-based alternative metal band System of a Down had released their album *Toxicity* the year before. It was inescapable, producing a string of massive hits that were all over cable music channels and terrestrial radio. And I was a fan. In the soaring outro of their hit single "Chop Suey!," Serj Tankian sings, "Father, into your hands / Why have you forsaken me? / In your eyes forsaken me." Feeling abandoned by God stirs up heavy emotions of hopelessness and isolation. I don't remember deciding to borrow that idea for my lyrics to "Vigil"; it happened naturally because I was listening to System of a Down a lot while writing a song about feeling betrayed by the church and by the government. Artists often write about what's floating around in their psyche without tracing where it came from. In this case, I referenced "Chop Suey!" as a defiant confrontation to a God and a government that would allow these things to happen.

Sickness to you my master. Here's to getting worse. Hope it
kills you faster.

Show me how it hurts to rot from the inside out.
This vigil burns until the day our fires overtake you.
Our Father we forsake you.
Blessed be his name. Nothing now the same.

Randy was honing his lyrical skills too. In "11th Hour," he candidly confronts the progressing unmanageability of his own addiction, personifying alcohol as a beguiling mistress.

Sweetly she draws me into her arms. A liquid embrace to
  chase the day away.
Sedate, numb, deaf and dumb.

Randy's lyrics for Willie's musical composition "Boot Scraper" reference alcoholism as well, only this time framing it into the beaten-down perspective of the toiling blue-collar worker. In between tours, Randy had worked for a couple of the same roofing companies that I had. He observed the resignation of some of our coworkers who, unlike us, had little distraction or escape from their hard labor besides alcohol.

Watch the broken, common man drown his sorrows at
  un-Happy Hour.
Dirty and sweaty, with just enough to get by.

By this time, both our lyrics and our music had gotten better. The songwriting dynamic between Willie and me was better established. We knew what to expect from one another, confidently toggling between Willie's abstract, highly technical riffs and my heavy, swaggering grooves. Our songs became notably more structured, with definable verses, choruses, and bridge sections. These conventional components to songwriting were new to us since we had usually used more of a stream of consciousness approach. Willie and I usually brought in song ideas first, but we worked them out on the rehearsal room floor as a fully assembled, live band. We shared a collective feeling of engagement and creative investment into our songs, which created unity and excitement around the new material.

With a new batch of songs, we began making arrangements for recording. Chris was lobbying hard for us to hire Devin Townsend to produce the project. Just like with our previous producer Steve Austin, I wasn't very familiar with Devin's work. I knew that he had worked with guitarist Steve Vai, was the leader of the Canadian metal band Strapping Young Lad, and had also released several solo projects, but that was about it. On Chris's recommendation, I dug into Devin's discography and was impressed. His work was diverse, spanning from the heaviest thrash metal to ambient, new age soundscapes and soaring operatic opuses. I was all in. The rest of the band agreed that Devin would likely provide a fresh perspective on our sound. The label liked our choice because Devin's own visibility as an artist would help raise intrigue among press and fans who hadn't yet heard of us. Devin wanted to take on more outside production projects and Lamb of God had a little buzz building, so it was a great fit for him too.

At the end of 2002, we set up in Richmond's Montana Sound studio to record *As the Palaces Burn* with Devin Townsend producing and engineering the project. The mood of the sessions was typical for Lamb of God: lots of bickering, criticism, sarcastic comments, and general infighting. But our confrontational personalities and the grueling day and night schedule of the sessions quickly took a toll on Devin. He had never been around us in person and apparently hadn't been warned. Shellshocked and overworked, Devin trudged through the sessions in a professional manner, but he wasn't having much fun.

179

Despite the tense atmosphere, though, we captured some great performances. There is a fiery energy in the tracks, particularly in the guitar takes, that I can still hear today. Devin is a master guitarist. He pushed Willie and me to the edge of our abilities. Not only did Devin improve our playing, but he taught us how to listen and evaluate our recorded performances. Some inconsistencies add character and life to a track, while others just make it feel loose and sloppy. Devin Townsend taught us how to differentiate between the two. We carry that lesson with us to this day.

Devin moved the session to his hometown of Vancouver to mix the album after the recording sessions ended. Chris and I went along to oversee the mix. Our live sound engineer Dennis Solomon joined us. Lamb hadn't been doing much touring. Winter weather had left my construction jobs scarce, and I'd just spent a couple weeks unpaid in the studio recording the album. This meant I was flat broke. The album budget paid for my travel expenses but not much else. Before we left for Canada, I sold a large bin of copper scraps that I'd been collecting from roofing jobsites to a recycling yard to help pay my bills. I also sold about a third of my CD collection. In Vancouver during the mixing process, I lived on free hotel bagels for breakfast and Minute Rice and canned beans for dinner.

Once the record was finally recorded, mixed, and mastered, it sounded, well, kind of bad and definitely weird. The guitars and vocals were pushed and overdriven in an exciting way, but the rhythm section sounded washy and thin. The whole mix sounded very low fidelity. Given our bigger budget and the sound quality of Devin's previous projects, I had been certain that we were going to get great results. However, once again, I'd ended up disappointed. And it wasn't just me. Everyone was disappointed, including Devin.

I've had several conversations over the years with some of the people involved in that recording regarding how and why that album sounded like it did. Without throwing anyone under the bus, I'll just say this: the mistakes that were made in our process could've likely been prevented with better communication. Nonetheless, we were proud of the songs. And despite that album having a weird, blown-out character to its sound, it *did* have character.

Lamb of God's *As the Palaces Burn* was scheduled to be released on May 6, 2003. Encouraged by our momentum, our label provided us with a budget to make several music videos. MTV had been shifting its focus toward the new "reality TV" trend, so to compensate for this shift away from music, their spinoff network MTV2 was aggressively collecting music videos to fill out airtime. Even better, they were planning to relaunch *Headbanger's Ball*, a heavy metal focused video show hosted by Hatebreed front man Jamey Jasta. It would be the perfect platform to promote our new release.

The first video we shot was for the album's opening track and lead single "Ruin." The video features the band performing on a harshly lit stage in a makeshift Los Angeles storefront church. After being introduced in Spanish by a seedy priest, we launch into the song while the ragtag congregation appears confused and overwhelmed by the spectacle. As our fury builds, the churchgoers start going into fits of rage, panic, and emotional meltdowns, ostensibly brought on by the music's intensity. It was simply shot but well edited, and the actors and directors made it feel authentic. The "Ruin" video was a huge step for the band because it was immediately on all the relevant video platforms and was giving us valuable exposure.

With our "Ruin" video getting airplay and a release date set for the new album, we hit the road for a two-month tour with Chimaira, another up-and-coming metal band from Cleveland. We had been getting a lot of attention; there was a buzz in the industry about us potentially moving up to a bigger label. We were still bound by our contract with Prosthetic, and we had a strong relationship with them.

But everyone understood that, under the right circumstances, jumping to a bigger label could benefit both us and Prosthetic.

The tour started in upstate New York and moved to our old stronghold of Philadelphia, where we always had a big turnout of rowdy fans who considered us their own. The third night of the tour was a stop at the legendary Brooklyn rock club L'Amour, which had held shows by such bands as KISS, Motörhead, Quiet Riot, and Slayer. The L'Amour show had, by default, turned into a label showcase for us. Nearly every major record label had an office in Manhattan, and it was no secret that scouts from several different labels would be there to see if they wanted to sign Lamb of God away from Prosthetic. We understood that we'd be under a microscope that night and that it was important to create a positive first impression.

The truth is that we genuinely didn't give a fuck. We treated it like any other show. In hindsight, I don't know if we would've done anything differently even if we *had* given a fuck. We were an entirely unpretentious band. There was no stage show, no costumes, no production. Just us. But it probably would've been wise to not get shit-faced drunk before we went on.

In the first ten seconds of our opening song "In the Absence of the Sacred," Randy, drunk and overcome by his punk rock spirit, jumped off the stage into the moshing crowd. As he dove, his foot caught the brass rail that bordered the front of the small stage, compromising his intended arc. He fell straight to the hard floor and was instantly knocked out cold. We stopped the show and, along with a few friends and fans, tried to revive Randy. He eventually came to but was now delirious in a perfect storm of drunk and concussed. Randy was carted away to the nearest hospital to be evaluated for head injuries and spent most of that process badgering—without success—anyone within earshot to prescribe him Percocet.

While our singer was busy shaking down the hospital for narcotics, we were left to limp through our big industry showcase show without him. Sympathetic to our plight, Chimaira's singer Mark Hunter attempted to fill in, but being unfamiliar with our material, the most he could do was scream randomness over the top of our songs. That lasted a couple of songs before Mark called it quits. A fan from the audience known locally as "Lurch" then took the stage with us and more adeptly handled a few songs. He knew the material and his voice actually wasn't half bad. Lurch wore out after a few more tunes, so we finished our abbreviated nightmare showcase with a couple instrumental versions of songs from our upcoming album.

Randy returned with a lump on his head as tour carried on. Our New York show had been a disaster. We'd convinced ourselves before we went on stage that we didn't care how the show was going to go. But when our reckless side bubbled over and blew the whole thing up in our faces, we were disappointed. Regardless, we had a new record coming out and a long tour ahead of us to focus on.

A few days after our debacle at L'Amour, we got an email from an A&R representative at one of the labels in the audience that night. He told us that his boss, the CEO of the label, had also been in the crowd and spent the whole next day in the office raving about the incredible show he'd been to the night before. "That was the best and most dangerous thirty seconds of rock 'n' roll I've seen in years!" he told anyone who would listen. "We need to sign that band!"

He wasn't the only one who felt that way. By the time the tour was over, with our new record having been out for less than two weeks, we were receiving big offers from multiple major record labels. Lamb of God was now in a bidding war. From the beginning of the onslaught of contract offers, Epic Records was always our favorite option. They were early to the jump, arranging a meeting with legendary A&R representative Kaz Utsunomiya, who had previously signed Korn and Ozzy to the label. Kaz made it clear to us that Epic understood we had our own unique identity as a band and that the label did not intend to alter it. But he did offer guidance and suggestions, and Kaz's impressive track record of bands he'd signed had our instant respect.

Kaz felt like we didn't reach our potential on our first couple of albums and that pairing us with the right producer could be the next step toward elevating the band. He gave me a copy of Clutch's *Blast Tyrant*, telling me to give it some listens and to pay particular attention to the mix and production. I was loosely familiar with Clutch but had never listened to an entire album of theirs. *Blast Tyrant* blew me away. It blended blues, punk, metal, and classic rock into well-written songs with fierce swagger and comically clever lyrics. It had been produced by a young producer-engineer who went by the name Machine. Kaz envisioned Machine producing the next Lamb of God release. It speaks to Kaz's vision that he wanted to pair us with a young, ambitious talent instead of a safer, older, proven one. He was looking to break new ground and develop rising talent, not plug us into a predetermined mold.

Epic Record's campaign to sign the band was aggressive, and we were convinced that they believed in us. Their offer gave Prosthetic Records generous financial compensation for releasing us, money Prosthetic could use to sign and develop more new bands and grow their own label. It also provided us with ample funding for future recording projects, with enough left over to pay ourselves a sufficient salary to live on. It wasn't the most lucrative offer we'd received, but it was substantial and we felt that Epic trusted us creatively more than the other options did.

On July 3, 2003, we played a sweltering show at New York City's Knitting Factory attended by several Epic Records executives, including label president Polly Anthony. Standing in a dim corridor of the club after our set, still in our sweaty stage clothes, Lamb of God, with our attorney's oversight, signed with Epic Records. A few weeks later, our signing advance was processed. I checked my bank balance and there was $25,000 in my checking account. I'd never had anywhere close to that much money in my life. It meant that I could now focus entirely on music. I didn't have to worry about picking up roofing jobs or building stage sets at theme parks.

We didn't stop to celebrate for very long. We headed over to England for our first appearances immediately after signing with Epic. Having caught wind of our major label bidding war, Slayer manager Rick Sales knew we were leveling up. He offered us the support slot for Slayer's two sold out nights at the historic London Astoria as a chance to explore the idea of working together. We crushed both nights and Rick was very gracious, but we decided to go with a smaller boutique management firm.

Shortly after returning home from England, we started a two-week tour with Anthrax. In just a month's time, we had signed a worldwide major label record deal and played on two different continents with two of metal's most legendary bands. We were moving quickly and it was thrilling, but it took some getting used to. My mind often raced as I tried to process everything. I'd analyze and rethink every choice we made, trying to learn and understand the options and ramifications of each decision. To slow down my thoughts, I also drank a lot. One night on the Anthrax tour in Peoria, Illinois, as the buses were loaded up and running, our driver was doing a final walk around at 2 a.m. before pulling out for the drive to the next show. He found me outside, passed out drunk and propped up against the double rear wheels of our tour bus.

"Hey! Damn, wake up man!" he shouted over the rattle of the idling diesel engine. "I sure am glad I saw you. That could've been real bad," he said as I labored up the stairs of the bus and staggered back to my bunk.

I escaped being run over by my own tour bus, and we completed the Anthrax tour and headed home for a short break. At the end of October 2003, we embarked on our final tour of the year, an eight-week run with fellow up-and-comers Killswitch Engage and Shadows Fall. Branded the "MTV2 Headbangers Ball Tour," the tour received heavy marketing and promotion from the video music channel in an effort to position all three bands as the cornerstone of a rising metal scene that journalists had named the New Wave of American Heavy Metal. Each band had huge industry buzz, but the synergy of us all on one bill expanded that excitement exponentially. The venues were packed, and fans were starting to recognize that they, too, were part of a growing movement that the entire music industry was noticing.

Epic Records was thrilled to see our success building on the road. But as happy as they were, the label wasn't in the concert business. They were in the recording business. They'd made a substantial investment into our band's recording future and wanted to see some results. Even though *As the Palaces Burn* had only been out for nine months, Epic was ready for us to start working on a new record—their record. We hunkered back down at home and turned our focus back to writing.

CHAPTER 14

GET READY
FOR THE
SUCKER PUNCH

"SPIRIT DITCH"
SPARKLEHORSE

No band sounds more like Richmond than Sparklehorse. While founder and songwriter Mark Linkous lived mostly outside the city in a rural part of the state toward the rolling hills that climb up to the Shenandoah Mountains, much of the band's activity and band members were deeply rooted in Richmond's music scene. Sparklehorse's 1995 debut album Vivadixiesubmarinetransmissionplot is the sonic embodiment of the lazy, careless, slacker-cool attitude that dominated Richmond in the 1990s.

187

The dreamy waltz of "Spirit Ditch" sounds like a slow stroll along the quirky, dilapidated, and ramshackle blocks of Richmond's Oregon Hill neighborhood where I lived for a time in the '90s. Poor, white, barely working-class neighborhood culture collided with art school slackers into an oddball and sometimes volatile mix of personalities. Confederate flags hung in the tall front windows of raggedy, neglected row houses where generations of longtime Oregon Hill residents lived next to patched-up rental houses that VCU students and dropouts used as off campus housing and often didn't leave. It was a uniquely Richmond setting. It was a time in my life flooded with possibility. Sparklehorse was a constant soundtrack.

This is about the time Lamb of God loaded into Richmond's Sound of Music studio to record our major label debut, Ashes of the Wake. *Our hired producer, Machine, was not from Richmond, and he was not impressed with the studio. It didn't look to him like the place to make a modern, heavy metal record with its outdated gear and shabby decorations. But to us it looked and felt like home. And for me, what was even cooler was that Sparklehorse had recorded there.*

Signing to a major label changed my life. I was now a professional, full-time musician. I could maintain a reasonably comfortable standard of living while focusing solely on my music career without worrying about a day job or a side hustle. It was a dream come true. But I soon found that my new career came with new stresses.

Epic was eager to get us back in the studio. This was an odd situation. On one hand, we were thrilled to be with a new label and grateful that they were excited about getting new material from us. But we had only just recently put out an album. We were proud of the songs on *As the Palaces Burn* and had devoted all our creative energy to it. We'd anticipated touring to support that album for at least a couple years, but that process was cut short when we changed labels. Epic had little interest in waiting for us to finish a tour cycle supporting a different label's release. They wanted an album's worth of material as soon as we could put it together.

Until this point, writing Lamb of God songs had been a process of collecting ideas as they popped up. Creativity is a strange phenomenon because it's difficult to schedule. Artists can put themselves in settings that may be conducive to working. They can deliberately eliminate distractions and surround themselves with stimulating environments. They can use instruments to find their flow. But if there's no artistic spark, no entry point into that magical current of creative inspiration, none of the other stuff matters.

With polite pressure from Epic to put a new album together, none of us had the luxury of writing the way we were accustomed to. There would be no gathering ideas as they fell from the creativity tree. We were going to have to shake that tree as violently as we could, scooping up every leaf that fell and hoping there would be enough. It was scary. And the pressure we felt was compounded by the fact that this was our first major label record. Everything was going to be higher profile with higher stakes. The budgets were bigger. The expectations were greater. There would be more eyes scrutinizing our work than ever before.

With no songs written and under the gun to write the most important album of our lives as quickly as possible, we set up in our rehearsal space on West Moore Street in Richmond's Scott's Addition neighborhood. Not having day jobs meant we could practice five or six days a week. We took full advantage of that time. We wrote and rehearsed new song ideas during the afternoons and evenings. After rehearsals, I stayed up late into the night, drinking beer after beer in the den of my small East End home, coming up with new guitar riffs and scribbling down lyric ideas to work into the new songs.

Despite new pressures and deadlines, my songwriting process remained constant. Song ideas were often an amalgamation of influences rooted in the music I was listening to or hearing around me. It's almost never deliberate. It's rare that I'll hear a song and think to myself, "I'm going to borrow that." It happens on its own. The creative part of my mind catalogs things I hear and files them away. When I write, those things sometimes pop up unexpectedly.

One of the new songs I was working on was a simple, up-tempo, heavily punk rock influenced song called "What I've Become." I was trying to explore new styles and feels. A straightforward punk song would feel fresh in contrast to the heavy groove and thrash metal style we were most often associated with. The song describes a state of disillusioned apathy. Themes of disconnection from one's dreams, confusion, resentment, and a general feeling of defeat weave through the twists and turns of the riffs.

> *Suffered consequence, It's been so long since*
> *any piece of this made any kind of sense.*
> *You anoint the king, I'll burn everything down to ashes*
> *You giveth, I taketh away*
> *It's a system now, intertwined*
> *Take your place in the line*
> *to be ground by the gears of the masterpiece*

I was describing my own conflicted relationship with our new-found success. Things weren't quite as bad as I was making them out to be in the song. I exaggerated some for intensity and dramatic effect.

But the emotions were genuine. I'd been wrestling internally with the notion of whether we'd screwed up a good thing by allowing ourselves to become a part of the major label music industry machine.

Queens of the Stone Age had recently released their *Songs for the Deaf* album. I listened to that album all the time in the year before we wrote *Ashes of the Wake*. In "First It Giveth," Queens' front man Josh Homme laments the fickle nature of addiction, "First it giveth, then it taketh away." It wasn't until years later that I realized I'd referenced their song in my lyrics for Lamb of God's "What I've Become." It had snuck in without me even noticing.

Another song I'd been putting together was centered on a classic thrash-style riff with a rolling 12/8 time feel that we were becoming increasingly comfortable working in. The main riff had been sounding off in my head for some time to the point where I eventually grabbed a guitar and deciphered what I'd been hearing in my head. It was as if I was figuring out a song from a cassette deck like I used to do when I was just learning to play. I brought the idea into rehearsal. The rest of the band loved it, so we built a song around it.

I'd also been working out some lyric ideas. Once again, a relatively minor argument was the catalyst for a flood of scathing vitriol that made for great heavy metal lyrics. My New York City girlfriend and I had broken up some time back. The distance had gotten to be too much for me to keep up with. I was now seeing a woman at home in Richmond who was a nerdy cool, punk rock librarian type. She was attractive and funny with an adventurous spirit. We were generally kind to each other but we both drank a lot, which sometimes created chaos.

One morning, after some inane and likely drunken argument with her the night before, I scribbled down some lyrics on a scrap of paper that characterized my emotionally immature disdain for what I'd perceived to be some kind of self-centered slight against me.

Console yourself, You're better alone
Destroy yourself, See who gives a fuck
Absorb yourself, You're better alone
Destroy yourself

When my petty, drunken-fight-with-my-girlfriend lyrics were paired up with our new 12/8 time thrash song, Lamb of God stumbled onto what would become one of the biggest songs of our career. "Laid to Rest" was born. The song felt special as soon as it came together. It's impossible to quantify exactly what sets "Laid to Rest" apart from the bunch. As songwriters, we invest the same amount of effort and care into every song we write and record. The goal is always to try to make each song the best version of itself. But sometimes a song will appear with an extra layer of excitement about it, an undeniable energy that elevates it above the others. "Laid to Rest" had it. Sometime later, as had happened with "What I've Become" and many other songs I'd written, I became aware of the influences that had guided me in the creation of "Laid to Rest."

As a young music fan and aspiring guitarist, I was a big fan of San Francisco Bay Area thrash metal pioneers Testament. I'd seen them in concert at least four times as a teenager, and though I loved Alex Skolnick's shred-style lead playing, it was Eric Peterson's heavy-handed, groove-filled rhythm guitar riffs that spoke loudest to me. The bounce and swagger of his driving riffs epitomized the Bay Area thrash sound that became a global phenomenon with lasting influence on metal musicians around the world, including myself.

In light of my deep love for Testament, maybe I shouldn't have been so surprised when, long after recording and releasing "Laid to Rest," it dawned on me that the intro riff I wrote the song around was strikingly similar to the Testament classic "Into the Pit."

This was never an intentional move on my part. In fact, it's similar enough that had I realized it when I was writing the song, I likely would've changed it. But at the time I didn't realize where it was coming from.

"Laid to Rest" had some outside lyrical influence as well. Shortly before we began writing the material for our Epic debut, Eminem's soundtrack to his film *8 Mile* had practically taken over the world. For more than a year after it was released, the lead single "Lose Yourself" was everywhere. My repeated, largely involuntary exposure to Eminem's hooky chorus eventually programmed my brain, and Eminem's "Lose Yourself" lyric inadvertently spawned Lamb of God's "console yourself / destroy yourself / absorb yourself" lyrics. It was all an accident: Bay Area thrash legends Testament and Detroit superstar rapper Eminem conspired to help Lamb of God write one of the biggest songs of our career. Over the years, Lamb of God has toured extensively with Testament. I've joked several times with Eric Peterson that every time we play "Laid to Rest," I owe him twenty bucks. The guys in Testament have always been very gracious, and we still value their influence as musicians, mentors, and friends. But we still haven't met Eminem.

The pressure of this new writing and recording schedule had us all on edge. But it became a lesson in trusting our own artistry. Willie and I churned out riffs, and together the band was whipping them into songs as quickly as we could bring our ideas into the rehearsal room. Randy and I were splitting the lyric writing. We had plenty to write about. The United States had invaded Iraq the year before, and a handful of our new songs waded into political themes. I wrote the lyrics for a song called "Hourglass," which described the escalating doomsday feel of the time and included the phrase that would become the title of our forthcoming album, *Ashes of the Wake*:

It's only getting worse, not worth a moment's regret
Each dawn another curse, every breath a twisting blade
What will be left behind in the ashes of the wake?

After seeing Tami Silicio's startling photo of the flag-draped caskets of US soldiers lining the cargo hold of a military plane, I added a line that took a harsh stab at the Bush administration's misrepresentation of the facts justifying the invasion. This misrepresentation cost thousands of US servicemen and women their lives, many who had believed in the cause they thought they were fighting for. I also added a reference from Kurt Vonnegut's novel *Slaughterhouse Five*. This reference was pure happenstance. There was a tattered copy of the book in a room at Water Music, the Hoboken, New Jersey, studio where we recorded drum tracks. Flipping through the novel, which I'd never read, I noticed Vonnegut's recurring line "So it goes." The matter-of-factness of those words was powerful in the context of the horrors of war. So I borrowed and repurposed the line for our heavy metal song.

You finally made it home
Draped in the flag that you fell for
And so it goes
The ashes of the wake

During our work, we'd finalized plans to record the new album with Machine. We first recorded drum tracks at Water Music then moved the sessions to Richmond, where we set up at David Lowery's Sound of Music studio. I was familiar with Sound of Music from sessions there with Corntooth and Avail. The studio was in an old, three-story building on West Broad Street. Other than the mixing boards, tape machines, and outboard recording gear assembled in each of the two control rooms, Sound of Music looked more like a hip, downtown loft apartment than it did a recording studio. The casual, threadbare vibe was part of Sound of Music's character, and regardless of its humble aesthetics, it had been the site of sessions from a diverse range of artists like Hanson, Daniel Johnston, and the celebrated Virginia-based indie rock band Sparklehorse, whose debut LP *Vivadixiesubmarinetransmissionplot* was one of my favorite indie rock albums.

With our new producer calling the shots, the sessions were efficient. But there was a bit of a creative tug of war between Machine and the band. As producer, he had expected to come into the project able to make adjustments to the songs and to add creative elements. But we resisted. Even though we'd worked with producers before, neither of our former hires had been heavy handed when it came to changing the songs. Machine was creatively ambitious and excited to take risks with our music. He lobbied for more melodic vocals, looped rhythm samples, and atmospheric layers in the tracks. Many of the techniques he was suggesting were part of his own signature production style and had been employed on some of the reference recordings we had used to get familiar with his work. However, once we heard those same techniques applied to our own music, it made us uncomfortable. It was out of our creative comfort zone, and combined with the anxiety we already had about the timeline and new label relationship, we pushed back. Machine was a professional, and sensing our collective apprehension, he backed off and dutifully made a very clean and conservatively produced Lamb of God album.

In preparation for our album release, we'd secured a slot on that summer's Ozzfest, an annual traveling heavy metal festival that took more than twenty bands on three stages all over North America. Ozzfest's 2004 lineup was strong, featuring a reunited lineup of Black Sabbath that included all four original members. Also on the tour that year were Judas Priest, Slayer, and a host of newer and more contemporary acts like Slipknot, who were well on their way to becoming one of the biggest bands in the genre. The smaller bands on the Ozzfest bill shared rotating slots on the second stage, but with a little help from our new label, Lamb of God was given a fixed time slot every day, playing right before Hatebreed, who were in turn direct support to the second stage headliner, Slipknot.

The tour lined up perfectly with the release date of our album. Actively touring as an album comes out is one of the best ways to promote visibility and generate sales. And Ozzfest was the highest profile tour we could dream of being on. We spent that summer playing to massive audiences and gaining new fans with every show. We understood that we were being catapulted to a new level of success, but we figured it would not last very long. Nonetheless, we celebrated. And we partied. Hard.

My daily routine on Ozzfest looked like this:

- **9:30 am:** Wake up in my bunk on the bus, usually painfully hungover and startled by the sound of whatever band was unfortunate enough to play the first of the rotating slots on the second stage that day. To this day, whenever I hear Lacuna Coil's "Heaven's a Lie," I think about waking up with my head splitting from the night before and the walls of my bunk vibrating to their early morning set.
- **10 a.m.:** Wander around until I find catering for desperately needed coffee.
- **10:30 a.m.:** Find a portable toilet to take my morning dump. The temperature will already be over 90 degrees inside the portable toilet, and flies will be swarming. I will attempt to find one that hasn't already been thoroughly obliterated by tour staff. (The stage crew gets up early.)

- **11 a.m.:** Find a "shower." There were usually a couple shower trailers behind the second stage. It was a bit like showering with a garden hose, but it was better than nothing.
- **11:30 a.m.–12:00 p.m.:** Find the Miller Lite tent and start drinking. Miller was a tour sponsor, and every day there was an air-conditioned tent with endless cold beer. It was an oasis of awesome for a young, ambitious alcoholic like me. There was nothing quite like an ice-cold beer on an empty stomach for breakfast.
- **12:00 p.m.–2:30 p.m.:** Drink beer, hang out, watch other bands. Ozzfest 2004 had a great roster of bands. Thoroughly representing the scene we were a part of. Some good friends on the tour were playing those rotating slots earlier in the day, including members of Throwdown, DevilDriver, Unearth, and our brothers in God Forbid. I tried not to get all the way drunk, just sufficiently buzzed enough to be in what I thought was a good "zone" for our show. This was always a moving target, so the results were entirely unpredictable.
- **2:30–3 p.m.:** Play our show. A half hour set was all the time we were given. That's six songs if we didn't rush the space in between them, and seven songs if we did. The short set time didn't bother me. I found the circumstances to be ideal for putting on an explosive show that grabbed the audience's attention and left them wanting more.
- **3:30 p.m.:** Maybe hose off again, maybe not. Head back to catering, this time for something to eat for the first time that day. I've battled weight most of my life, but the Ozzfest lifestyle was keeping me thin.
- **4 p.m.:** Crawl into my bunk for a nap. Sleep off my six-beer, half-drunk, postshow fatigue.
- **5:30 p.m.:** Wake up from the afternoon nap. Crack a fresh beer and start waking up for the night's activities.

- **6:45 p.m.–10:30 p.m.:** Hang out, drink beer, watch bands. Over at the main stage, Slayer went on at 6:45 p.m., Judas Priest at 7:55 p.m., and Black Sabbath at 9:30 p.m. I was a huge fan of all three bands and usually tried to catch a little bit of each set, but I rarely ever missed Black Sabbath. They are the godfathers of heavy metal. My love and respect for them runs deep. I knew that getting to see them with all original members was a huge honor and I took full advantage of it.
- **10:30 p.m.–2 a.m.:** Drink and hang out. Crawl into my bunk.
- **REPEAT.**

In conjunction with the marketing and promotion of the Ozzfest tour, MTV had created a reality-style competition game show around the tour called *Battle for Ozzfest*. Contestants from young, relatively unknown bands competed in a series of challenges, with the winning prize a slot on the following year's Ozzfest. Lamb of God was featured on several of the weekly episodes, including one in which Randy was particularly harsh with one of the young contestants during their challenge. Of course, this being reality television, the interaction was edited to exaggerate the drama. In a later episode, we brought the young man along to ride with us to a headlining show to "make up for" Randy's ruthlessness during the challenge. It made for good television, and the high visibility of MTV was good for our promotional campaign.

Another notable development of my Ozzfest 2004 summer was that I met a young woman I would eventually marry and have children with. She was a production assistant and had been working on Ozzfest for several years. We were introduced early in the tour and realized that we shared some mutual friends. We struck up what began as a very platonic friendship. I'd hang around watching bands, and once the show was over, I'd wander over to the office area and wait for her to pack up her desk and be done with work for the night. We'd split a bottle of wine and smoke a joint, talking freely and easily until it was time for our buses to leave for the next town. She was a Southern girl with a laid-back personality. We laughed a lot. I was still dating someone back home, so I had no intention of finding a new relationship. But over the course of the summer, I started looking forward to spending more time with my new friend. We texted each other during the day, and I was excited to see her each night. We were falling in love.

Ashes of the Wake was released on August 31, 2004, just as the Ozzfest tour was winding down. The album was easily our most successful to that point, selling 35,000 copies in its first week and landing at number twenty-seven on the Billboard 200 album chart. It was a respectable showing for any band, but even more impressive for a band as heavy as we were.

When I returned to Richmond following the tour, I broke up with my girlfriend there. It was inevitable, but I wanted to do it in person because she deserved it that way. I'd started a new relationship on tour, so there was no point dragging it out.

After a monthlong break, Lamb of God headed out again. We followed up our high-profile summer with a six-week run of North American dates with Fear Factory. Immediately after that, we headed to the UK for a two-week tour headlining clubs to close out the year.

Beginning on the tour with Fear Factory, we added videographer Doug Spangenberg to our traveling crew. Doug was an independent video director and editor who'd been making a name for himself in the metal and hardcore scene. His job with us was to film anything and everything. Doug was easy to be around. He was funny, with a sarcastic wit that fit right into our collection of personalities. Doug quickly gained our trust and was able to film at will without us feeling self-conscious or even being aware of the camera. He filmed throughout the North American and UK tours.

We'd been working hard. It had been a monumental year for the band, and the growth was thrilling. But we were tired. Constant, close-quarter living and a grueling touring schedule can be exhausting. The road can give you a negative attitude. Most of us were drinking daily and excessively. Randy and I both fell into that category.

Just one week before our last show of 2004, we played in Glasgow, Scotland, at The Garage. As usual, we'd started drinking well before our set. Doug was filming in the dressing room immediately after our show as I opened a fresh bottle of Glenfiddich scotch provided by our tour rider to keep the festivities rolling. Randy was hanging out with some local friends that night and invited me to join them as they headed out to hit a few neighborhood bars.

Randy had spent much of the day doing his best to imitate the harsh Scottish accent native to Glasgow. It started out as a funny, playful gag. But as Randy became increasingly more drunk, his ridiculous put-on accent began to stick. By the time the night was halfway through, he was talking like that constantly. Randy had evolved into an extremely drunk, fake Scottish dude. Somewhere along the way, he'd even put on a kilt, which made the whole scenario even more outlandish.

Our night out drinking was nothing more than a couple of American band dudes in Glasgow getting hammered with some locals. No big deal. I tapped out a little earlier than the rest of the guys. I was getting pretty shit-faced and I could tell that if I kept going it was going to turn bad quickly. There were few things I liked less than laying in my coffin-sized tour bus bunk trying to pass out with the spins. I walked back to the bus, ate a sandwich to soak up some of the booze I'd been guzzling, and crawled into my bunk.

Sometime later, I woke up to the sound of yelling and arguing coming from the front lounge of the bus. That wasn't an entirely unfamiliar occurrence, so I tried to ignore it and get back to sleeping off my drunkenness. But it kept escalating. The commotion was Randy, shouting belligerently and indiscriminately at anyone in his field of vision. He was wasted and aggressive. I had seen this behavior in him before when he drank himself into oblivion, and I always dismissed it as simple drunken idiocy. But on this night, something in me snapped. My frustration of being cooped up in a tour bus for weeks at a time, my feelings of isolation and missing home, my exhaustion, the stress and uncertainty, the commitments I'd made to touring and to the label became more than I could shoulder. It all ignited into a rage that I channeled directly toward Randy, who was still spewing his drunken vitriol in the front lounge.

I rolled out of my bunk and walked toward the front of the parked bus where half a dozen band and crew members were congregated, trying to calm Randy down. Intuitively sensing a storm brewing, Doug had pulled out his camera and started filming the chaos. Without much thought, I pushed my way straight to the front of the bus where Randy stood berating his audience. I swung hard and punched him squarely in the jaw. "Who fucking hit me?" Randy bellowed, staggering backward and still speaking in his absurd attempt at a Scottish accent.

Seconds after I punched him, I was picked up off my feet and forcefully pulled backward. Our tour manager, Boz, had been trying to deescalate the situation from the beginning. He was well accustomed to our drunken stupidity and was almost certainly looking forward to getting through that last week of shows as smoothly as possible and getting away from all of us for a nice, long break. Boz was a big dude. He had been a lineman on his college football team and though his days as an athlete were long behind him, he could've picked any of us up with one hand and tossed us around like a pillow. Which is exactly what he did after he watched me hit Randy.

Boz hoisted me up from behind and started carrying me toward the back of the bus. Now completely off my feet and in Boz's arms, I lunged forward and swung again, this time even harder. I connected, punching Randy hard in the face. "Oyy! He hit me again!" Randy shouted, still using his Scottish accent. "You fucking asshole!" He now realized it was me who hit him, and he was appalled that this was how I repaid his generosity. "I bought you a drink tonight! Come on laddy, let's fight!" he yelled from the front of the bus to the back. (Yes, he really called me "laddy.")

"Let's go!" I answered eagerly.

"Mark Morton, get ready for the sucker punch!" The comedic value of telling someone to get ready for a sucker punch didn't sink in until later.

I went out the side door and Randy went out the front. We met on the sidewalk alongside our tour bus and started grappling, with the other members of our tour entourage following behind us to witness the spectacle. Randy and I were still plenty drunk, but he was worse off. We tussled around awkwardly and both lost our balance. As we fell, Randy rolled me to the side, and we landed hard on the concrete sidewalk with the momentum of our fall and the weight of both our bodies slamming down on my left shoulder. We stood back up and I tried to negotiate a truce as Randy threw multiple wide, swinging haymakers at my head. None of them landed. We grappled a bit more and as we struggled, Randy headbutted me hard in the face. I hadn't really felt the fall to the sidewalk. My adrenaline had overridden that pain. But the headbutt to the middle of my face hurt. And it pissed me off.

After a few more seconds of tussling, Randy swung again, and this time he connected to the back of my head. Enraged, I reacted with a series of wild, flailing swings and pushed him hard toward a small set of stairs leading up from the sidewalk just behind us. Our drum tech protectively yanked our merch girl, Angie, out of the way. Randy and I hit the stairs, and I immediately flipped him around, slamming him back down on the sidewalk. The back of his head cracked audibly against the concrete. As he landed on his back, I punched him twice in the center of his face before noticing that he was knocked out cold. I stood up and headed down the sidewalk while the others revived Randy, who chuckled defiantly as he came to. I walked aimlessly for a few minutes and actually cried a little, overcome with a flood of emotions as I processed everything that had just happened.

When I returned to the bus, I walked into the front lounge and saw Randy sitting by himself in the dark at the table drinking a beer. I grabbed a cold beer for myself, cracked it open, took a huge swig, and sat down with him. We looked at each other and started laughing. Boz and the rest of our band were in the back lounge of the bus discussing what to do next and how we could keep the tour going to get to the end. Randy and I sat up front, drinking and chuckling about the chaos we'd created.

The next morning I woke up to the sound of my own loud groans. I could barely move my left shoulder. The pain was excruciating. I was also pretty sure I had a broken a finger on my right hand, but that felt barely noticeable compared to my shoulder. We had driven overnight to Liverpool for our next show at Carling Academy. Once the gear was unloaded, I tried strapping on a guitar, but I could barely hold it, let alone play. The pain was too extreme. I went to see a doctor, and the X-rays determined that I'd torn cartilage in my left shoulder, which happened when we first hit the sidewalk. I'd also broken my finger punching Randy. The doctor gave me a sling for my arm and several sleeves of unadulterated codeine pills.

"These are very strong," he warned me. "Take one every four to six hours, and do not drink any alcohol with these." Upon returning to the bus from the hospital, I opened a bottle of red wine and swallowed three of the pills with my first gulp.

"What'd you get?" Randy asked me excitedly, walking in from the bunk area of the bus.

"Codeine," I replied, guzzling more wine.

"Well hook a brother up!"

His eye was dark blue, and one side of his face was noticeably swollen. He grinned at me, his hand outstretched and open, waiting for his cut of the painkillers. I happily obliged his request.

That night, with my arm in a sling and drunk on wine and high on codeine, I watched from the soundboard as Lamb of God performed without me. It was uncomfortable. I was rooting for them, hoping they could pull off a great show. They did their best. Many bands would've cancelled, but that wasn't our style. And we also needed the money. I watched three or four songs but couldn't stand it any longer. I went back to the bus for more codeine and wine. I sat alone in the back lounge listening to the Mars Volta's *De-Loused in the Comatorium*, a brilliant concept album about a man in a drug-induced coma. The irony of the album's theme was lost on me as I faded in and out of consciousness in an opiate haze.

By the next show at Clwb Ifor Bach in Cardiff, Wales, I rejoined the band. Loaded up on painkillers and beer, I limped through our set. A couple days later, I woke up on the bus the morning before our show in Brighton, England, to a series of texts from my girlfriend back in the United States. One of my biggest guitar heroes, Dimebag Darrell of the bands Pantera and Damageplan, had been murdered on stage in Columbus, Ohio, along with one of his crew members, an audience member, and a venue employee. We were stunned. We had met Dimebag just a few months before and were thrilled to find that someone who'd been such a huge influence on our band was a genuinely sweet dude. He talked to us like equals and hung out and partied as if we'd been friends for years. He and I had exchanged phone numbers, and he made it clear that I could call him anytime for advice or just to chat. Dime's murder was a devastating loss to the entire music world.

We finished the last of our UK shows and flew home for a much needed break. Randy and I had quickly burned through all my codeine pills. I was wishing they'd given me more of them.

CHAPTER 15

CRUISE CONTROL

"I NEED A MIRACLE"
GRATEFUL DEAD

When I was growing up in James City County, Virginia, the closest real city was nearby Williamsburg, but by anyone's practical standards, Williamsburg was, and still is, a town. The closest bigger cities were Hampton and Newport News, about forty-five minutes away. If you wanted a mall, a car dealership, or fashionable clothes, you had to go there. Hampton Coliseum was also the center of my teenage universe for live music.

The first concert I saw at Hampton Coliseum was Van Halen in May 1986. I was thirteen years old and had just started playing guitar. Eddie Van Halen was my hero. I bought every magazine I could find with him in it, and I listened to his records over and over, marveling at his acrobatic guitar technique. My older brother was twenty years old, and though he was only a casual Van Halen fan, he supported my musical ambitions. He was happy to take me and my friend Mark Wisniewski, also a beginning guitarist and Eddie worshipper, to see the show. I was *in awe. I couldn't believe I was in the same room with my hero, listening to him play guitar in real time.*

My parents soon started letting me to go to shows in Hampton without my older brother as a chaperone. Throughout high school, I saw Aerosmith, Ozzy Osbourne, Iron Maiden, and Judas Priest. As I became a more accomplished musician and began playing in bands, going to concerts was like going to school for me. I paid as much attention to how the show was set up as I did to the show itself. I'd find a spot far to the side of the stage to see how Joe Perry's amps were set up and how many guitars Zakk Wylde had for the show.

On April 10, 1992, when I was a nineteen-year-old college sophomore, I saw Metallica at Hampton Coliseum. They were spectacular. A month earlier, I saw the Grateful Dead in that same building with Williamsburg native Bruce Hornsby on keyboards. Walking past ticketless Deadheads holding signs saying "I need a miracle"–Grateful Dead parking lot code for "I need a free ticket"–I couldn't have imagined that one day I would tour alongside some of my heroes and play concerts of my own in Hampton Coliseum.

Our intense touring schedule wasn't letting up. We were working harder and more often than we ever had before. Our manager, Larry Mazer, continually reassured me that staying on the road was how bands got bigger, so he kept us on tour as much as he could. Larry was an old-school, blue-collar manager. He'd worked with legends in the industry, managing Cheap Trick and KISS. He oversaw the rise of Cinderella in the '80s and managed them throughout their most successful years as a chart-topping arena band. Larry was the antithesis of the slick, stereotypical Hollywood types that permeated the industry. Middle-aged, slightly disheveled, and often prickly and cantankerous, he was aggressive with his strategy for growing the band. But as hard as he worked us, it was always clear that he had a much bigger vision for Lamb of God. Few people believed in us as much as Larry Mazer did. He saw no limit to our possibilities, and his leadership in those early days was instrumental to our rise through the ranks. His schedules were exhausting at times, but I couldn't argue with the results because it was working.

In March 2005, as we continued to tour in support of *Ashes of the Wake*, we set out on our first arena tour in support of Slipknot. This was huge. Growing up and going to concerts, the biggest bands and biggest shows I'd seen were in Hampton Coliseum, about a forty-five minute drive from Williamsburg. I saw bands like Van Halen, Mötley Crüe, Iron Maiden, Ozzy Osbourne, and Aerosmith. Touring arenas with my own band, even as a support act, was a dream come true. Even more mind blowing was that the tour made a stop *at* Hampton Coliseum, the very building where I'd seen so many of my heroes play and where I dreamed of one day playing.

I was living like I thought a rock star was supposed to live. I drank every day, keeping it fairly tame before our show but letting loose after. The codeine painkillers I'd been prescribed in England had awakened my fondness for opiates. In the mid-2000s, Vicodin and Percocet painkillers containing synthetic, pharmaceutical opioids as their active components were widely overprescribed. And on tour, painkillers were passed around like sticks of gum. Fans, groupies, industry people, and road crew almost always had a couple pills to share. Beer, weed, and a couple Percocets was my favorite after-show routine. I loved the buzz. And I didn't feel like I was anything close to out of control.

Some of us were having a more difficult time. Soon after the tour began, I learned that Slipknot bassist and songwriter Paul Grey was leaving. I had only just met Paul when the tour started, and we'd hung out a couple times. He didn't seem like someone in trouble. Paul was gentle and sweet. He was humble in a way that you might not expect from someone who'd seen that much success.

But Paul was struggling with his own substance abuse. It had reached a point of crisis, so the decision was made to send Paul to treatment. The tour continued with various crew members and opening band members filling in on bass. Slipknot drummer Joey Jordison asked me to play bass on two songs he had picked out for me, "Everything Ends" and "Duality," the latter of which was a massive hit for the band. I was honored and happy to accept. The afternoon before my first performance, Joey and I sat in a dressing room while I learned the songs from a small CD player.

That night after Lamb of God's set, I quickly showered, changed clothes, and rushed back up to the stage to be ready for my songs. There was a bass guitar and a small audio monitor behind the stage backline, a few feet away from Joey's massive drum kit and out of the view of the audience. In the break before my two songs started, I grabbed the bass from the crew member who'd played a few songs before me and strapped it on. Joey turned back just before he counted off the start of my first song, put his fist up in the air, and gave me an exaggerated nod from behind his mask that he wore as part of his stage costume. Four counts on his high-hat cymbals and we were off. Yes, I was playing bass for Slipknot, but I hated why. Nobody wanted Paul to be away.

After the Slipknot tour, we headed to Europe for a quick run of festivals beginning at Germany's Rock am Ring and finishing a week later at the massive Download Festival in the UK. Then, it was back to the states for a six-week North American tour as headliners on the Sounds of the Underground festival, an Ozzfest-style tour that featured newer acts from the hardcore and metal scene.

While we were out on the Sounds of the Underground tour, Epic released our first full-length concert and documentary DVD, *Killadelphia*. The video featured footage from two back-to-back 2004 shows in Philadelphia. The title referenced a slang term for the city of Philadelphia and its high homicide rate. Philly has always been a second home to us, so it felt right to have filmed the footage there. Woven throughout the film was behind-the-scenes footage that Doug shot while traveling with the band, including the fight between Randy and me. Our goal was to accurately represent our tour life. When we started the project, we hadn't planned on releasing footage of a fist fight between band members, but we left the fight footage in the final edit. Randy could've easily had it removed; everyone would've understood why he wouldn't want that public. It was unflattering to us both, plus he'd gotten knocked out cold on camera. But Randy didn't give a shit. It was more important to him that we be *real* than it was to protect whatever bruise to his ego the footage may have caused. It says a lot about Randy's character and personality that he didn't ask for that scene to be left out. Make no mistake about it: Randy is punk rock as fuck. *Killadelphia* was certified Gold in Australia and Platinum in both the US and Canada.

After a few months' break, during which we began assembling some new material, we ended the year with a three-week headlining tour in Europe to capitalize on the exposure we'd gotten from our festival appearances there earlier that summer.

The *Ashes of the Wake* album cycle had been grueling, but our band's profile had grown exponentially. Everyone involved agreed that there was momentum, and Epic was ready to start planning for a new album. As usual, Willie and I had been steadily compiling riff ideas on our own in between tours. We felt confident that we had the beginnings of what could be a strong new batch of songs.

We spent the first half of 2006 writing and recording the *Sacrament* album. Once again we hired Machine to produce. This time, however, Machine had a stipulation: he insisted that he be allowed to actually *produce* the album. He had walked away from the *Ashes of the Wake* sessions feeling like his hands had been tied and that much of his creative input had been shot down. Not wanting to repeat that, Machine made clear that he intended to be hands on this time, pushing us out of our comfort zone both creatively and sonically. We agreed that it was time to take some risks. Machine had gained our trust.

We set up once again at Sound of Music studios. Assisting Machine with the sessions was a young engineer from New York City named Josh Wilbur. Josh had spent several years as an assistant to legendary engineer Andy Wallace and had only just recently set out on his own. Josh had initially been hired just to engineer the drum tracks, but when we all realized the scope of the work we had in front of us, he stayed on to assist in guitar tracking. I wound up recording most of my guitar parts on the album with Josh. Over the course of those sessions, we became good friends.

One of my favorite submissions for the album was a song called "Walk with Me in Hell." During the *Ashes of the Wake* sessions, Machine had turned me on to Muse and their album *Absolution*. They had great songwriting and production, with heavy guitar riffs and huge anthemic chorus hooks. The songs "Stockholm Syndrome" and "Hysteria" both stood out as fantastic guitar-driven compositions with twisting, slinky, high-energy riffs. Around the same time, Velvet Revolver had a rock radio hit with their song "Slither." Anchored by a bouncing, overdriven guitar riff that wound its way up and back down the fretboard, "Slither" was exciting in the same way the Muse songs were. Those influences inevitably impacted my writing. Although it wasn't a deliberate strategy, the intro and verse riffs of our new song "Walk with Me in Hell" reflected my intrigue with the Muse and Velvet Revolver songs. As I've mentioned, my writing is never too far away from what I'm listening to at that time.

I had plenty more song submissions for the *Sacrament* album. One was a song called "Redneck." Normally, song titles are derived from the lyrical content, but "Redneck" was "Redneck" before it ever had a single word assigned to it. It just sounded to us like, well, a redneck. Another song I brought in was "Descending." To break out of our norm, the music for "Descending" was intentionally simple. It relied heavily on a repetitive, hypnotic riff to lay the landscape for the dark, introspective lyrics I'd written referencing my feeling of doom related to my progressive substance abuse issues.

> *The river I'm bound to be found in, a rope chosen, bound*
>   *for the hang,*
> *When I'm blinded I think I see everything, convincing*
>   *myself again,*
> *This God that I worship, this demon I blame*
> *Conspire as one, exactly the same*

I was excited to present it to the band, but I was met with blank stares and confused looks. Our drummer Chris hated it, and he wasn't shy about letting me know.

Incensed by the reaction I'd gotten to "Descending," I went home after rehearsal and immediately started crafting a new, snarling riff that pushed, pulled, and swung with a confident swagger. I was redeemed. The band loved this new song instantly. I later added some vague "fuck you"-style lyrics that collectively referenced a handful of distasteful personalities I'd encountered in my life. But the first line, *"So goddamn easy to write this,"* is an ode to the original motivation behind the riffs.

We went back on the road as soon as we finished the album. We toured throughout June and July of 2006 supporting Slayer on their Unholy Alliance tour, then on to a full North American tour supporting Megadeth. In the short break between those tours, *Sacrament* was released, debuting at number eight on the Billboard 200 chart and selling 63,000 copies in its first week. It was our strongest chart debut to date, propelled in part by the success of "Redneck," which was nominated for a Grammy the following year. We closed out 2006 with an extensive tour of Europe once again supporting Slayer, who had taken us under their wing for a bit. It was a good fit. Although the Slayer audiences were notoriously intolerant of opening acts, we were going over well with their crowd. Winning over Slayer audiences worldwide was a big step in developing our own core fanbase.

In the beginning of 2007 during a quick break between tours, I married the woman I'd been dating since Ozzfest. We'd been living together for a couple of years at that point, though I'd been away on tour for much of it. Such was the rock 'n' roll lifestyle. After taping a television performance for *Late Night with Conan O'Brien*, Lamb of God continued touring with a headlining run of North America and a string of dates in Australia, Japan, and Europe. We returned home for two weeks and headed out again on our second Ozzfest tour, this time as direct support to Ozzy on the main stage. We finished our year back in the UK supporting Heaven & Hell, a reunited Black Sabbath lineup featuring Ronnie James Dio on vocals.

As you can probably tell, our work schedule was relentless. It had begun to feel like we were in constant motion. We jumped from tour to tour and continent to continent, landing at home just long enough to put a new batch of songs together and start the cycle over again. But we were seeing results. The band was exploding worldwide, and we were making great money. I was generally happy. My life and career were on cruise control. My schedule was laid out for me by my manager, and I followed along without much protest. My wife had worked for years in the music industry. She was familiar with the traveling and commitments that were required of me. She also valued her own independence and time to herself. It was working for us.

After touring most of the world to support *Sacrament*, we stopped to catch our collective breath. I bought an eight-acre piece of land in a rural area east of Richmond and began to build a new home there. My wife and I started making plans to have a baby. All the touring and the associated madness had me yearning to establish some stable roots.

Standing still was a welcome change, but work continued. We started putting together our next album, a process that took up most of 2008. Despite the success of *Ashes of the Wake* and *Sacrament*, we decided to work with a new producer. But the person we chose wasn't even officially a producer yet.

During the making of *Sacrament*, we had been blown away by Josh Wilbur's efficiency and work ethic. He was easy to work with and had a knack for keeping whomever he was recording relaxed and productive while they worked. We knew Josh was a world-class engineer, but he had never officially produced a project. Nonetheless, we offered him the job, which he nervously accepted. Josh traveled to Richmond with a carload of his recording gear and set up for several weeks of preproduction sessions in our rehearsal room. On the first day, we played our new songs for him in the room, a private concert for a one-man audience. When we finished, with our ears still ringing, I looked at him and said sarcastically, "Okay, produce." And with that, we started working.

We recorded the drum tracks for *Wrath* in New York City at Electric Lady Studios, a historic studio built by Jimi Hendrix. Led Zeppelin and the Rolling Stones had recorded there. We recorded the guitar and bass tracks at Studio Barbarosa, a beach house converted into a recording studio in a secluded area of Mathews, Virginia, on the Mobjack Bay. I drank constantly. I held it together just enough to stay sufficiently productive, but my drinking was compromising my performances. While the results were still good, it was taking me more tries to get them. Josh was quietly annoyed. He knew why I wasn't performing at my peak.

In contrast to our previous album's heavy-handed production that used rhythm section loops and heavy editing, Wilbur chose an approach that was more natural sounding. The recordings felt raw and real. Imperfections were often left unfixed. We wanted it to sound almost like a live performance. The picturesque setting of our guitar sessions inspired an impromptu intro on the album's closing track "Reclamation," in which Josh captured a live recording of Willie and me playing acoustic guitars on the back deck of the beach house with the soft waves of the Mobjack Bay rolling in and out behind us.

Randy hung around the sessions while we recorded guitars. It wasn't his turn to record yet, but he sure as hell wasn't going to pass up a free stay at a beach house. Josh and I recorded in the upstairs control room with its huge bay window overlooking the water, and there was Randy on the horizon, slowly paddling by in a kayak to check the crab pots he'd set the day before in the hopes of catching dinner. It was hilarious because normally Randy hates being anywhere near a studio session. He loathes recording. But this felt more like a vacation. He also drank the whole time. Attempting to outmaneuver the specter of alcoholism, Josh arranged for the vocals to be recorded separately at Dizzyland Recording in Rochester, New Hampshire. He thought that putting Randy in an unfamiliar and distraction-free environment would keep him more focused and easier to record. It didn't work, but his vocal takes still came out sounding phenomenal.

With *Wrath* wrapped and set for release, we did what we always do next: hit the road. But this time it was special. We'd gotten an offer from Metallica to be direct support for them on the North American leg of their World Magnetic tour. Metallica was the biggest band in metal and easily one of the biggest bands in the world, regardless of genre. It was a massive opportunity. I was a huge Metallica fan growing up and never dreamed I would wind up playing shows with them. And there was no better way to promote our forthcoming album than opening for one of the world's biggest bands.

As the tour got going, I was happy to see that the dudes in Metallica were down-to-earth and cool. I'd toured with stars of their caliber before who were guarded and who mostly stayed secluded unless they were on stage. And that's cool too because some people are just private and want to be left alone. But the Metallica guys were social. I spent time chatting with all of them, but Kirk Hammett and I talked the most. We most immediately bonded over music and gear. He'd recently started getting into collecting vintage guitars, so I was curious to learn what he looked for in an older guitar and how he found them. Kirk was always approachable and sometimes even invited me to head out with him after their show for dinner or drinks.

A week or two into the tour with Metallica, on an evening when we had an off date and were playing our own headlining show in Chico, California, I got a call from my wife back home in Virginia. She was pregnant. We'd been trying for a while and were ecstatic.

My life now felt like a dream. My career was at an all-time high. We were touring the world and making great money. I was building a beautiful new home out in the country. I was married to a woman I loved. And best of all, I had a baby on the way. A couple months later, while we were on tour in Australia, our sixth studio album, *Wrath*, was released. It sold 68,000 copies in its first week and landed at number two on the Billboard 200, second only to Taylor Swift.

CHAPTER 16

THE UNTHINKABLE

"FADE TO BLACK"
METALLICA

Heavy metal music tends to have very dark lyrics. It's a tradition and part of the genre's culture. Black Sabbath, who most agree invented heavy metal, wrote songs in the early 1970s that referenced taking Lucifer's hand and Satan spreading his wings. Judas Priest sang about street-stalking murderer Jack the Ripper. Slayer referenced the atrocities of Josef Mengele and Ed Gein. Heavy metal's morbid fascination and preoccupation with dark, haunting themes is well established. To the uninitiated it can seem shocking and scary. And that may be part of the attraction. But most real metal fans see the lyrics as fantasy: dark storytelling seen from the same perspective as one might view a horror movie.

When I was in high school, my friend Jeff Hightower wrote all the lyrics to Metallica's "Fade to Black" on the front cover of one of his class notebooks. Metallica was one of our favorite bands, and the song's somber, introspective lyrics about hopeless isolation felt profound to our teenage minds. But when Jeff's English teacher noticed his notebook decoration, Jeff was sent straight to the guidance counselor's office for a psychiatric assessment. They thought the lyrics were his cry for help. We thought it was hilarious.

Decades later, while developing material for Lamb of God's Wrath LP, I wrote the lyrics to a song called "Dead Seeds." The words are essentially a compilation of pseudo-biblical sounding phrases that don't have a lot of direct meaning in and of themselves, but when compiled together abstractly reference a doomsday vibe. Among the phrases is the line:

You will not comprehend, or find words that will describe
The will of God and man until you watch someone die

I was thinking about someone I knew who had passed away when I wrote that line. But more than anything else, I thought it sounded like a cool heavy metal lyric. I couldn't have imagined that less than a year after releasing "Dead Seeds," I would find those lines all too painfully accurate after watching my infant daughter die in my arms.

I don't believe those events are related. I refuse to believe in a God that would punish me and take the life of my firstborn child for writing some spiritually arrogant lyrics. But I can say that the experience of losing Madalyn was a catalyst for me to rethink the purpose and the value of the energy that I put out into the universe.

was overjoyed at the thought of becoming a father. But almost all my excitement would have to take place on the road. The band was in full swing, playing shows all over the globe in support of our new album, *Wrath*. While my wife was at home, alone and pregnant, I spent seventeen of the first twenty-five weeks of 2009 completing multiple headlining tours in the United States, United Kingdom, and Asia. We also continued supporting Metallica on their World Magnetic tour throughout Australia and Europe.

I felt like I was being hypnotized. We would fly from a two-week run of Europe straight into an Australian tour, then directly to a string of shows in Japan. From there on to Indonesia, where crowds of fans waited outside the airport, hoping for an autograph or even just to catch a glimpse of us climbing into a van to be whisked away to a hotel. Sleep schedules were impossible to maintain. Days and weeks melted into an indiscernible blur. We moved fast. It was disorienting. I would drink a few beers and a couple shots of whiskey before the shows to loosen up, then continue drinking during and after the show. I made friends with some crew guys who worked for bands we'd been touring with. They'd hook me up with a few oxycodone painkillers whenever I asked. I looked forward to scoring pills, and I didn't feel any shame about it. I wasn't addicted. I just loved that feeling of spacing out and letting my thoughts drift off aimlessly. All the stress and anxiety evaporated as the pills kicked in. I tried not to ask those guys for pills too often because I didn't want to burn out that connection. But I still wound up asking quite a bit.

While supporting Metallica in Europe, with the baby's due date approaching, I made plans to leave the tour so that I could be home for her birth. We'd already found out we were having a girl. I was relieved when I'd gotten that news. The thought of raising a son would've terrified me.

Buz McGrath from the band Unearth was going to fill in for me beginning in Denmark, where we had two shows in a row at the Forum Copenhagen. I played the first night as he watched the show to get familiar with the stage set up. Buz was a professional and had learned our material inside and out, but Metallica's production was in the round. They'd designed an unconventional, oval stage in the middle of the arena, which made things awkward for us to navigate as an opening band. Having learned all the songs in our set and seen a show firsthand, Buz confidently stepped in and took over for me. On July 28, 2009, I flew home from Denmark. My daughter was due in a little less than a month.

Arriving home was a relief. Our tour schedule had been overwhelming. I'd been drinking a lot and adding painkillers to the mix more frequently. The constant travel, long distances, and time zone changes left me feeling isolated. Drinking and getting high was an escape, but it left me disconnected. When I got home, I slowed down. I still drank every night, but it was much less than my tour intake. I took a few pills here and there too. But it wasn't every day.

My wife and I had recently moved into our new house. Having a few weeks at home before the baby arrived gave me a chance to spend some time taking it all in. It was a beautiful home, tucked into the woods and out of sight from the road. There were large front and back porches and a huge, paved patio in the back. I had a separate, detached garage in the back corner of the long driveway with a music room on the second floor.

We set up a nursery for the baby. My parents brought us a crib and nursing chair, and my dad was excited to put them together for his new granddaughter. We hired one of my favorite local artists to paint cartoon owls perched on trees along the walls of the baby's room. There was a baby shower with gifts of clothes and blankets, car seats and toys. We were ready.

On a hot, quiet, late afternoon in August 2009, my wife woke up from a nap realizing her water had broken. Knowing it could happen at any time, she'd already packed her bags for the hospital. She had to calm me down as I scurried to get our things loaded in the car for the twenty minute drive into town.

We checked into the hospital, and she was settled into her room. Her regular obstetrician was not on duty that day, so we were assigned the doctor on call, who with the assisting nurses did some initial checking. All was well. Things were calm. My wife was in early labor but still likely hours away from giving birth, so I relaxed. I chatted with her and sent dozens of text messages to family and friends announcing that the time had come. The baby was on the way! Early into the night, I fell asleep in a chair next to her bed.

I was awakened abruptly by a flurry of activity in the hospital room. Machines were beeping. Nurses had concerned looks. I didn't know how long I'd been asleep or what was going on. I was told that there was a problem but wasn't given much explanation. They did tell me that the baby's heart rate was climbing too high. My wife didn't look well at all. She was lethargic and confused. Her temperature was well above one hundred degrees.

She was taken away to the operating room for an emergency C-section. I was hurried into a prep room, where I sanitized my hands and got dressed in a hospital gown and a mask before being led into the operating room. The surgery was already underway. A couple of minutes later I heard the cries of my daughter, and I was relieved. She was born. She was alive. I could hear her. Everything must be okay.

But none of the hospital staff looked relieved at all. The umbilical cord was quickly cut and the baby was taken to a table where she was cleaned up. I could see her lying on the table. Her legs were kicking. She was blue. I could still hear her crying in short, rapid, muted wails.

"Is everything okay?" I asked nervously. Nobody replied. I waited for what seemed like a long time but likely wasn't. "Tell me what's going on! Is she alright?"

The head nurse spoke in a measured, professional tone that instantly meant things were not okay. "Mr. Morton, your daughter has very low oxygen levels," she explained. "She has a high fever, and her heart rate is extremely elevated. Your wife also has a very high fever. We are getting them both stabilized so we can figure out exactly what's going on as quickly as we can."

The nurse turned back to the table where Madalyn was laying, still moving, still blue, still crying. Soon after that, she was taken to the neonatal intensive care unit of the pediatric ward for further tests and evaluation. The head nurse said they would update me as soon as they had fully assessed the situation. I wasn't told much of anything else. I felt totally helpless.

My wife was taken back to a recovery room after her C-section. She was heavily medicated from the surgery. Soon after, a nurse stopped by to tell me they were running tests on the baby. She assured me that the baby was being well cared for and to let them know if we needed anything. After that, my wife and I were left alone in that room. We waited for two hours. There were no updates. There were no reports. Nothing.

Slowly my wife began regaining consciousness as the anesthetics wore off. "What's happening?" she sobbed. "Where is she? Why won't they tell us anything?" I sat still staring at the floor. I was full of rage and fear and adrenaline. But I couldn't say or do anything. I was terrified.

After a long wait, a different doctor came in. He introduced himself as the head physician on the neonatal intensive care unit. He explained to me that during labor, my wife and the baby had both come down with an infection, the origin of which was not yet entirely clear. It had taken them some time to figure that out. Now that they knew, the baby was going to be airlifted by helicopter to the University of Virginia Medical Center in Charlottesville about seventy miles away. He said they were better equipped to treat her and that she would be getting the best care there.

I watched from the sidewalk in front of the emergency room as they wheeled my daughter to the ambulance that would take her on the short ride to the helicopter. As they lifted her into the back of the ambulance, I ran to my Toyota 4Runner in a nearby lot.

I raced down I-64 west from Richmond to Charlottesville as fast as I could maneuver through traffic. I felt outside of myself as if I were watching a film. Pulling into the hospital parking lot, I saw a helicopter making its approach toward the landing pad on top of the building. I'd beaten them there. "I should have fucking driven her myself," I said out loud to nobody.

I was met by an attentive staff of the neonatal intensive care unit at the hospital. They'd been expecting me. I was directed to a private room down a long hallway. It was quiet, separated from the din of everyday hospital activities. As I sat down and tried to collect my thoughts, a doctor came in and introduced herself. She looked remarkably young, maybe in her early thirties, but more likely late twenties. She was very petite, not much over five feet tall, which added to her youthful appearance. She was wearing a flight suit. "Mr. Morton, I'm Dr. Vallas," she said, shaking my hand firmly. "I'm the flight transport physician. I'm very sorry that we have to meet under these circumstances." She spoke gently. Her eyes were kind and compassionate.

"Can you tell me what's going on? I still don't even know what's wrong with her."

"Mr. Morton, your daughter and your wife became very ill during labor. They were exposed to an infection that quickly overcame them both," she explained. "We don't entirely know why or how that happened. Your wife's life was likely in danger as well, but she had more strength to fight the infection. The baby was more vulnerable."

I struggled to process what she was telling me. I understood what she was saying. It just didn't feel real. The doctor continued, "What I can tell you right now is that we have her stabilized. The oxygen level in her blood had gotten dangerously low. Her heart stopped twice during the flight, but I was able to bring her back. We now have her hooked up to machines correcting those levels. I can't speculate to what extent that oxygen deprivation damaged her brain, but I do suspect there will be some issues. If and how those present will have to be determined further down the road. This is going to be a process."

Dr. Vallas told me that an overnight room was being prepared for me. She then led me into the large neonatal care room where Madalyn was stationed. I walked over to her and saw her sleeping. Her small platform sat in front of a wide, glass window that looked out toward the rising Shenandoah Mountains. Her color looked entirely different than it had in the Richmond hospital. The bluish tint to her skin had disappeared. Her skin looked like mine. There were several tubes coming out from her neck and arms. I watched her chest rise and fall as she breathed. My child was alive.

A nurse brought me to my overnight room. I shut the door and fell onto the bed. I lay there looking up at the ceiling as my mind began to register all the events of the day. I sent texts to all my friends who had been asking for pictures and details, hoping to celebrate Madalyn's arrival. I rolled over, buried my face into a pillow, and cried.

That evening, my brother Allan made the two-hour trip from Williamsburg to Charlottesville to be with me. I was grateful that he came. Things at the hospital had settled down for the night. Madalyn was stable and would continue to be assessed. Allan and I went out for sandwiches near the hospital. We sat and talked calmly. I was relieved that Madalyn was getting great care and that things felt less chaotic. The panic had ended. That night, I slept deeply.

The following morning, I woke up early to a bright summer sun streaming through the window. Once I got up and got myself together, I walked over and spoke to the nurses on duty that morning. I sat with Madalyn for a while. She looked the same as she had the night before. *Stable* was the word I kept hearing regarding her condition. Stable is better than not stable, I thought. I was relieved.

The layers of emotions I felt in that situation were complex and confusing. The uncertainty of Madalyn's prognosis was terrifying. What kind of damage had been done to her brain? Would she be catatonic and bound to life support machines? Would she be blind or paralyzed? Would it be even possible for her to make a full recovery? There was no way of knowing. I didn't even know what would be realistic to hope for. But I was relieved that there was any hope at all. I worried about my wife, recovering from the infection and emergency surgery. How had they gotten so sick, so fast?

The head nurse on duty pulled me aside and spoke with me. "As you know, we've stabilized Madalyn. Now we're in a period of observation and assessment. If we get her through the next couple days, we'll have a clearer picture of what we are dealing with and how best to proceed. You're likely going to be here with us for a while. I don't know how long. But I do suggest you make a trip home and get together some clothes and whatever else you need to stay for a week or so."

Again, I felt a wave of relief and hope. They were actively getting a plan together. This was progress. And finally there was something I could *do*. Going home to pack a bag for the week was a task; it was something I could do that made me an active part of her treatment. It made me feel less helpless.

Making the long drive home that morning from Charlottesville to Richmond, I spoke to God. I didn't have much of an idea who God was, but in that moment, I didn't care. I asked God to let Madalyn live. I made a promise that whatever disability this situation resulted in, I would happily accept. I was committed unconditionally to doing anything and everything she needed. "God, just please don't take my daughter from me," I said out loud.

I arrived at my empty house. As soon as I got inside to start gathering some clothes, I received a call from the hospital. It was the nurse I'd been speaking with earlier that morning. "Mr. Morton, I'm sorry but I'm calling with some very bad news. Your daughter has begun to deteriorate rapidly. Her brain and organs are beginning to shut down," she told me in flat, serious tone.

"What are you going to do?" I asked in a panic.

"I'm sorry, Mr. Morton. There's nothing left we can do. She's transitioning. I do believe she has a little bit of time left. Maybe several hours. I urge you to get back here to the hospital as quickly as possible so that you might spend that time with her."

I went numb. Something switched off in my brain. I didn't cry. I didn't punch the wall. I just felt empty. In that moment, I learned what total hopelessness feels like. I drove back to Charlottesville. I don't remember anything about the drive at all.

When I arrived back at the neonatal intensive care unit, the room felt still. The normal bustling activity of the nurses was missing. There was a chair set out for me by Madalyn's station. As I walked over, the supervising nurse stopped me. She put her hand on my shoulder.

"Mr. Morton, I don't want to scare you, but I do want you to be prepared. As your daughter transitions, you may see what appears to be struggling or discomfort. It can be unsettling if you aren't expecting it. It's just sometimes what dying looks like."

I looked her in the eye as she spoke, but I couldn't bring myself to respond. I sat down in the chair in front of my daughter. A nurse had already begun disconnecting her from the life support machines that weren't going to save her. The nurse picked Madalyn up from her small elevated hospital crib, swaddled her in a hospital blanket and laid her in my arms. She was warm. I watched her chest rise and fall. My child was alive.

I cradled Madalyn in my arms, rocking her in the chair and staring out of the window at the edge of the Appalachian Mountains. It was a gorgeous day. I touched the soft hairs at the top of her forehead. I ran my fingers over her hands and across the tiny knuckles of her fingers. I bent over and smelled her head. She smelled familiar. She was my daughter. I spoke softly into her ear, telling her how sorry I was that this world had made her so sick. I told her about how I'd dreamed of teaching her to play guitar. I told her about the wide green pasture that was the front yard at her house and how one day I'd planned to teach her to drive the tractor that I used to mow it. I told her about her room and how it was all ready for her with owls on her walls. I told her that I loved her. Her breaths were getting further apart. Her color was changing. A small trickle of blood fell from her left nostril. I wiped it away gently with her blanket and then wrapped her up a little tighter. I glanced up and noticed several of the nurses crying softly. I sat for some time longer, staring out the window. I eventually looked down and saw that her color was changing to a shade of purple. She wasn't breathing. My daughter Madalyn Grace Morton had died in my arms. She was two days old. I was numb. I stood up and handed the blanket with my dead daughter wrapped up in it to a nurse.

CHAPTER 17

DRUGS

"NUTSHELL"
ALICE IN CHAINS

My heroes have always been alcoholics and drug addicts, drunks and junkies. For me, becoming so captivated by music at an early age meant inevitably wanting to be like the people creating that music. Jimi Hendrix, Jimmy Page, Stevie Ray Vaughan all wound up strung out on drugs. While I was aware of that as a young fan, I never gave it too much thought. Addiction just seemed to be a common thread among many of the musicians I admired. I didn't understand why that was.

As I got older, I began to view drinking and drugs as a component that came along with the lifestyle of being a musician. Guns N' Roses, Nirvana, Jane's Addiction, Alice in Chains, and so many of the other bands I listened to all had public struggles with drugs and alcohol. Many of them referenced addiction in their lyrics, often warning about its perils. For a very long time I shied away from hard drugs because I had seen what they'd done to a lot of my heroes. I listened to the stories they told. But I didn't listen close enough.

Eventually, I found my way to drugs, becoming a casual user. It was normalized in the environments I was in. Partying was all around me, and drugs were simply a part of it. But when genuine tragedy hit, it wasn't a party for me anymore. The role of drugs in my life immediately changed. They became the solution to my problem. And in short time, the drugs themselves became the problem.

Musicians and artists are sensitive. Our gift keeps us open to the endless possibilities of our creative process. We share our emotions through sound and color, and we find joy and relief when we can speak in the language of our art. But our gift also comes with burdens. Emotions hit extra hard and can carry an unreasonably heavy psychological weight. We hold on to trauma and pain. Our most painful experiences often become the inspiration for our most poignant work. It can become a self-destructive cycle.

When I returned home from the hospital in Charlottesville, my mother was waiting for me. She hugged me and cried quietly as soon as I walked inside. She too had lost her first-born child. I knew she understood, but I was still numb. We sat quietly together in rocking chairs on my front porch overlooking the woods and field that make up my front yard. It's a beautiful property full of singing birds and soft, audible breezes. After a little while, I stood up and walked down the hallway and into the room that we'd set up as Madalyn's nursery. Standing alone in what was supposed to be my daughter's room, I looked at the owls painted on the walls, at the blankets, stuffed animals, and clothes, all neatly arranged in anticipation of her arrival. I walked over to the crib that my dad had assembled, pushed up against the wall with a battery-powered mobile above where Madalyn would have slept. I pressed the button on the mobile, and it started softly playing Brahms's "Lullaby." I stared down into the empty crib, my hands trembling as I clutched the side rail. As I looked up at the mobile spinning and listened to the lullaby play, the cold, detached numbness that had been holding me up drained away. It was replaced by an all-consuming despair that was unlike anything I'd ever felt before. The emotional weight of Madalyn's birth, illness, and death fell onto me so intensely that my knees buckled. All at once, I felt everything. I collapsed to the floor sobbing.

Within a couple days, my wife returned home from the hospital to continue recovering from her illness and surgery. She laid in bed crying for days on end. I won't tell her story for her. It's not my place. But I've never witnessed such deep sadness as I saw in her in those first few months after Madalyn died.

One afternoon, a day or two after we'd gotten home, I suggested we take a ride. I didn't have a destination in mind; I just knew we needed to get out of the house. My wife reluctantly agreed. I helped her gingerly descend the back porch stairs and then climb slowly into the passenger seat of my truck. She was still in significant physical pain from her surgery. It was warm outside and drizzling. We headed out aimlessly down Route 5, a historic rural road that connects Richmond and Williamsburg. Twisting through the turns past sprawling farms and historic pre–Revolutionary War plantations, we barely spoke. We'd exhausted all our words and now simply existed quietly together in our unimaginable grief. We drove across the county line separating Henrico County from Charles City County, and the horizon in front of us opened to a massive pasture. As the road wound its way into the clearing, the clouds parted, and a bright ray of sunshine beamed through the windshield. A vibrant rainbow appeared over the field as we drove by, arcing from the horizon, high over the trees and back down to the ground. There wasn't another car in sight. I felt a powerful sense of peace. I was sure that Madalyn was letting me know that everything was okay. Maybe I was believing what I wanted to believe. Maybe I was assigning supernatural meaning to a random, everyday occurrence. But the sense of relief I felt was very real, albeit fleeting. It didn't eliminate my sadness. It didn't make what had happened any easier to process. But I felt a message of love from the soul of my daughter who had died in my arms. And I clung to it.

My wife and I were friends with a man named Brian who was a mortician. Brian was a huge heavy metal fan, and I'd found it a bit comical that he was a metalhead running a funeral home. It seemed like a silly cliché. But after Madalyn died, we decided to have her cremated, and Brian generously offered his services. It seems strange to find any kind of relief in converting your child's body to ashes, but it was comforting knowing that a trusted friend was the person carrying that out. When the cremation was completed, we met with Brian at his funeral home to receive the urn with Madalyn's ashes. It was wrapped in a green velvet drawstring bag. It was an emotional exchange. Brian was a father himself and his sympathy for us was genuine. On the way home from the funeral home, we stopped at a grocery store. As we walked across the parking lot into the store, I felt uncomfortable, like I shouldn't be leaving Madalyn's ashes in the back of the car unattended. When we returned, I loaded several bags of groceries into the back of my SUV next to the ashes. We drove home silently.

The tour with Metallica had been on a short break but would be resuming soon with dates all over North America. Before the loss of Madalyn, I had anticipated joining back up with the band for the start of that next leg, but I decided to take some more time away. My wife was devastated. I didn't want to leave her home alone, still healing physically and still coming to terms with the loss of the baby. Friends and family had shown lots of love and sympathy. For the first couple weeks after Madalyn's passing, the house was showered with cards and flowers. An extended network of friends had organized home-cooked meals dropped off on our front porch. It was a beautiful gesture. But as the days and weeks passed, things got more still. The phone rang less. The flowers wilted and the cards stopped coming. People got back to their regular lives. But our lives were changed forever. The house was silent and depressing. I did my best to be a source of love and support for my wife. And to some degree, her overwhelming grief offered me a distraction from my own.

There was, however, another distraction from my sadness: I also dove headfirst into drugs and alcohol. I'd been drinking alcoholically for years, and my fondness for opiate painkillers was also well established. But the loss of Madalyn and the depression that followed was the catalyst of my addictions taking off like wildfire.

My wife had been sent home from the hospital with a large bottle of Demerol, a strong opioid painkiller prescribed to treat her post-surgery pain. But I started using it to treat my own emotional pain. Between the two of us, we used that prescription up quickly. When she requested more a short time later, her doctor obliged without hesitation. In addition to helping myself to my wife's medication, I started hitting up all my drug contacts around town, sourcing more pills from dealers and friends who were regular users. I had made a conscious decision; I didn't want to feel any more pain and sorrow. Drugs made my despair easier to navigate. The pills left me detached and blank, which felt much better to me than the crushing grief and anger that I felt without them. I took painkillers and I drank beer. All day, every day. I knew that the way I was living was dangerous. I didn't care. I knew that the drugs were potentially addictive. I didn't care about that either.

My entire life, I'd believed in God without understanding what God was. I'd never had an active "faith" or religion and had never cared to have one. But I did believe, in a very general sense, that there was some kind of force or power behind our human existence. When Madalyn was dying, I begged God to spare her. In desperation, I'd tried to bargain with a God that I hadn't spoken with much before. But I didn't get what I asked for. And I became resentful of God. How could some supposedly loving and compassionate higher power let an infant baby die in her father's arms? Religious people commonly say, "God has a plan." Was it God's plan to kill my daughter? "Well then, fuck God," I thought.

The band headed back out on the Metallica tour with our friend Doc Coyle from God Forbid capably filling in for me. I stayed home, drunk and high. We'd built a beautiful home on a picturesque piece of property, all timed to coincide with the baby's arrival. But now it just felt like a graveyard. My depression wasn't lifting. Nothing seemed to change or get better. I had a small collection of guns that I kept mostly just for target shooting. I'd been having intrusive thoughts and suicidal ideations. The idea of escaping my new reality was attractive. But I knew I wasn't thinking straight. I called a friend to come over and take my guns away.

Over the course of working together for several years, my manager Larry Mazer and I had developed a close friendship. He was checking in with me by phone daily. He could tell things weren't getting any better. "Mark, you've got to get moving. You can't just sit in that house suffocating in sadness." He urged me to get back out on the road. "You're a musician, Mark. It's what you do. You've got to force yourself to get back to living your life. Getting back out and playing music is going to help you heal."

I didn't have any better ideas. I didn't think being back on the road could be much worse than spending days upon days drunk and high and not leaving the house. We arranged for me to rejoin the tour. My wife would come with me. The band offered us the back lounge of the tour bus to have as our own space. It was a generous and compassionate gesture. Privacy and space are limited on tour, but they knew we would be needing both to maintain any kind of sanity.

On October 1, 2009, just forty-eight days after losing Madalyn, I played my first show back with Lamb of God, opening for Metallica at the BankAtlantic Center in Sunrise, Florida. Rejoining the tour was difficult. As a performer, my job is to entertain. But it was difficult to do in the depths of extreme grief and depression. Looking out into the audience, I could see that people were thrilled to be at our shows. They were smiling and cheering. Meanwhile, I was devastated and hopeless. The joy of the crowds just made me feel more alienated and alone.

The dynamic with my band was awkward as well. My bandmates are like family, and their sympathy for my situation was never in question. But my emotional trauma wasn't theirs to navigate. Regardless of how profoundly Madalyn's death impacted my life, my bandmate's lives were in a different place. They were having a different experience. Lamb of God was in the middle of a world tour with the biggest metal band on the planet. We were playing to huge audiences, and the rest of the band were having the time of their lives. There was endless laughter and partying. I just wanted to disappear.

My wife didn't last long out on the road. After a couple weeks, she decided it was more productive to be home and to start regaining some sense of a normal life. I completely understood. She would still come out to shows close to home or meet up with me on convenient days off, but her time touring with me was finished. We began to grieve the loss of our daughter separately.

With my wife back at home, my mindset changed. She had been my partner. We were companions in our grief. The trauma of losing

Madalyn had taken over as the cornerstone of our relationship. We traveled together and got through the shows, both understanding how cruel it felt for us to have to pretend to be okay while everyone and everything around us was in full rock 'n' roll celebration mode. With her out of the picture, I felt alone. I resented my manager for suggesting I rejoin the tour. I resented my bandmates for having fun. I hated playing the songs. I hated pretending to be okay. My sadness turned into anger. I didn't want to feel the way I was feeling, and drugs and alcohol provided me with a solution.

Alcohol was easy. Touring bands typically get a rider, which is a list of the daily supplies to be provided at each show. Riders commonly include coffee, tea, soft drinks, snacks, and basic food stock for the bus refrigerator like bread, lunch meats, cheese, and peanut butter. They also usually include alcohol. And our rider included a lot of alcohol. At every show we got three or four cases of beer, a large bottle of bourbon, and a large bottle of either vodka or tequila. We liked to alternate. My preshow drinks had changed from beer to liquor. I'd fill a red plastic Solo cup up with ice, then pour straight vodka in until it was about an inch from the top, leaving just enough room for a healthy splash of Gatorade. It worked quicker than drinking beer. I'd start with vodka, then continue drinking during the show and long into the night after we were done. I'd usually switch to beer at some point to plateau my intoxication level, but not always.

Finding drugs was more challenging than finding alcohol, but I had resources for that too. In my travels, I'd made the acquaintance of quite a few drug dealers all over North America. They were almost always the same. At their core, they were *fans*. They wanted to be as close to the action as they could get, and they had learned that the drugs they sold would often get them access. They always wanted multiple tickets to the show and backstage passes if possible. Sometimes they'd even ask for free T-shirts. As a support act on a tour as high profile as Metallica, my ability to provide that type of access was limited. But I'd always try my best, because I knew the better I made the experience for my connection, the more motivated they would be to supply me with what I wanted. Rarely did I actually like hanging around these people. A few were cool, but most of the drug connections weren't people I'd normally spend time with if they weren't providing what I was looking for. I tolerated them and serviced their requests as best I could, because doing so meant I could get high. And getting high was quickly becoming my favorite thing to do. I liked it better than playing music. I liked it better than hanging out with my wife. I liked it better than doing anything. When I was high, I didn't care about anything anymore. I loved that feeling.

The North American leg of Metallica's World Magnetic tour was ending with two nights in a row at New York City's Madison Square Garden. It was a monumental event for everyone involved. We never would have dreamed that our extreme, underground, basement metal band could end up at one of the world's most famous arenas, playing with the one of the world's biggest bands. Several nights before, I'd linked up with a drug dealer friend of mine. He was one of the few dealers who I actually liked being around. We hung out most of the night, catching up and watching some of the Metallica set. While we were together, he sold me eight 80 mg Oxycontin pills for $500. That was a decent price. Oxycodone-based painkillers like these could sometimes sell for as much a $1 per milligram. But this guy was a friend and didn't price gouge me. The pills he'd sold me were among the strongest opiate-based painkillers available. They were typically only prescribed to patients with a terminal illness or to chronic pain patients who'd been on narcotic painkillers for so long that their tolerance to the drug necessitated an extremely heavy dosage. I had a reliable source for the same pills back home in Richmond, so I was accustomed to them. I didn't ask my dealer friend where he'd procured these. I didn't care. These were among my favorite scores.

Over the next couple days, I paced my drug use. I went through three of the 80s in two days which, for me at that point, was a steady trickle of staying reasonably high. I'd take 40 mg in the morning and drink a couple beers with it to catch a little buzz to start my day. I'd nap in the afternoon, which would reset me for the show. An hour or so before our set, I'd start drinking again. If I didn't have any strong pills, I'd drink vodka. But with something heavy like these, I'd stick to beer. After we finished playing, I'd take another 40 mg or so...half an 80...and then another half after that kicked in, to keep it going. My goal was to stay functionally high as often and as long as possible.

By the time we got to New York City, I was down to five of the pills I'd scored. Leaving the tour bus early that afternoon to check into our swanky, five-star Manhattan hotel, I shoved a T-shirt and a change of underwear into my backpack, along with a bottle of Absolut Vodka and a few beers from our bus's small refrigerator. When I got up to my room, I took half a pill and drank a couple beers, figuring I'd ease into my usual buzz. But it wasn't kicking in like it normally would, so I took another half pill about an hour later. That evening, I went out for drinks with a friend named Justin, who was in town to hang out and see the show the next night. Before I left to meet up with him, I took another half a pill to keep my buzz rolling.

Hanging out with Justin, I was distracted. We'd been close friends for a long time. Justin was very successful in professional motorsports and was transitioning from being a driver to building his own team. Our busy schedules had prevented us from being able to hang out together for quite a while. I hadn't seen him or even talked with him much since Madalyn's death. We had a whole lot to catch up on. But I struggled to carry on a conversation. I couldn't stay focused. I wanted to be interested and present with my friend, but my mind was elsewhere. My buzz was fading. I just wanted to be back alone in my room so I could get high again.

Sensing something was up, Justin leaned in.

"You doing alright, man?" he asked. "I know you've been through a lot. Is there anything I can do? Just say the word. Whatever it is, I've got you."

"I'm alright man," I answered. "Just a little burned out from the road."

We hung out for forty-five minutes, then parted ways, agreeing to catch back up the next night before the show.

"Get some rest, brother," Justin said, as I walked down the sidewalk back toward my hotel.

Back in my room, I was relieved to be alone. I poured vodka into a Solo cup full of ice and took a huge swallow. The night turned into a blur. Over the next few hours, I took two more 80s and drank vodka until I blacked out. Sometime later, falling in and out of consciousness, I struggled to stay upright in my chair. My heart was racing, my breathing erratic. My arms and legs felt prickly with pins and needles sensations. I was terrified and pouring sweat. I laid down on the bed and passed out until I was startled awake by the sensation of vomit burning the back of my throat. I stumbled to the shower and leaned against the wall under cold water trying to shock myself into coherence. With a little focus regained, I walked back over to the bed and passed out, soaking wet.

The next two nights we opened for my childhood musical heroes Metallica at Madison Square Garden. At the time, it was easily the biggest moment of my career. I barely remember being there.

CHAPTER 18

DESOLATION

"MY MICHELLE"
GUNS N' ROSES

The first time I saw Guns N' Roses was probably on MTV. The video for their debut single from 1987's Appetite for Destruction *was seemingly everywhere. Its depiction of a young, naive, straight-from-the-boondocks Axl Rose stepping off a Greyhound bus onto the seedy streets of Holly-wood was a spot-on portrayal of my own rock 'n' roll dreams and the shared dreams of millions of other kids just like me.*

Guns N' Roses appeared out of nowhere, blending the classic blues rock components of the Rolling Stones and Aerosmith with a New York Dolls–influenced glam aesthetic. And they delivered it with a reck-less punk and metal musical edge that made it feel dangerous. I was instantly a fan.

The album is laced with the groovy, churning riffs of guitar duo Slash and Izzy Stradlin, slinking in and out of step with one another while orbiting drummer Steven Adler's swinging but dependable pocket and Duff McKagan's smart and simple bass lines. Axl Rose shrieked and crooned dark, detailed narratives of sex and drug-fueled debauchery in the underworld of Los Angeles. Songs like "My Michelle" immortalized characters from their circle of friends and coconspirators, shamelessly referencing heroin and cocaine. They held bottles of whiskey in their press photos, and they often appeared wasted in interviews, slurring their words and mumbling nonsensically without a care. My fifteen-year-old imagination was captivated: this is how a rock star is supposed to be.

In time, I found my own way into a rock 'n' roll wasteland. I drank myself into alcoholism and became desperately addicted to drugs. But I never managed to do it quite as cool as my teenage heroes in Guns N' Roses. And I could never have imagined the irony that years after I idolized his band and their reckless debauchery, Slash would offer a hand of support in my journey to get clean and sober.

What Slash had learned before me, and what I would later come to learn, is that the drug-fueled, mythological rock 'n' roll lifestyle is unsustainable. Some of us might get away with it for a time, but it always turns on us eventually. Strung out rock stars either die or get clean.

After finishing the North American leg of the Metallica tour in New York City, we took a few weeks off before heading back out for a quick run of shows in Australia. I returned home to Virginia just in time for a very somber Christmas. The band stayed off the road through January 2010. During that time at home, my wife and I got some incredible news. She was pregnant again. I was ecstatic. But my joy came with a complicated mix of emotions. Still grieving the loss of Madalyn, it was a strange feeling for me to be simultaneously navigating despair and elation. And I was scared.

After the traumatic experience we'd just had with Madalyn, my wife and I were both terrified at the possibility of something like that happening again. But even during our grief and fear, our overriding feeling was one of joy and hope.

Once again, we did most of the celebrating and processing of emotions around a new baby separately. Lamb of God left in early February for a five-week headlining tour of western Europe. We quickly moved on to a tour of Asia, including a show in Thailand; shows in China; as well as dates in Singapore, the Philippines, and Japan. We stopped home for a few weeks then started another monthlong run of international shows beginning in Bangalore, India. It was our first ever appearance in India, and the turnout was massive. The excitement surrounding the show landed us on the front cover of *Rolling Stone* India. From there we headed straight to Istanbul, Turkey, where after our show rowdy fans swarmed around the van transporting us to our hotel. Hundreds of our own fans rocked the vehicle back and forth so hard I thought we would tip over. We continued on to shows spreading throughout Eastern Europe, which included stops in Slovenia, Croatia, Slovakia, Hungary, Czech Republic, and Poland, plus two shows in Russia. After playing Moscow and Saint Petersburg, we flew to Tel Aviv, Israel.

We arrived in Tel Aviv the day before our show, and the promoter generously arranged for us to take a day trip to nearby Jerusalem. I've never been a follower of organized religion, and my feelings about God during our first trip to Israel were as conflicted as they'd ever been. I was angry at God. And I was scared of the concept of a God that would have me hold my dying child. But when I got to Jerusalem, I felt a positive energy. It's possible that just knowing that the city is considered holy by three different religions made me feel spiritually connected. Regardless, I felt an undeniable sense of calm. Our guide took us to the Western Wall, one of

Jerusalem's holy sites where there is a custom of scribbling prayers onto scraps of paper, folding them up tightly, and tucking them into the small spaces between the stones. I wrote a short prayer for the child we were expecting and pressed it into a tiny opening in the wall.

From Israel we continued to Athens, then back into western Europe for more headlining shows and festival appearances. We ended the run with a return to England's massive Download Festival at Castle Donington. The touring schedule was exhausting. Our manager and booking agents were focused on expanding the profile of the band which, in fairness, was their job. And it was working. Lamb of God was getting bigger opportunities and bigger paydays than we ever had before. But the continuous travel and waking up not remembering what country I was in yesterday; the lack of sleep; constant jet lag; and in my case, alcohol and drug use were all taking a heavy toll. We were tired and grumpy. Relationships within the band and crew were strained. We were burnt out from the road.

Our personal relationships back home were being tested as well. My wife was navigating a trepidatious pregnancy by herself. I tried my best to be supportive with regular phone calls from the road, but the distance, time zone differences, and lack of dependable cell service left us disconnected. I felt like I was living two separate lives. By the middle of June 2010, we'd played fifty-three shows in twenty-nine countries. And we kept going. In early July, we started a twenty-six show run in North America, supporting co-headliners Korn and Rob Zombie on the Mayhem Festival. It was an important tour for us. Although we'd already toured in arenas and amphitheaters on Ozzfests and as a support act to Metallica, Megadeth, and Slayer, the Mayhem Festival had more of a mainstream feel than any of our previous tours because

Rob Zombie and Korn were proven rock radio acts. For us, mingling among hit terrestrial radio bands was new territory.

As exhausted as we were from constant touring, being back in the United States was a morale boost. It gave us a collective sense of being at least sort of "at home." I was particularly relieved to be back in America because it meant I'd have a much better chance of linking up with my drug connections. Sourcing my drugs of choice had been difficult for the first half of the year; international touring makes it challenging to be an active pill junky. I managed to score occasionally, but mainly I drank a lot. Rather than use those periods of involuntary abstinence from narcotic painkillers as an opportunity to steer myself away from them, once we got back to the US, I leaned into using even harder than I had before. My opiate addiction was making up for the time I'd spent away from it.

Aside from the issue of my escalating drug use, the Mayhem tour was a great experience for the band. We went over well opening for the radio-friendly headliners, which was encouraging considering that much of their audience was seeing us for the first time. Korn front man Jonathan Davis and I often ended up chatting together on the venue loading docks at the end of each night. He and I both liked to smoke cigars before the buses pulled out for the next town. The docks became our meeting point and the site of some meaningful conversations. We discussed some of the things I'd been through in the last year, and I talked about the anxiety and excitement I felt about having another daughter on the way. Jonathan was a father himself. He thoughtfully shared his insights with me. He was a kind and gentle dude. I liked him a lot.

The Mayhem tour ran through August 14, which was less than two weeks away from my wife's due date. I'd been gone for most of her pregnancy, away on tour while she handled doctor's appointments and home preparations herself. We'd found out early on that we were having another girl, and I couldn't have been happier. I again arranged to leave the tour early so that I could be home well before her due date. I'd been using pretty regularly over the course of the tour. I started trying to slow my intake a bit, but it was challenging.

On August 10, 2010, our friend Paul Waggoner, guitarist for the band Between the Buried and Me, flew in to join the tour in Tampa, Florida. Just like Buz McGrath had done the year before, Paul watched our set from a side stage that night to help him prepare to take over for me at the next show in West Palm Beach. Earlier that evening as I'd packed up my things to fly home for the birth of my daughter, Jonathan Davis walked up to my bus with a huge box in his hands.

"I know you're heading home after the show tonight," he told me. "So I got you this! Throw it on the bus and have one of your guys bring it to you when they get home in a couple weeks. It'll be right on time!" Jonathan smiled and handed me the big colorful box. It was a motorized baby swing. "We had one of these same swings when my youngest was a baby," he explained. "Your daughter is going to love it. It'll put her right to sleep, and you're about to learn how truly valuable that is!"

I was touched by his gesture. I knew that we'd connected during our late night loading dock talks, but for Jonathan to go through the trouble of getting a gift for the baby while we were out on tour meant the world to me. I gave him a hug and thanked him for the gift and for having us out on the tour.

"Congratulations, brother. And don't worry. It's going to be great," he reassured me.

That night after our set, I took the last of my stash of oxycodone pills. I'd been using every day for a while, but I managed to time it just right so that I wouldn't run out until I was headed home. I hung around for a while that night after the show and drank some beers before heading to an airport hotel. My flight home was the next day.

By the time I got home the following afternoon, I wasn't feeling well. I had no energy and my joints were aching. My stomach was churning, and I was making frequent trips to the bathroom with aggressive diarrhea. By evening, I was shivering and sweating at the same time, laid out on the couch, miserable.

"You okay?" my extremely pregnant wife inquired suspiciously.

"Not really," I groaned. "I think I have the flu." I was pretty sure I did not have the flu.

"The flu, huh?" she asked sarcastically. "You come home from a month on the road and all of a sudden you just happen to come down with the flu?" She wasn't naive. She knew that I'd been using for a while. I hadn't made much of an effort to hide it since the baby died. She knew I was in withdrawal. "We're about to have a baby. You'd better get your shit together."

She shook her head in disappointment and walked out of the room. She didn't say much else about it, which I appreciated. But I knew she was right. I needed to get my head straight. I had a daughter due at any time. I spent the next few days in bed and on the couch, shivering and squirming, withdrawing from oxycodone.

Opiate withdrawal is like the worst flu you've ever had combined with a crushing anxiety attack. I couldn't sleep. I had painful muscle spasms, aching joints, and extreme restlessness. I was nauseated and couldn't eat. I had violent diarrhea and cold sweats. This would be the first of countless full-fledged opiate withdrawals I experienced over the next several years.

After a few days, the doom cloud of my withdrawal gradually lifted. As always, I continued to drink daily, but even that slowed down noticeably to barely a six-pack of beer a day. My wife and I prepared ourselves and our home as best we knew how for the arrival of our daughter. The nursery room that had been set up for Madalyn had been closed and locked for the better part of a year. But with a new baby coming, it was opened and freshened up. The furniture, crib, and accessories that had been assembled for Madalyn now awaited the birth of her sister. And we kept the owls on the wall.

In late August 2010, just a few days past what would've been Madalyn's first birthday, my wife gave birth to a healthy, beautiful baby girl. When they placed her in my arms right after delivery, I repeatedly asked the nurses if she was okay. They assured me she was fine.

The band had a two-week tour of South America booked that began the last week of that September. Paul Waggoner continued to fill in for me while I stayed home and settled into our new life with a baby. I felt loved and supported by my bandmates. They put no pressure on me to rush back out to touring. Nonetheless, I rejoined the band for our last leg of Metallica's World Magnetic tour on October 13, 2010, at Auckland, New Zealand's Vector Arena. From there, we finished our year with a string of dates supporting Metallica across Australia. It was during that Australian tour that my close friend, lead singer, drug scoring partner, and drinking buddy Randy Blythe got clean and sober. I did not have a single drop of faith that it would last.

At the end of 2010, after what had been a marathon of world touring on the *Wrath* album, Lamb of God took a year off the road. It was a welcome break for all of us. We were exhausted. But we didn't stop working entirely.

In February 2011, we set back up in our Richmond rehearsal space and began writing songs for what would become the *Resolution* album. Eager to build on the success of *Wrath*, we brought Josh Wilbur back as producer and head engineer. He sat in on our writing sessions, helping us to organize our rough ideas and build song structures.

Guitar riffs have always been the initial building blocks for Lamb of God songs. Willie and I both came into the writing sessions with stockpiles of riffs that we'd been compiling in what little spare time we'd had since the last album. And we had plenty of time to sift through them. With no touring on our schedule and Josh fully committed to the process, time seemed to be on our side.

With stable time at home to spend with my wife and baby, along with relaxed writing and preproduction schedules for our new album, 2011 could've potentially been a turning point for me. If I'd taken the proper steps to navigate my grief correctly and had used my time off the road to reset my perspectives on my home life and my career, I might have avoided a lot of the chaos that lay ahead of me. But what I understand now—and didn't know then—is that I was already too deep into my addiction to get out on my own.

Addiction is a cunning affliction. Some casual users can stay casual users. Some drug abusers fizzle out of their drug use, chalking it up to a phase of their life that they grew out of. Others become full-bore addicts, trapped in a web of drugs and/or alcohol long before they ever even realize it's a problem. In my case, opiates and alcohol enabled me to change the way I felt about myself. They became my solution. Drinking and using was my means of avoiding anxiety and emotional pain. I used them so I could function comfortably and be free of those obstacles. But over time, the solution I'd found for my problems began to evolve into a problem all its own. And it became a huge problem.

I was starting to rely on drugs to function. I was unmotivated without them. Nothing was fun or desirable to me without first getting high. As a result, my friend circle got smaller. The friends I'd had who didn't "party" with me came around less. For several years I'd raced at a local drag strip as a hobby. I was pretty good at it, and I'd become a part of the community at the track. But my race car had now been sitting in the garage for a couple years, collecting dust. You can't exactly race when you're drunk and high. And I chose drugs over racing.

My addiction was progressing. Being at home in Richmond for an extended period meant I had regular access to a reliable network of dealers, so I was staying high as much as possible. Black market pharmaceutical opiates are expensive and my tolerance and habit had grown, which meant I was spending hundreds of dollars a day on drugs. Inevitably, my sources would sometimes dry up, and I'd go into withdrawal. Getting dope sick was becoming a condition that was all too familiar.

I did my best to keep it together at home. I tried to act present and available for my wife and to help with our daughter. But I wasn't fooling her. One evening as I gave our baby a bottle before my wife put her back down to sleep, she walked into the living room and found me on the couch, folded over. The baby was laying in my lap and still sucking on her bottle. I had nodded out while I was feeding her.

Drinking and using was affecting my work too. We kept consistent Monday through Friday hours in our practice space as we worked to compile new material. Saturdays were reserved for shorter sessions, earmarked for one-on-one time that anyone might need to work on an idea. As new instrumental song outlines were established, Josh would record the whole band playing the new idea until we got a decent take to use as a reference. Facing away from the band and watching his computer monitor while he recorded us, Josh often noticed one guitar getting increasingly sloppy and then going silent altogether. He'd spin around in his office chair to see what the issue might be and find me slumped over my guitar, nodded out in the middle of a take. Willie would shrug his shoulders and shake his head in disappointment, continuing to play the new song without missing a note.

In spite of my deteriorating condition, I made several good creative contributions. "Straight for the Sun" was a heavily downtuned dirge that I'd written the music and lyrics for on my own. It was short, slow, and doomy, referencing the churning and fuzzed out riffs of Eyehategod and the Melvins. It was so radically different from anything we'd ever recorded that I initially thought it didn't feel appropriate to be considered a Lamb of God song. To my surprise, when Josh and the rest of the guys heard my rudimentary demo of the idea, they loved it. It became the first track on the *Resolution* album.

"Desolation" was another of the roughly half a dozen songs I initiated for the album. In contrast to the warped crawl of "Straight for the Sun," "Desolation" had a rolling, up-tempo pace and a series of note-filled riffs that spanned the entire length of the guitar neck. My lyrics for it directly referenced my drug use. It's clear to me now that I was beginning to get honest with myself about how bad my addiction had gotten.

Around that time, one of my drug suppliers was providing me with 80 mg Oxycontin pills. They were one of my favorites. He told me where he was sourcing them: an older man he knew with terminal lung cancer. The guy didn't have too long to live and had been put into hospice care. He was prescribed the strongest of painkillers and apparently found he didn't need them all. I never asked what the terminally ill man used the money for, but he'd sell half of his prescription to my contact every month. Most of those pills ended up in my hands.

I was thinking about those relationships when I scribbled the lyrics that would become the bridge section to "Desolation" into my notebook:

The dying man might take me with him
Until then, I'll split the difference
All that for nothing, what a fucking waste of time

Randy later insisted on replacing the word *me* in the lyrics with the word *you*. He'd been staying clean and sober and was well into his first year of recovery. He didn't want to take ownership of my addict confessions. I didn't care if he changed the words or not.

For the studio recording of *Resolution*, we returned to the Mobjack Bay studio in Mathews County, Virginia. We loved the atmosphere, and it was close enough to Richmond that we could get home if we really needed to. It was also far enough away that we could stay focused on recording without being distracted. One evening as we finished up a preproduction session, Josh pulled me aside. "I really need you to be sharp for these recording sessions we have coming up," he said.

Of course, I knew what he meant. He was asking me not to be fucked up while we tracked the album. And I felt ashamed that I'd put him in the position to have to request that. Josh and I had become good friends, and I admired him both professionally and personally. I told him that I understood and that I would not let him down.

I kept my word for the most part. Before packing up and heading off to the studio, instead of scoring enough Percocets and Oxycontins to get me through the session, I found a dealer to sell me some Suboxone. It's a harm reduction drug prescribed by doctors to treat opiate addiction. It's also sold on the black market. It keeps cravings and withdrawals at bay without getting the user high. I found that I could take Suboxone and function normally. Oddly, I found myself less inclined to drink heavily on Suboxone as well. The result was that I was active and engaged in those recording sessions. I enjoyed recording the album. But as soon as the sessions were wrapped, I went home and dove headfirst back into my using.

Lamb of God's seventh album *Resolution* was released on January 24, 2012. It debuted at number three on the Billboard 200 albums chart. Coinciding with the album's release, we did a short run of shows up the East Coast to help promote sales the first week. I was using the whole time.

A couple weeks later we left for another tour of Asia and Australia. I intended to kick pills again by the time we left for the first show in Seoul, South Korea. But an addict's best intentions rarely work out. It's a common theme: always "just one more high, just one more day." It's what Perry Farrell sings in the Jane's Addiction song "Jane Says": "I'm gonna kick tomorrow."

I boarded the plane in Richmond feeling okay. I'd weaned down a bit over the previous few days and hadn't used at all since the night before. I'd arranged to meet a friend outside the airport during our layover in Chicago. The plan was for him to give me a few Oxys to take for the flight to Seoul; this would at least ensure that I'd be comfortable for the long trip. But my plan fell through because he canceled at the last minute. I was terrified. I knew what was coming next.

By the time I was in my seat for the flight to South Korea, I was pouring sweat. My legs were cramping and restless. I couldn't sit still. A couple hours into the fourteen-hour flight, my withdrawal got even worse. I was stricken repeatedly with aggressive waves of diarrhea. It was pure misery. Fortunately for me, the flight wasn't very crowded. There was almost always a bathroom available, and I was the only person in my entire center row. Knowing withdrawal would be imminent at some point, I'd been smart enough to pack some antidiarrheal medicine. Once the medicine eased my guts, I laid down and stretched across three seats, shivering and sweating all the way across the Pacific Ocean.

For the first half of 2012, we toured around the world in support of the *Resolution* album. From South Korea we returned to China, then on to Taiwan, the Philippines, Singapore, Japan, and Australia. In South America we performed in Brazil, Argentina, Chile, Ecuador, Colombia, Venezuela, and then Mexico. Then we went back to Israel and India. We carried on with shows throughout the UK and Europe.

On June 27, 2012, after appearing at the Hovefestivalen in Arendal, Norway, the night before, we flew to Prague, Czech Republic. As we exited the plane in Prague, there was an issue at the end of the jet bridge. I noticed several officials checking passports before letting passengers into the airport. Among them were a handful of towering armed guards with military-style rifles in their hands and masks covering their faces. It occurred to me that there must have been some kind of fugitive on our flight. When we reached the end of the jet bridge and our passports were collected, our entire tour party, both band and crew, were detained. We were taken to a back room and advised that we were being held for questioning.

Over the next few hours we were made aware that a couple of years earlier, a nineteen-year-old fan named Daniel Nosek had attended a 2010 Lamb of God show in Prague and was injured after falling from the stage. Weeks later, Nosek died of a head injury he sustained during the incident. This was the first time that anyone in our organization had been notified that someone was injured at the show. A Czech prosecutor had put together a case accusing Randy of being responsible for Nosek's injuries.

After we were all interrogated by Czech investigators, Randy was arrested and charged with manslaughter. The court considered him a flight risk, so he was held for over a month in a Czech prison. Randy was eventually released on $400,000 bail and returned home, awaiting a trial to fight the charges.

Aside from the shock and sadness of knowing that a fan died from injuries he'd received at our show, one of my biggest take-aways from this incident is that I was a terrible friend to Randy. I wasn't supportive at a time when he needed all the support he could possibly get. This was never my intent. Randy and I have a broth-erly relationship. We can be competitive, and sometimes we argue. Sometimes we even fight. But even when we're at odds, we always know that we love each other. That's never once wavered. And as well as anyone, I know how sensitive and emotional he can be. We're alike in that way. I knew he was scared and hurting. But I was so caught up in my addiction that I wasn't present for him. He couldn't count on me for meaningful emotional support during one of the most difficult times in his life.

In late 2012, while Randy awaited trial, Lamb of God toured the United States. I drank heavily and was strung out on pills. When we returned home after the holidays, I enrolled myself into a Richmond area methadone clinic to get off opiates. Every morning, I'd drive across town at 6 a.m. and stand in line to wait for my little plastic cup of cherry-flavored methadone syrup to keep me out of withdrawal for the day. One morning I was in line next to a young man who hap-pened to be a Lamb of God fan. He recognized me. "What are you doing here? Don't you have to go out on tour soon?" he asked. "How are you going to do that without getting dope sick?"

I didn't have an answer. I was just grateful that we didn't have any shows coming up too soon. I lasted about a month in the methadone program and was soon back to my same old routine: spending thou-sands of dollars a month on prescription painkillers and drinking beer by the twelve-pack.

In March 2013, Randy was acquitted of all charges related to Daniel Nosek's injuries and subsequent death. Meanwhile, my addiction progressed. Later that year I used heroin for the first time. I had hoped it would be a stronger high than the heavy painkillers that I'd gotten so used to. It wasn't.

Not long after Randy's acquittal, the band was booked for a European tour, ending with an additional two dates in South Africa. By then my addiction issues had reached unmanageable extremes. As the tour approached, I was constantly hitting up my dealers and stockpiling methadone pills, determined to make it through the monthlong run without getting dope sick. I had multiple premonitions of my own death. I had a clear vision that if I left, I'd be returning home from that tour in a body bag. Two weeks before the tour began, I told my manager and my bandmates that I would be skipping the tour. I'd decided to check myself into rehab. Last minute arrangements were made for Paul Waggoner of Between the Buried and Me to fill in during my absence. Giving them such short notice was crazy, but this decision was rooted in a palpable fear: as miserable as my condition was, I didn't want to die. My daughter was now three years old, and she meant everything to me. I wanted to be better.

I entered an addiction treatment facility in Williamsburg on December 22, 2013. I took methadone and oxycodone pills the morning before I left for treatment. When we took the exit off the highway that led to the rehab facility, I told my wife to stop at a convenience store so that I could buy a beer to drink in the parking lot before checking in. I didn't see my daughter that Christmas. Her mother made the forty-five-minute drive to see me for a few hours that day, but she left our daughter at home with family. We had agreed that it would be best to tell her that I was at work.

Shortly after entering treatment, I received some horrible news. Up to this point, my father had been living energetically with a slowly progressing and closely monitored intestinal cancer. But while I was in rehab, he was admitted to a hospital that was only about a mile away from my rehab facility. He was having complications resulting from his cancer, but he was expected to fully recover after a routine procedure. But a few days later, my father's prognosis got much worse due to an infection, and his condition quickly deteriorated. It soon became clear that his illness was terminal. The staff at the rehab center was sympathetic and gave me day passes to go visit him. This wouldn't typically be within the routine of their treatment program, but it was a unique situation; the only other options were not to see my dad or to check myself out of treatment completely. I was grateful that they made that exception. I wanted to stay clean, and I knew that remaining in treatment was essential to that end.

As heavy as all of this was, I took solace knowing that I was present and engaged with my dad for those last days we had together. We had been slightly distant during my early childhood. I didn't have the same sort of connection with him that I'd had with my mother. But as I became an adult, we grew close. He was my biggest role model and my best friend. For several nights in the hospital, I sat next to him, touching his arm and telling him how grateful I was for all the things we had done together. I bristle at the thought of how different it would've been had I not been clean and sober for those weeks. I would've been distracted and erratic, self-absorbed and disconnected from the reality of what was happening. It was a gift that I was able to be with my dad in his last days. On the afternoon of January 4, 2014, my dad, Raymond Morton, died while my mother, his wife of fifty-two years, took a nap on the couch nearby. He was seventy-four years old.

I completed my residential treatment program after thirty-three days. I can't say that I felt reborn or in any way sure of myself. In fact, being newly clean after decades of drinking and years of using left me scared and unsure. I felt like damaged goods, like I had a blinking neon sign on my forehead that said "Addict." It felt like everyone around me wasn't sure how to act or what to say.

Following treatment, the first order of business was my dad's funeral. It was a small and subdued affair befitting his quiet and dignified nature. Just a couple of weeks later, the band had an event scheduled around the debut of a documentary film we had been making with the talented Don Argott. *As the Palaces Burn* began as a tribute to the loyalty and enthusiasm of our fans, but it ended up becoming a gripping documentary detailing Randy's trial. I'm a haggard mess throughout the film, but by the time it debuted in February 2014 at Philadelphia's Trocadero Theater, I was fresh out of rehab and newly sober. The event was an awkward experience to navigate sober. I stuck very close to Randy.

Other awkward and uncomfortable results came with my new attempt at sobriety. One of the most frightening was a strained and confused relationship with music. I was suddenly terrified to pick up a guitar. It had been many years since I created music sober. Drinking and drugging had been an ingrained part of my creative process, freeing me from the barriers of self-doubt and inhibition. Could I even do it without being fucked up on something? I tried picking up a guitar and riffing around, but everything felt empty and lame. What had once been a natural, free-flowing relationship between my instrument and me now felt stiff and unfamiliar.

I asked around for some insight and help, as I had been advised to do in rehab. A mutual friend put me in touch with Slash from Guns N' Roses, who had gotten clean some years earlier. Slash graciously called me one afternoon and patiently listened to my tale of creative insecurity and fear. "You're putting too much pressure on yourself," he told me sympathetically. "It's unrealistic for you to think that you can tap right back into your creative element so soon after the shock of getting clean. You're learning a whole new way to live. You're going to have to prioritize staying clean over everything else right now if you want it to stick."

I hung on for a few more days after speaking with Slash. As grateful as I was for his insight, I soon got high again. It wasn't a decision I thought much about. I don't remember any of the details regarding where I was or what I used, but once I started, it was immediately back to my usual routine. Using again after a relatively short term of abstinence was like putting on an old, worn-out sweatshirt: comfortable and familiar. The sad byproduct of this was that I began writing riffs and song ideas as resource material for our next album. Using was of course the wrong choice. I was again in active addiction, using regularly and complicit in the progression of my own mental, physical, and spiritual self-destruction.

CHAPTER 19

THE ALPINE OPIUM CAPER

"GOD OF WINE"
THIRD EYE BLIND

An interesting part of being a songwriter is the inevitable change that occurs once a song you've written gets recorded and released. That song no longer belongs to you. The life experiences that may have inspired each line of the lyrics, the personal reasons behind specific words, and the particular points of reference laced throughout the music all fade into obscurity when the song opens up to the audience's interpretation.

It's a bittersweet feeling. A song can feel very personal and sacred. It can be difficult to expose your inner feelings honestly. As songwriters, we often feel protective of our emotions and confessions, even in the face of releasing them into the world. I've heard people compare writing songs to raising children. It's a worthy metaphor. As parents and

263

songwriters, we are tasked with helping the child and the song grow into what they're meant to be. But in the end, they don't belong to us. They never did.

I've read that Stephan Jenkins's heartbreaking lyrics to Third Eye Blind's "God of Wine" weren't directly written about addiction. But as a fan, it's hard for me to imagine any other interpretation. As I hear it, the lyrics of that beautiful song speak so directly to the desperation of active addiction and the impact it has on the people who love the addict. I wouldn't ever want to consider any other meaning.

A s Lamb of God reconvened to work on new material in the summer of 2014, the morale of the group was at an all-time low. Personal relationships between the band members were deteriorating. It's hard for me to pinpoint why. I won't speak for anyone else, but my continuing substance abuse issues and the chaos that had enveloped my daily life had left me angry and guarded. I wasn't having fun. There was little interaction within the band outside of the rehearsals and business meetings, which were required to keep our work schedule moving. Our conversations with one another had become stiff and disjointed. The writing sessions in our dingy, fluorescent practice space were awkward and tense. And my drinking and drug use had again gotten out of control. As had become the norm, I showed up to the sessions late and high on painkillers, often distracted. I had what I thought were some quality song ideas to contribute, but I had little patience and enthusiasm for working on them.

Compounding my creative disconnect was Randy's newfound reluctance toward accepting my lyrical submissions. Usually when I envision a song idea, a vocal pattern and lyric idea come to me as I'm working out the instrumental part. Ever since I was a teenager writing my first songs, I've always written lyrics and vocal parts along with the music, and this had been part of my process in Lamb of God since the early days. Some of Lamb's more popular songs were conceived this way, like "Redneck," "Walk with Me in Hell," and "Now You've Got Something to Die For." By the time we began working on *VII: Sturm und Drang*, most of my lyrics had been reduced to dreary, uninspired meanderings about how fucked up my life had become or some other nonsensical romanticization of my despair. Randy wanted no part of that anymore. I had been writing about my own downward spiral for a couple of albums at that point, and Randy, now several years sober, was sick of singing about it. "I'm the one that has to sing this stuff," he told me. "And I don't relate to all this drug and doom stuff. It's boring. I don't live that way anymore."

At the time, my self-absorbed mind saw that as an ego-driven power trip on his part. But now I can see it for what it was: a sensible, sober man holding a sensible, sober boundary of not wanting to sing about some bullshit that he no longer related to. A few of my lyrical contributions did end up making it on to the album, including "Embers," cowritten with Randy, which directly references the passing of my daughter Madalyn and features a haunting guest appearance by singer Chino Moreno of Deftones.

Despite the tension in the room, or perhaps as a result of it, the band worked up an album's worth of songs, once again produced, engineered, and mixed by our longtime creative partner and friend Josh Wilbur. We wrote and rehearsed in our Richmond practice space, with Josh helping to direct song structures, tempo changes, and vocal patterns. Once the songs were well established and some-what rehearsed, we moved the recording sessions to several studios in the Los Angeles area. We recorded the guitar and bass tracks at the nondescript Suburban Soul Studios in nearby Torrance. I set a goal of remaining sober during the recording, even bringing out a sober friend for support. Though I had been plenty fucked up for the writing and preproduction sessions, this was the first time in the band's history that I ever recorded anything clean and sober. I made it through the two weeks of tracking guitars without drinking or using, but it didn't stick. As soon as I got home from California, I got back to my regular bullshit. A couple weeks of abstinence had done little to quell my appetite for opiates and alcohol. Nonetheless, in retrospect, little flirtations with sobriety such as this were the earliest signs of my showing a potential willingness to change.

Though *VII: Sturm und Drang* was not a concept album, its advance tracks "Still Echoes" and "512" both referenced Randy's time in Prague. Our loyal fans welcomed the new music after all that heavy, emotional turmoil as a reason to celebrate the band's return to creative productivity. No matter what we may have thought of the album ourselves, music journalists found the comeback narrative easy light to cast the album in.

Sturm und Drang, which means "storm and stress," refers to a period of eighteenth-century German literature, music, art, and the-ater when the themes of tragedy, conflict, and extreme emotion were prevalent. Any heavy metal band ought to find those concepts to be comfortably within their creative wheelhouse, but given the experi-ences Randy and I had navigated over the previous few years, we felt it to be particularly appropriate for an album title. The rest of the band was less enthused, but nobody else could suggest anything better. The debates and eye rolls eventually fizzled out, so we titled our album after a German phrase that very few of our fans or band members could even pronounce.

It's worth mentioning that Lamb of God has always struggled to build an audience in Germany. There has always been some disconnect. I say this with great respect and appreciation for the German fans we do have, but we've never quite caught on there like we have in other parts of Europe. I've often wondered why. It could be that we're just too American. The joke inside our camp became that we were so desperate to gain some ground in Germany that we gave our album a German title. It must've worked: *VII: Sturm und Drang* became our strongest debut in Germany, landing at number twelve the week of release on the Offizielle Top 100, though still well short of our number three debut position on the US Billboard 200 chart that same week of July 24, 2015.

The release of *VII: Sturm und Drang* coincided with a flurry of worldwide touring, starting in 2015 with a tour across Australia as part of the once great but now defunct Soundwave Festival. We were billed alongside more mainstream hard rock acts like Soundgarden, Incubus, and Faith No More. In addition to sharing the stage with these heavyweights, we also shared quite a few rowdy flights packed with band members and crew from the traveling festival. The Qantas flight attendants were exceedingly patient with our idiocy. A grim joke was made that if one of these planes happened to go down, we were going to make rock and roll history, like the whole Ritchie Valens, Buddy Holly, Big Bopper tragedy.

On one particular show—a festival appearance in Auckland, New Zealand, called West Fest—Lamb of God played the main stage, followed by Judas Priest, Soundgarden, and Faith No More. I was thrilled to even be mentioned in the same breath with those bands, but to play shows with Soundgarden was extra special. I had been a huge fan since hearing them as a teenager. Their gargantuan, plodding riffs, layered with Chris Cornell's soaring vocals and Kim Thayil's abstract, off-kilter guitar, hit me in a way very few bands ever could. Soundgarden has always struck me like a modern Led Zeppelin. I have always held them in the highest regard.

Shortly after playing our set, a member of our stage crew and my main tour companion, Stu (not his real name), slid into a spot with me behind the monitor mixing desk, located stage left, to watch Judas Priest's last few songs. Even well into his sixties, Rob Halford's blistering high-pitched vocals sounded as strong as ever. As we soaked in the moment from our side stage vantage point, we noticed Soundgarden guitarist Kim Thayil walking toward us. Stu and I made quick eye contact, acknowledging what was about to unfold. This was about to be the coolest thing ever: he was heading over to join us! Watching Judas Priest from twenty feet away with Kim Thayil was going to be one of those amazing rock 'n' roll moments that Stu and I would brag about forever.

We kept it super cool, giving Kim a simple, quick nod of acknowledgement as he approached. But just as he was about to round the corner of the monitor desk to join our spot, our cool kid moment was crushed. A sort of famous guitarist from a sort of famous band that had played earlier in the evening dashed up, seemingly from out of nowhere, with his girlfriend in tow. Judas Priest's stage volume prevented us from hearing exactly what they said, but context and facial expressions made things easy to interpret. It was something along the lines of:

"Hey Kim, I'm [insert name] from the band [insert name]!"

"Yeah cool, man."

"I'm a big fan! This is my girlfriend. Can we grab a quick picture?"

"Uhh, yeah. Sure thing, man."

Kim dutifully posed for the picture with guitarist dude and his girlfriend. As they stared at him, clearly hoping some kind of conversation would continue, Kim smiled and walked away. I looked at Stu and shook my head. He leaned over and shouted, "Man, Kim Thayil was comin' over to hang out with us 'cause we're fuckin' cool, and that dumbass fucked it all up!"

After the Australian run, we got home for a short break and, in anticipation of the release of *VII: Sturm und Drang*, headed to Europe for a monthlong tour built around a number of festival dates. By this point, my addiction had fallen back into a predictable and dismal routine. But tours, particularly international ones, bring a complication: jumping from continent to continent and city to city doesn't lend itself to sourcing a raging, insatiable opiate addiction. The constant bag checks and border crossings made carrying any kind of stockpile of pills or dope unrealistic. I had my tricks, but there are only so many methadone pills you can crush up into dust and load into emptied out Tylenol capsules. No matter how many I managed to prepare, they never lasted long enough to get me through a tour. I wasn't able to regulate my intake. I'd binge until my stash was gone, deluding myself that something else would pop up to get me through. I had a few dealers and drug contacts overseas, but scoring anything worthwhile when I was out of the country was unpredictable. Tours outside of the US always entailed a nasty withdrawal, either just before or during the first week of a tour, followed by weeks of involuntary abstinence from my drugs of choice.

There were occasional, desperate Hail Mary–style options for mitigating my condition. Some of the countries we toured sold low-dose opiate painkillers at pharmacies over the counter. I became familiar with what was available wherever we were, and I scheduled my free time around collecting whatever crumbs of relief I could scrape together. During a couple days off in France, for example, most people spent the day strolling through quaint, winding streets and alleys, sampling local food and culture. But not me. I spent my time visiting half a dozen or more pharmacies in search of codeine pills and codeine cough syrup, which I knew were available at the pharmacist's discretion. I'd walk in, put on my best fake cough and try to look as pathetic as possible, which wasn't that difficult to do given my lifestyle. It usually worked. Back at my hotel with my pathetic score, I'd swallow codeine pills with mouthfuls of codeine cough syrup and then chase it all down with beer from the minibar.

In other countries, it could be more complicated. There were several tour stops where I knew I could get low-dose, over-the-counter codeine pills that were inconveniently mixed with ibuprofen. The amount of codeine in the pills was so low that they had very little abuse potential for an experienced pill junky like myself. My tolerance was simply too high to even notice any effects from a handful of them. Taking a whole box of them wasn't really an option because the amount of ibuprofen would wreak havoc on the kidneys. But I found a way around it. Thanks to the internet, I'd learned a way of crushing up the pills and separating the codeine from the ibuprofen. Empty boxes of the over-the-counter codeine painkillers were scattered around my hotel room, and the desk was covered with crumpled coffee filters and glasses full of ibuprofen paste left over from my extraction process. My tour companion Stu referred to my technique as "squeezin' 'deines" because of how I twisted the filters to extract the water-soluble codeine from the crushed pills. Stu had a way of finding dark humor in fucked up situations.

In addition to my tours of city pharmacies and hotel room lab experiments, alcohol was, of course, always around. And though I drank more or less constantly, it did little to soothe my jones. Cocaine was also available, a fact that I found annoying because I really didn't like the effects of it. I always found it particularly obnoxious that cocaine had a level of social acceptability that my preferred drugs of choice most definitely did not. Nonetheless, whatever distaste I may have had for cocaine certainly didn't stop me from doing it when it was around, but it always made everything worse. Cocaine seems to have little effect beyond making the user obnoxious and obsessed with doing more every thirty minutes. I call it instant asshole powder. As anyone around me at the time could confirm, I was a miserable fuck, constantly obsessed with trying to find some narcotic solution to my physical and emotional discomfort.

In hindsight and through the lens of my recovery, I can see one of the great ironies of my life in addiction. My quest for comfort and solace led me on a perpetual crusade to escape an existence that I wasn't particularly present for in the first place. I was trying to blot out a reality that I wasn't even willing to observe or appreciate. My life had become a pathetic, lonely run on a gerbil wheel: a continuous effort to avoid any involvement in the events around me, most of which were things that I had long dreamed of accomplishing. My perspective was the opposite of mindful and the antithesis of grateful, but even more than that, it just made for a wretched and undignified way of life.

Despite the ongoing drudgery of my self-imposed misery-go-round, I had moments of genuine levity. Even in the trenches of full-fledged active addiction, there were comically absurd situations that I still laugh about. As our world tour meandered through Europe in the summer of 2015, we stopped in a small Alpine village for a day off before our appearance the following day at a large, multistage festival nearby. The surrounding scenery was majestic, and the town was quaint and idyllic. I watched local farmers march their herds of cows right down the center of town, bells ringing and hooves clicking. If fräuleins had rolled out a maypole and a bunch of dudes in lederhosen pulled up and started yodeling, it wouldn't have seemed out of place.

We checked into our hotel in the center of town, a cross between a giant doll house and an antiquated youth hostel. I dropped my bags and surveyed my new digs. The wood-framed twin beds, the low ceilings, the grandma-style decor, and the lack of air-conditioning made it feel like a church youth summer camp. I knew that the odds of stumbling across any sort of narcotic enhancement on my day off were zero. Once again, I'd have to make do with alcohol.

After settling in, I texted Stu. We worked closely together on show days, and I had always been impressed with the pride and precision with which he performed his job. On days off we usually hung out and, whenever possible, found some kind of trouble to get ourselves into. This was one of those days.

Born and raised in West Virginia, Stu grew up riding motorcycles through the mountains and huffing spray paint out of paper bags to get high. "Silver paint works best. I don't know why," he once told me. He grew up watching his neighbors make crystal meth out of cold medicine. "You can do it in a Gatorade bottle. Just gotta know how to burp it right." Stu was raised in a world of Pentecostal churches with snake-handling preachers and convulsing worshippers speaking in tongues. It was also a world with little exposure to the outside: he once told me that he had never seen a Black person until middle school. "I mean, I saw them on TV, but not in real life," he explained.

Despite his rural and secluded upbringing, Stu was one of the most curious and open-minded people I'd ever met. He was also one of the smartest. He was a voracious reader and was particularly interested in quantum physics, often trying to explain theories to me that my squirrel brain couldn't even begin to grasp. He had a thorough understanding of mechanical and aerodynamic engineering, particularly as it applied to stock car racing. He was a devoted husband and father. I never heard him say anything disrespectful about anyone's race, gender, or sexual orientation.

Stu had plenty of his own personal experience with drugs and alcohol. He'd done it all and wasn't intimidated by anything. But he was one of those rare drug users who could keep it in check. He'd never gotten strung out on anything. Drugs and alcohol had never been a source of despair or presented any serious consequences for him. He certainly enjoyed partying, but ultimately, he could take it or leave it.

Stu was my homie, so on this day, like most days off, I hit him up. We met downstairs in the lobby and decided to head out in search of some lunch for him and some drinks for me. As we strolled through the picturesque Alpine village, we joked about being on another one of our "dates." We always made it a regular practice to flaunt to our wives all the romantic settings we found ourselves in while on tour: dining on mussels by the Mediterranean Sea, strolling around the Eiffel Tower, evening walks in the moonlight through Amsterdam.

Here we were again, adding to our impressive list. As we walked down a winding lane, I stopped dead in my tracks, mouth agape. "Do you see that?" I said, suddenly hushed.

Stu's eyes grew wide. "Is that what I think it is?"

We backtracked a few yards and gazed beyond a small fence that ran along the sidewalk in front of what appeared to be a preschool or kindergarten. Small benches and chairs were thoughtfully arranged among neatly trimmed bushes and vibrant, colorful flower beds. On the right side of the walkway was a small playground, and on the left, tucked directly against the front fence, was a row of raised garden beds full of meticulously nurtured *Papaver somniferum*: poppy pods.

"Holy shit, man."

"Are those the right ones?"

"I think so, dude."

"You're not thinking about..."

"How are we going to do this?"

"We're not really going to do this, are we? It's a fucking kindergarten, man."

We didn't have a formal education in the botanical sciences, but we knew enough to know that opium came from poppy pods. And that meant an irresistible opportunity had just fallen into our laps.

We composed ourselves and quietly continued our short walk to the restaurant. Over his pizza and my beers, we discussed the comic absurdity of attempting to harvest opium from a primary school in Switzerland. We spoke in hypotheticals—because this could never happen. We could not possibly follow through with the plan. "We ain't scumbags!" Stu declared, nervously laughing. I raised my eyebrows and laughed along, questioning that assessment. But even as we dismissed the ridiculous mission, we planned the details. Sort of joking, sort of not joking. For Stu, this may as well have been a mindless prank. It didn't matter to him if it worked out or not. But I was already counting on it because once getting high was on my mind, I became obsessed.

As we joked, it became clear that this was going to happen. It would take two trips. On the first we'd score the pods by making cuts to the outer skin, after which we would allow time to let the fluid inside the pod seep out. On the second trip, we'd collect the secretions to be dried and smoked. These secretions were essentially opium. It was not exactly a textbook harvest technique, but our window of opportunity was narrow. It was a school, after all, in the middle of town. This would all be pretty conspicuous. We had to work quickly. And with that, it was confirmed: we'd stepped across the threshold into the realm of complete idiocy.

We had to decide who would score the pods and who would keep watch. Neither Stu nor I blended in with the locals. Stu looked like a touring heavy metal crew dude from Appalachia. I looked like Chris Stapleton, if Chris Stapleton were a homeless, alcoholic pill junky. Stealth was not on our side. We agreed that Stu should do the skilled labor. He was always calm and cool, in contrast to my constant anxiety. We both knew that he was also generally better than me at anything except playing guitar. I was demoted to the task of nervously standing lookout.

The next few hours consisted of a ridiculous pair of trips between the hotel and the unsuspecting school. Stu scored the pods by making a series of cuts on the outer skin while I stood lookout. For what, I wasn't sure. What would I have told people if anyone asked what we were doing? Trip number one was a success, so we sauntered off feeling like little kids playing bank robber.

We waited for nightfall to complete trip two. We dared not speak of our mission because loose lips sink ships. In a last-minute change, Stu smartly decided it was best that he make the last trip alone. He realized that it would be a big problem if Lamb of God had to cancel our major festival appearance the next day because the guitar player was in a village jail, charged with trespassing (at a preschool no less) and conspiracy to manufacture drugs. He also likely realized that two dirtbags were twice as conspicuous as one. Now I was just along for the ride, chewing my nails and hoping for the best.

While Stu ventured out to complete the mission, I waited anxiously back at the hotel. When he got back, he was stone faced. "I got it. It ain't much. But I got it," he said. We scurried down the narrow hall and into Stu's room, quickly locking the door behind us. Stu unveiled a crumpled coffee filter with several small blobs of milky, gooey secretions from the poppy pods. "That's all I could get, man. It was sketchy as fuck, and I don't think we waited long enough for the cuts to seep out, but we got us a little something!"

"Hell yeah it's something!" I laughed, still marveling at the absurdity of it all. We impatiently dried out our sad little score, using a hair dryer to speed the process of transitioning our precious blobs into a smokeable condition. With expectations dwindling but a ray of hope remaining, we grabbed a butter knife from the empty hotel bar, took it back to the room, and held a lighter under it until it was scorching hot. Placing the small gooey blobs on the tip of the heated knife, we took turns taking long, cross-eyed hits through a straw and holding in the faint billows of smoke as long as we could.

"You gettin' anything?" Stu asked optimistically. I couldn't really tell, but I could taste it. "It tastes like the real shit. We just ain't really got enough to do anything," he sadly concluded. Stu was right. We waited a few minutes for a buzz that never came. With a final deflating exhale, our day's expedition had reached its pathetic end. We'd spent an entire day off in one of the most beautiful settings in Europe wasting our time in a futile quest to catch an impossible buzz. It was a microcosm of my life.

CHAPTER 20

ANESTHETIC

"PHANTASMAGORIA BLUES"
MARK LANEGAN

The first time I was in a room with Mark Lanegan was in April 1993. He didn't know I was there. I was a twenty-year-old college student, and his band, Screaming Trees, was headlining The Boathouse in Norfolk, Virginia. The Screaming Trees' throwback, psychedelic guitar rock packaged as the "grunge" trend of the day checked all the boxes for me: heavy riffs, bluesy leads, great songs, and underground cool. But what really made them great was Mark's distinctive voice. His low, raspy growl sounded tattered and raw, but it carried soaring melodies. His lyrics were dark and genuine.

Well over two decades later, still a fan of his extensive catalog of post-Trees work, I reached out to Mark to see if he'd be interested in collaborating for a song on my first solo album, Anesthetic. It was a shot in the dark. We had never met and had no connection other than me being a fan of his work. To my surprise, he was open to the idea, asking to hear the song and then agreeing to work with me. The result was a song called "Axis," featuring Mike Inez of Alice in Chains (bass), Steve Gorman (drums), and Marc Ford of the Black Crowes (lead guitar).

Mark and I would later cowrite two songs for his 2020 solo album, Straight Songs Of Sorrow, *recording them with the stunningly talented Alain Johannes. Whenever I work with those guys, it feels like that first time in high school when you get invited to sit at the lunch table with the older cool kids: I listen, learn, and try not to look too excited. My solo work has given me the opportunity to work with some amazing artists I have long admired. Mark Lanegan is high on that list. Mark and I stayed in touch until his untimely passing in 2022. I remain a massive fan of his work.*

O n it went. What had started out as a solution to my problems had evolved into the biggest problem of them all. When I was a teenager, alcohol was a source of comfort and confidence. It told me I was good enough. It told me I was acceptable. Then weed became an added voice of validation. And those vices were sufficient for a long time because they worked for me. They were close friends. As time went on, I learned that narcotic painkillers worked even better, soothing me in the face of tragedy and sorrow. But eventually, it all turned on me. Drugs and alcohol had long since stopped providing any emotional relief. Now the only relief they brought was from the symptoms of withdrawal that I felt without them. I was in a hole that I didn't know how to climb out of.

As our intro music to a headlining show in Penticton, British Columbia, played, I stood on the side of the stage, agitated. From before the venue opened and right up until our set, I'd been on the phone trying to figure out the status of an incoming drug delivery. Fortunately, I was not in withdrawal. We'd been on the tour for quite a while, long enough that any physical symptoms I'd felt from being without opiates had passed. But I was anxious: knowing that drugs were on the way had me pacing the floor, impatient and fidgety.

A few days earlier, I'd reached out to Nik, an Eastern European hustler I knew in Canada. I asked him if he could help me score something. Nik was another one of my connections I actually liked. He wasn't really a drug dealer, but he was well connected to a black market network and could usually find anything. Through his contacts, Nik arranged for a prostitute who worked in the area to come to the venue where we were playing and deliver me some heroin. She was supposed to have arrived hours before the show, but she still hadn't shown up.

"Where the fuck is she?" I barked into the phone. "We're on in a half hour and she still isn't here!"

"Bro, relax! She's on the way, I promise. She'll hit you up by the time you get off stage."

As we ended our set with the last chords of "Redneck," I couldn't get off stage fast enough. I immediately checked my phone that was sitting on our guitar workbox off stage left. A text had just come in from a local number. "It's Rianna. Nik's friend. I'm outside the concert. Where are u?"

I threw a hooded sweatshirt over top of my sweat-soaked stage clothes and walked straight out of the side stage door to find her. Fans were already pouring out of the building, still energized and cheering from the excitement of the show. I pulled my hood up and stared down at the sidewalk, hoping not to be recognized as I called Rianna to find out where she was. We met down the block from the venue in a covered doorway next to a parking garage. "Are you famous or something?" she asked with a curious smile.

"Don't worry about that," I snapped. She kept grinning, unfazed by my shitty attitude. Rianna was young and attractive, probably twenty-six or so. But she looked haggard. There were dark circles under her eyes, and she wore too much makeup. It was caked up in the pockmarks on both of her cheeks. She was thin and was dressed unremarkably in blue jeans and a jacket.

"I couldn't really find anything on such short notice," she explained. "But Nik said to take good care of you, so this is from my roommate's personal stash. I didn't do any of it, but I think it's pretty good shit." She pulled a small plastic bag from her jacket pocket and slid it into the palm of my hand. Inside the bag was a gram of heroin. We both looked around. Nobody was paying any attention to us. I handed her a rolled-up wad of Canadian dollar bills that she quickly shoved into the front pocket of her tight jeans.

"I put a little extra dough in there for you. Thanks for hookin' it up."

"Hey!" she suddenly blurted, louder than she'd been talking before. "Can I take a picture with you? Is that weird? I promise I won't ever post it anywhere! It's just for me. I really promise!" Her eyes were bright and kind. She seemed like a sweet girl.

"Okay, yeah fuck it," I relented. Rianna and I stood under the light of the parking garage doorway, arms over each other's shoulders, and took a selfie on her phone.

That night, instead of riding on the band tour bus like usual, I took the crew bus to the next city. I stayed up all night in the back lounge snorting heroin and watching '90s music videos. Rianna was right. It was pretty good shit.

Shortly after I got home from that tour, my wife packed up her things and left, moving into a rental house about fifteen minutes away. There's no question that my alcoholism and drug addiction played a significant role in damaging our relationship. But it was not our only issue. We were living separate lives. My touring schedule had turned our marriage into a long-distance relationship that was often reduced to daily phone calls to check in. We grieved the loss of Madalyn independently. When I *was* home, I was emotionally distant: I was drinking and using, but I was also disconnected because we were apart so often and for so long.

Our daughter, who was about to turn six, started going back and forth between her mother's new house and mine. Despite my substance abuse issues, I had remained an engaged and devoted father. At the time, I would've claimed to be a "good" dad. I'm not sure I would say that now. My daily dependence on drugs and alcohol affected my judgement and focus. It's impossible to be authentic and emotionally present for a child when you're under the influence of drugs or alcohol. Still, I was the best father I knew how to be given my condition. Birthday parties, play dates, beach trips, amusement parks, kindergarten assemblies: I did all those things happily. For a time, being her dad was the only thing keeping me alive.

Around the time that my wife and I split, I got the opportunity to do something that I'd been dreaming of for a long time. My friend and producer Josh Wilbur had been consulting with an investor who was seeking projects to help get a new record label off the ground. Josh knew that I'd been compiling material that was creatively exciting but that wouldn't fit into the Lamb of God repertoire. Josh pitched some demos we'd recorded to the new label. They loved it, and we signed on to record my first solo project.

The timing of my solo album couldn't have been better. It gave me something positive to focus on. Breakups are always difficult. The breakup of a marriage, even an unhappy one, comes with a lot of emotions. It's even more complex when children are involved. Writing songs, and writing lyrics in particular, gave me a destination for my anger, resentment, fear, and sadness.

During the downtime between Lamb of God commitments, I'd fly out to Los Angeles and work with Josh on song ideas. Some of them were pieces of music that I'd been working on at home, others were built from improvised riffs freestyled in musical brainstorming sessions. We'd talk about a certain vibe or groove we were looking for and tinker around with ideas until we were on to something. I had written a lot of lyrics, so we recorded vocal ideas as well, usually with me singing. I'm not a great singer, but I'm decent enough to get a demo idea down.

Working with Josh had a positive effect on my lifestyle. Ever since he'd pulled me aside during the Lamb of God *Resolution* sessions and scolded me for letting my addiction get in the way of my music, I'd regulated my drinking and using around him. When I'd end up drunk or high around Josh, I felt ashamed. I respected Josh immensely, both as a creative partner and as a close friend, and I didn't want to disappoint him again. I mostly kept myself together during our sessions, but sometimes I'd find an excuse to wrap up early. I'd finish working with Josh, then make the long drive from his Long Beach recording studio up to Hollywood to score pills from one of my several established connections.

But there were also nights when I'd reach out to other addicts I knew who were in recovery. I'd learned from my time in rehab that the best support for an addict trying to get clean could be found in a fellow addict actively working a recovery program. In reaching out, I started to realize that something inside my spirit was starting to shift. It was a slow and inconsistent change. But I was just beginning to imagine what a life free from drugs and alcohol could be like.

As the songs for the solo project materialized, Josh and I talked about the best candidates to sing over each piece of music. One of the early instrumentals had a modern, active rock feel that we felt was perfect for Myles Kennedy. Having played numerous festivals together with Slash featuring Myles Kennedy and the Conspirators, Myles and I were friendly. I reached out to him about working together and was thrilled to hear that he was interested. We sent him an instrumental demo, which he loved, and he agreed to finish writing and recording the song "Save Defiance" with us. I had a similar experience with Jacoby Shaddix from Papa Roach. He and I played on several festival bills together and had become friends over the years. I'd written a song called "Sworn Apart" that Josh and I agreed would be perfect for Jacoby, and he signed on to sing it as soon as he heard the demo.

Not all the singers I reached out to were artists I had established relationships with. I took a chance with a couple cold calls as well. Mark Lanegan had been one of my favorite rock singers since I first heard him fronting the Screaming Trees back in the early '90s. I'd even seen them live when they opened for Belly. Mark's looming stage presence and raspy, tortured voice was as cool as I'd hoped it would be and left a lasting impact. I continued to follow his work with Queens of the Stone Age, and his solo album *Bubblegum* is one of my favorite rock albums of the twenty-first century. Mark's unique voice on one of my songs would be a dream come true, but I had no connection to him other than simply being a fan. We reached out, and to my surprise he was receptive. We started creating what would become the song "Axis," one of my favorite tracks on the album. As we worked, Mark and I also developed a genuine friendship, one that would last long after our song was completed.

The material for my solo album was inspired and energized by the raw emotions of my recent life experiences. Josh and I were happy with the songs and excited about the guest vocalists and musicians on the project. It was an all-star cast of musicians. Steve Gorman, Roy

Mayorga, Ray Luzier, Jean-Paul Gaster, and Alex Bent were handling the drums. Mike Inez, Paolo Gregoletto, and David Ellefson covered the bass tracks. Big name singers were signing on as well. Chuck Billy, Naeemah Maddox, Josh Todd, Alissa White-Gluz, and even Randy Blythe had also all committed to adding vocals.

One song, though, stood out. It had started with a simple chord progression that felt like it could support a strong chorus melody. Rather than just strum out the chords on guitar, Josh suggested I build a guitar riff around it, one that was a bit more technical but that still moved within the framework of the chord progression we'd established. Within a few minutes, I was freestyling a cool riff based on his prompt.

I also had some lyrics that explored many avenues of my personal life at the time. I used double entendres to simultaneously reference the sickness of my drug and alcohol addiction and the toxicity of my marriage; they explored my struggle to be free of them both. Josh and I paired my draft of lyrics to our new riff idea, and the song "Cross Off" was born.

> *Wasting away, a self-inflicted slow decay*
> *What should've been, what never was*
> *Became the end for both of us*

As soon as Josh and I laid down the first demo of "Cross Off," we'd instantly recognized that it was special. But who could sing it? We knew it had potential to be a big song, so choosing the right singer could make all the difference. "What if we got Chester Bennington?" Josh asked.

"Yeah, great idea. Let's ask Robert Plant while we're at it," I sarcastically replied. Linkin Park was perhaps the biggest rock band of the early 2000s and was still going strong. Chester Bennington was the voice of a generation. There was no way we could ever get a star as big as Chester to work with us on my solo album.

"What's the worst he can say?" Josh asked. "Is he going to tell us fuck off? We can handle that. Besides, I have a friend who's a friend of his. I think we can get him to listen to this demo pretty quickly. This song is great. Why wouldn't he want to sing on it? It's worth a shot!"

I thought Josh was out of his mind. But I couldn't bring myself to argue with his optimism. And he was right, the worst that could happen was we'd get a firm "no thanks" from Chester's management. We could handle that.

Josh and I polished our demo recording of "Cross Off" with a little extra attention to the mix and to the vocal takes, which I sang. The song wasn't finished lyrically, so we purposely left an open verse and bridge; this would give Chester room to write if he wanted to get involved. Josh made a couple phone calls to establish the connections, and we sent Chester the demo. He absolutely loved it.

A few months later, I was in the control room at NRG Recording Studios in North Hollywood, California, with Chester Bennington, finishing the lyrics for "Cross Off." He came with a lot of lyrics. We looked over his ideas and discussed how we related to each other's lyrical contributions. We were intuitively talking about the same things with our lyrics. Chester had lived with many of the same substance abuse and self-defeating psychological struggles that I was addressing in the song. He picked up on those themes and added to them, drawing from his own experience.

> *Fuck sanity, I wanna bleed*
> *Can't kill the pain, It's everything*
> *It's all I feel, It's what I breathe*

Standing over a table in the studio, Chester and I scribbled lyrics on a yellow legal pad, passing it back and forth for feedback. Even though we'd only just met, he was one of the most genuine and open creative partners I've ever worked with. There was no arrogance about him. Writing music with a partner, especially lyrics, requires trust. If the subject matter is going to be personal and have any real meaning, you have to be vulnerable. Chester and I instantly established that trust with each other. We connected over our shared experiences and bared our souls in that song. I'd come into the session with an immense respect for him as a singer and performer, and I was honored to be working with him. But the best part was that I got to see how authentic and driven Chester was as a songwriter and an artist.

That evening I sat at the mixing board in NRG as Josh recorded Chester's spectacular performance on "Cross Off." His technical ability as a vocalist was out of this world. I've never seen anything like it before or since. After the song was tracked, we hung out for an hour or so in the studio lounge. We discussed our children and what each of our bands had planned. Chester played me several songs from the new Linkin Park album they had just finished but hadn't released. He was so proud of their new material. We hugged as he left and thanked each other for the chance to work together. "Dude, let's do another one!" he said, smiling. "I'm serious!"

Three months later Chester was found dead in his home. He'd hung himself.

CHAPTER 21

THE CHANGE

"RELATIVELY EASY"
JASON ISBELL

I've always been motivated by what I thought was cool, and skateboarding seemed cool to me. The aesthetics of the skateboarding lifestyle–the clothes, the music, the haircuts–all were appealing. I wanted to fit into that world; unfortunately, I didn't. I sucked at skateboarding, and I didn't look cool posing like I was good at it.

When I figured out that I had a talent for playing guitar, it opened a new world. It was a world that could accept me, one that came with established role models and heroes. People like Jimi Hendrix, Keith Richards, Jimmy Page, Eddie Van Halen were all mentors I could look up to as cool. Most of them were also addicts and alcoholics. I didn't know it when I was younger, but I was too.

By the end of 2018, I'd already made several attempts at getting clean and sober. I'd been to outpatient treatment programs, methadone maintenance clinics, and inpatient residential rehabilitation facilities, but nothing ever stuck. I had also made my own attempts to manage my addiction by trying to drink more and use drugs less, or by substituting one drug for another. Those efforts were also unsuccessful.

It wasn't until I felt spiritually and emotionally dead that I became desperate enough to surrender my own delusions about being able to control my addictions. Fortunately, it wasn't long before I discovered some role models. And many of them had been right there all along in my familiar world of music.

After hanging around meetings for a little while, I began to recognize the language of recovery when I heard it, and I started noticing recovery references in songs I was listening to. While it was true that a disproportionate number of my heroes were drunks and junkies, it was also true that many of them had found recovery. As I picked up on the messages of hope in some of the music I loved, like Jason Isbell's "Relatively Easy," I started understanding that recovery could, in fact, be very cool. It wasn't the punishment or the sentence to a lifetime of boredom I thought it would be. I found people I wanted to emulate who were living the serene and productive lives that I aspired to have. I became willing to listen and learn from them.

W orking with Josh on my solo album motivated me to keep my drug and alcohol issues in check. It wasn't a solution, but our periodic writing and recording sessions provided opportunities for some calm in the storm.

At the end of 2017, I got the chance to do more music apart from Lamb of God when my old friend and producer Machine contacted me about working with him on a project. He was producing an album for an up-and-coming band from Long Island called Moon Tooth, and he thought I'd be a great match to help them develop some of their material. He sent me a few demos. I liked what I heard. I'd always enjoyed working with Machine, and I was learning that staying busy with music benefited my well-being. I was happy to join in. I offered my home studio as a space for us to work on songs. I spent the week between Christmas and New Year's Eve 2017 with Machine and Moon Tooth at my house writing and recording. I wasn't sober, but I was keeping myself in check as best I could. We had a fun and productive week.

Machine and Moon Tooth left to go home on the morning of New Year's Eve. I'd made plans to go to Williamsburg that night and jam with my friend James's band, Blind and Dirty. They were a cover band that played mostly classic rock songs with a lot of Grateful Dead in the set. James had invited me to sit in with them for a handful of tunes at the hotel convention center where they were playing. Blind and Dirty was a popular regional act, drawing hundreds of people to their shows. I was excited to jump in with them for a bit, and they'd even gotten me a room where the gig was.

When I arrived at the hotel that evening, I settled into my room for a few minutes before heading down to check out the stage and set up my gear. I had a few Oxys with me, just enough to stay comfortable if I paced myself. I didn't want to get too loaded anyway because I was excited for the show and wanted to play well. Just before I headed down, James texted me, "YO! On your way down here, check out the bartender chick setting up. She's CUTE! Maybe you should holler at her."

I appreciated the heads up, but I wasn't in the mindset to socialize. I'd been casually seeing a girl out of state, a situation I liked because from my perspective it came without a commitment. Nonetheless, I followed James's suggestion to check her out. As I walked down to the stage, I took the long way, veering off to the far side of the room to get a look at the bartender setting up for her shift. She was young and beautiful: slim, with long, light brown hair and bright green eyes. She wore a tightly fitted black dress that was simple and classy. She had very little makeup on, but she didn't need it. She had a timeless, natural beauty that heavy makeup would've hidden. As soon as she opened the bar, I was naturally ready for a beer, so I walked over and started chatting with her.

"Hi, I'm Mark. You're probably going to see a lot of me over here tonight, so I figure we might as well be friends."

"Oh, *you're* Mark? You must be the special guest I've heard about," she was smiling playfully and making eye contact. "I'm Brittany," she said, extending her hand. "It's nice to meet you. Since you're with the band, you get free beer."

"You may end up rethinking that after an hour or two," I replied with a smirk.

That night I could barely take my eyes off her. I made sure not to stare because I didn't want to make her feel uncomfortable. She was working, and she deserved the right to earn her pay without having to deal with me eyeballing her all night. But I was smitten. I found any excuse to go chat with her more.

At the end of the night, as Brittany broke down her bar, I invited her up to my room for a drink. There was one problem: I didn't have anything to drink. Lucky for me, not only did she accept my invitation, but she also had a bottle of rum in her backpack. That night we stayed up until sunrise talking and drinking her liquor. She drank hard. Maybe harder than me.

Brittany was twenty-six years old. She was surprised to find out that I was forty-five. "You don't look anywhere near *that* old!"

"Thanks?" I replied. I asked her out on a date. She laughed out loud. "That's not the response I was hoping for," I told her.

"No no no! I'll absolutely go out with you," she laughed. "You're just the first guy who's ever asked me out on an *official* date."

"What the fuck is wrong with those dudes?"

"Guys just always talk about hanging out or getting together. It's nice to be asked out for real."

The following week, I got tickets for us to see Zoso, a Led Zeppelin tribute band playing The National, a theater in Richmond. A few days before our date, I realized that because she was born in 1991, Brittany may not be familiar with Led Zeppelin. And that could make for a long boring evening. So I asked her if she had ever heard of them. "Led Zeppelin? Of course I've heard of Led Zeppelin!" she replied, much to my relief.

We had an awesome time at the show.

Brittany and I started dating. She was smart and fun to be around. She loved nature and music and had an open-minded curiosity for new experiences. I had become closed off and set in my ways, generally uninterested in things outside of my normal routine. Brittany liked going out and being around people. She loved being outside and in the sun. She pushed me to get up, get out, and do things with her. She was a good influence. And I fell in love with her.

Brittany didn't do hard drugs. As a partying teenager, she'd gotten in over her head with some friends doing some drugs that she wasn't familiar with, and one time she overdosed. She woke up being revived in an ambulance. After that, she'd sworn off hard drugs and mostly stuck to weed and drinking. She believed that would be a safer, more manageable option. But as time progressed, her drinking did too. And by the time I met her, Brittany drank a lot. She usually started her day with a couple of airplane bottles of whiskey to level herself out. Then she drank liquor on lunch breaks at work. And in the evenings, whatever she was doing almost always included constant alcohol consumption.

Brittany was a beautiful, vibrant, intelligent, active young woman. She was also an alcoholic. But to me that was actually a promising detail. The fact that she only drank and smoked weed struck me as a model of how I might mitigate my own addiction. I aspired to be more like her. Even though I drank a twelve-pack of beer daily, I'd never considered myself to be an alcoholic. I didn't wake up with the shakes. I'd never gotten arrested for drunk driving. I didn't think I did the things that "alcoholics" do. I assumed that I was somehow immune to alcohol addiction.

As I spent more time with Brittany, I began using opiates less often and drinking more. But I couldn't shake my pill addiction. On days that I wasn't hanging out with Brittany, I'd drink less but often binge on Oxys. And sometimes I still couldn't keep from using around her. On a trip to the Outer Banks of North Carolina in the summer of 2018, I nodded out at the table as a server took our dinner order.

By late 2018, any questions regarding whether I qualified as an alcoholic had been answered. In October, Willie Adler, Josh Wilbur, and I took a trip up to a small studio in Maine to demo some new song ideas for our next album. Willie and I had collected a lot of great riffs, and song outlines were materializing quickly. The sessions were inspired and productive, but I was drunk most of the time—still functioning, but drunk nonetheless. Most mornings, while Willie and Josh woke up slowly in the studio's residential cabin, making breakfast and coffee and chatting over the plan for the day, I took the keys to the rental car and drove fifteen minutes to the nearest liquor store, arriving just after they opened. I'd buy a few small bottles of whiskey to supplement the twelve-pack of beer I was drinking each day. I'd add a couple airplane-size bottles of Fireball to my purchase for the ride back to the studio. It paired well with my morning coffee.

I was also ingesting large amounts of kratom powder. Kratom is a plant native to Asia that had become popular for its effectiveness in staving off opiate withdrawal symptoms. In some ways, it helped by easing my symptoms. But ultimately, I'd just become dependent on the kratom until I started using opiates again. And my tolerance was so high that the amount of kratom I required for relief was unreasonable, causing severe gastrointestinal issues.

On November 1, 2018, Lamb of God started a tour of the UK and Europe supporting Slayer. The day before I left for the tour, a very close, lifelong friend of Brittany's passed away unexpectedly from a stroke at the age of thirty. Brittany was devastated. She reacted the way that an alcoholic reacts to pain: she drank heavily, even heavier than usual.

When I arrived in Europe, I called home to check on Brittany. She'd been preparing for her friend's wake and funeral, but she was clearly in the middle of a drinking binge, one that would continue for a week. By the end of it, she'd been blacked out for days and couldn't eat or even drink water without vomiting unless she drank liquor in front of it.

Meanwhile, I was on my own binge. During our first week in the UK, I scored some morphine pills from a friend. It wasn't enough. It's never enough. It wasn't working for me. I couldn't get high. I chased the morphine with vodka. But nothing was working.

The evening of our night off in Cardiff, I spoke with a drug dealer acquaintance about getting me some heroin. I gave him $400. He came back a couple hours later with cocaine. I was furious. I fucking hated cocaine. Of course, I spent that night and all the next day doing the coke and drinking whiskey. But it wasn't working. The drugs and alcohol weren't giving me the feeling I was chasing. They hadn't been for a long time. I'd do more and more, but I always ended up feeling worse, never better.

Following our show in Cardiff, Brittany and I spoke by phone. Her voice was trembling. She was depressed and exhausted. She said she felt poisoned and that her body was shaking. Her hair had been falling out, and she was dry heaving every morning when she woke up. She was completely defeated by her alcoholism. She wasn't sure what to do, but she was determined that she had to stop or she was going to die. I knew that feeling. I felt the same way. I suggested she go to a recovery meeting, and she agreed.

Brittany and I had both been to meetings of recovery fellowships before. I'd been to lots of recovery meetings during my time in rehab, and I continued to go sporadically as I explored the idea of getting clean. But I was never committed, so it hadn't stuck. Brittany had been to meetings when she was younger, but like me she hadn't been desperate enough to be willing to change. You have to be ready.

The day after our Cardiff show, we had a day off in Birmingham. I checked into my hotel room early that morning and started drinking beer from the minibar. Brittany had gone to a meeting back home the night before. I stared out of my hotel window watching people down on the sidewalk. I drank all four beers that were in the small refrigerator. I wondered how her meeting went. As I drained the last bottle of hotel room beer, I felt total emptiness. I was alone. I felt dead inside. I felt no joy. I had to get out of that room. I had to change my surroundings. I needed to do something to make me feel different.

I pulled up a map of the area and noticed a Buddhist temple nearby where there was an open, guided meditation in a couple of hours. I took a shower and walked to the temple. Inside, I met calm, friendly people. They drank tea and spoke softly with one another in a lounge area next to a larger room where the meditations were held.

When the time came for our guided meditation, I sat on a mat in the large room and followed along. It felt good. I had meditated before, so I wasn't uncomfortable with the setting. I was doing something positive for myself. On the way out, I stopped in the small gift shop and bought Brittany a wooden beaded bracelet.

For the next couple of shows, I continued with what had become my routine: drinking liquor and trying to score drugs, chasing a buzz that I couldn't seem to get. On November 10, 2018, I woke up late in the morning in my bunk on our tour bus. We were parked outside the Metro Radio Arena in Newcastle, England, where we were playing that night. I was hungover. But it wasn't the hangover you get after a night of too much fun. I was hungover from an entirely uneventful evening the night before. Nothing out of the ordinary had happened. I hadn't stayed up partying with another band or some old friends. I hadn't happened upon some elusive and exciting drug score. I'd simply played a show that I couldn't recall much of anything about and then drank until I passed out in my bunk. And I woke up feeling like shit. Again. I was exhausted and miserable. My body was bloated and aching. I hated being on tour. I didn't want to play any more shows. I didn't want to hang out with anyone.

That day I didn't drink. I don't remember what I did. I probably slept a lot, but I didn't drink. I still had to take kratom powder to hold off my opiate withdrawals. I knew that meant that I wasn't completely clean and sober. But I promised myself that I wasn't going drink. That night we played our show in Newcastle. Afterward, I showered and went straight to bed. And I didn't drink.

The next morning I woke up on the bus parked in front of our hotel in Glasgow, Scotland. I checked my phone to see if there were any recovery fellowship meetings nearby. I believed that I could derive strength from being around people who were changing their lives. I went to two meetings that day, one in the early afternoon and one later that night. When the chairperson in the first meeting asked if there were any newcomers or visitors, I raised my hand and introduced myself in the way that I had learned was customary for the fellowship I was attending.

"My name is Mark and I'm an addict," I said flatly. I knew that much was true.

"Hi, Mark. Welcome!" the entire room replied.

Later that night at the second meeting, I saw some of the same faces I'd seen that morning. A couple of people smiled when I walked in, recognizing me from earlier. One came over and greeted me. He remembered my name. The next morning I took a cab from the hotel to another meeting. I'd gone to three meetings in twenty-four hours. I would've gone to more if it was possible. I felt safe there. There was an energy and spirit in the room that I felt comforted and supported by. I was still using kratom because I didn't want to go through withdrawals on tour. But I promised myself not to use any other drugs. No pills, no cocaine, no heroin, not even weed. And I wasn't drinking. I knew that was a start.

I didn't tell anyone about the changes I was making. There was nothing to talk about. Nobody would've believed me anyway. I was defeated. I felt dead inside. I had become so miserable and desperate that I was finally willing to admit that my drug and alcohol use was likely my problem. It wasn't a loud, public revelation. I just quietly fizzled out and broke. I was emotionally blank and spiritually dead, but there was a tiny ember of hope. I had seen people change their lives. I knew that there were people living in recovery from addiction, and I knew that there were ways to be among those people and that it was possible to learn how they had changed.

I made it through the remaining four weeks of the tour without drinking, though I continued to use kratom powder to help stay out of withdrawal. I knew that meant I wasn't really clean and sober, at least not in the way that I aspired to be. But I also knew that I was actively working to get all the way clean.

Back home, Brittany was on her own path to sobriety. She'd quit drinking and quit all drugs. She even stopped smoking weed. She was going to meetings daily and had begun to actively work a program of recovery. We spoke by phone every day. We supported each other but didn't rely on each other to keep ourselves on the path. Our goals were congruent but not connected. I intuitively knew I couldn't count on her staying clean to get me clean. She knew that as well.

As was my common practice, I had tucked away a significant stash of pills in the house for when I returned from tour. Brittany knew they were there but didn't know exactly where I stashed them. She asked me where they were so that she could flush them down the toilet before I got home. I refused to tell her. "I want to be the one to do that! It's symbolic!"

"Mark, that's fucking stupid, and you know it is," she replied. "If you're serious about not using anymore, why not just let me get that shit out of the house?"

She was right. It was stupid, and I knew it. But the truth was that I still wasn't completely sure I was ready to stop. Maybe coming home to one more good pill binge would be a cool way to end it. I stubbornly held my ground, not telling her where the pills were. But by the time the tour was ending, I'd become more convinced that I genuinely wanted to change the way I was living.

On the way home from our long European tour, we landed in Washington, DC, in the middle of a snowstorm and got stuck there. Our short connection to Richmond was canceled due to the bad weather. After spending an unplanned night at an airport hotel, John Campbell and I rented a car and drove home the next day. Not long after getting home, Brittany and I stood in our master bathroom as I flushed 250 milligrams of oxycodone down the toilet.

A couple of weeks later, on December 26, 2018, after several failed attempts to stop, I took my last dose of the kratom powder. The next day, despite the onset of what would end up being a long, strange, drawn-out withdrawal, I stayed completely clean and sober.

THE LIFE
I GET TO LIVE

When I got clean in late December 2018, it wasn't because I didn't enjoy the feeling of being drunk or high anymore. I wasn't excited by the idea of getting sober. It felt like breaking up with a longtime girlfriend. I'd relied on drugs and alcohol for decades. They protected me from my insecurity and anxiety. They told me that I was good enough in times when I didn't feel like I was. Drugs and alcohol numbed my emotional pain, eased my fears, and had been dependable best friends to me. But over time, they became less dependable. They didn't work like they used to. And eventually, they became a bigger problem than the problems that I'd been using them to fix.

In the context of recovery, the concept of hitting "rock bottom" is often discussed. This refers to the notion that an addict must experience consequences so dire that they become desperate enough to change. At a glance, the consequences of my addiction weren't as severe as one might expect. I'd somehow managed to stay alive and keep my home; my career; and most important, my time and relationship with my daughter. I'm grateful that was the case, and I believe that had I not gotten clean when I did, I'd have lost all those things in a short amount of time.

Though I didn't have the insight to realize it then, I've come to understand that my "rock bottom" was spiritual in nature. I felt lost and alone everywhere I went. I was terrified by the way my addiction had progressed, but I was equally terrified at the thought of living without it. By the end, my every waking moment was haunted with a sense of impending doom. I lived in fear: fear of death, fear of withdrawal, fear of responsibility, fear of being found out, fear of losing what I had, and fear of doing what it takes to maintain those things. I'd fallen out of contact with almost all my friends. I'd given up on my hobbies and interests. My life was a miserable routine of trying to stay out of withdrawal and doing just enough to get by.

There were a few bright spots. I clung to my love for my daughter like I was clinging to a life preserver. I believe my love for her kept me alive. Brittany provided a source of hope for me as well. Despite her struggles with alcoholism and the challenges of her own journey into recovery, our relationship was loving and strong. And music remained a constant guiding light. There were times when that light dimmed and almost burned out, but music has always been my direct connection to some type of spiritual energy that I don't understand but that I know is real.

Getting clean and sober was not easy. But living drunk and high had become even more difficult. I'd been given the gift of desperation. I was so miserable and beaten down that I became willing to listen. I sought out and found other addicts who'd found their way into genuine recovery. I listened to their stories and saw that their lives looked calm and manageable compared to mine. I admired the way many of them carried themselves. When I asked for advice, they gave me suggestions, and I started staying clean a day at a time. Each morning, I'd wake up and promise myself that I wouldn't drink or use any drugs for just one day. The idea of "quitting forever" sounded overwhelming. But I was usually confident that I could make it through a day without drinking or using. Those days began to string together.

On January 8, 2019, "Cross Off" featuring Chester Bennington was released as a single in advance of my first solo album, *Anesthetic*. The song was embraced by rock radio and was celebrated by Chester's legions of fans. It had the biggest debut of any song I'd ever been a part of, staying on Billboard's Active Rock radio charts for weeks and peaking at number six. A couple of months later, with less than ninety days sober, I embarked on my first solo tour across North America. I stayed sober.

Lamb of God remained active too. In July 2019, we parted ways with our longtime drummer Chris Adler. It was a difficult and emotional split for everyone. Art Cruz joined the band as our new drummer. He was a welcome addition. We continue to write, record, and tour the world.

As my recovery became more stable, I developed a new relationship with my career and the people I work with. I found myself more grateful for the opportunity to live my life playing music. I began to appreciate the talent and commitment of my bandmates in ways that had never occurred to me. And best of all, I became present for the joy of the audience.

I've played thousands of shows in my life. But it wasn't until I got sober that I was able to experience the miracles that happen in front of me almost every night. I can finally see the depth of our fans' connections to our music. With their hands in the air, eyes wide with excitement, and voices shouting the lyrics at the top of their lungs, our fans show us what true joy looks like. At in-store appearances and meet and greets, they tell us how our songs have helped them through their own challenges. They show us tattoos of Lamb of God lyrics that are special to them and share important memories that they relate directly to our music.

As I write this, I am just short of five years clean and sober. Brittany and I have a two-year-old daughter, and we will be married in one week. I no longer wake up craving drugs or alcohol. I don't miss the feeling of being drunk or high. But I also know that I'm not immune from relapse. I don't believe that anyone can be completely cured of addiction or alcoholism. I don't assume that after staying sober for any length of time I can ever resume drinking or using drugs safely or normally. So I take consistent action to practice a recovery program. My life depends on it.

Today, I still get the opportunity to write, record, and perform music with my best friends. Knowing that our music goes out into the world and becomes a cherished part of people's lives is among the greatest joys of my own life. I'm eternally grateful to be a part of that system.

ACKNOWLEDGMENTS

Mark Morton

I'd like to thank the following people for their assistance and support over the course of this project:

My family, Brittany, Lorelei, Meadow, and Mom...for unconditional love and patience. Ben Opipari...for having the idea in the first place, for guiding me, and for teaching me how to write! My bandmates, past and present, for a lifetime of music and stories to tell. Brad Fuhrman...for your vision and for always believing in me. Ben Schafer for your trust, confidence, and friendship. Randy Blythe for lots of things, but for our purposes here, for taking my picture. Joey Huertas, Denise Koryicki, Michelle Spaulding, Jeff Seibert, John Partin, John Skaritza, and Abe Spear for photo contributions. Chris Marrow and Dave Harris for help with memory. Bob Johnsen and all at 5B Artist Management for having my back on all things, all at Hachette Books for working to make this a reality. Tim Borror for being a voice of reason...and bookings, Adam Mandell for legal assistance, Ed Gold for business management. Most of all, thanks to everyone who takes the time to listen to the music and read the book...I'm grateful.

Ben Opipari

I met Mark in 2014 after interviewing him for my *Songwriters on Process* podcast. I'd like to thank him for being a great writing partner and a great friend on this journey. We hatched a crazy idea on a back porch in Corolla, North Carolina, to write this book. I've become a better writer working with Mark, but more importantly I've become a better person listening to him. He told me once that "middle age is a privilege," and I joked that this should be a book title. Fortunately it isn't, but his story has taught me to see life like this. What made this collaboration so easy was that we always listen to each other. There were some deep conversations about what growth means to two middle-aged men. (We always seemed to have them on that back porch in Corolla.)

I'd also like to thank Adam Turla of the band Murder by Death. I haven't spoken to Adam in about ten years, and we've only spoken a few times. I'd be surprised if he even remembers me. Adam was the first interview for my Songwriters on Process site in 2010. It was backstage at Lincoln Hall in Chicago, and Adam was stretched out on a couch before the show because of a bad back, clearly uncomfortable. It would've been easy for him to cancel our interview, but Adam was kind, gracious, and thoughtful in his responses. He didn't have to be any of these things, given his condition. But because of his generosity, I thought it would be an interesting project to interview songwriters about their creative process and to hear them tell their stories. And that project led me to Mark.

You wouldn't be reading this book if it wasn't for Ben Schafer, our editor at Hachette. I'm thankful for his constant encouragement and feedback. Ben believed in two guys who had never written a book and who thought that they had a story good enough to tell. Thanks also to David Kostiner for his legal assistance and his advocacy.

I'd like to thank my mother for unwittingly jumpstarting my love of metal. I'm not sure what she was thinking when she let my friend Jeremy and me see AC/DC and Fastway by ourselves when we were barely fourteen, dropping us off at the entrance to the Capital Centre and letting us fend for ourselves in our Members Only jackets.

I'd like to thank my father for instilling a love of live music. He took me to my first concert when I was four: Loggins and Messina, with Jim Croce opening, at Pine Knob outside Detroit. I learned to read by asking my father to transcribe the lyrics to early Eagles, Traffic, and Chicago albums. I listened to them, the handwritten lyric sheet in front of me, with giant white headphones while the albums spun.

Most importantly, I'd like to thank my family. My wife, Kelly, has been nothing but supportive in all my pursuits related to music, whether it's going to shows, doing my podcast, or working on this book. She's always given me time to pursue my passion, which is not always easy when there are four kids in the house. And those kids—Annabella, Nicolas, Francesca, and Cristiana—keep me, well, somewhat cool. Their musical tastes vary, so I've kept up with what's good and what's popular—even when they remind me that most of the songs I like "are from the 1900s."